PAINT ALCHEMY

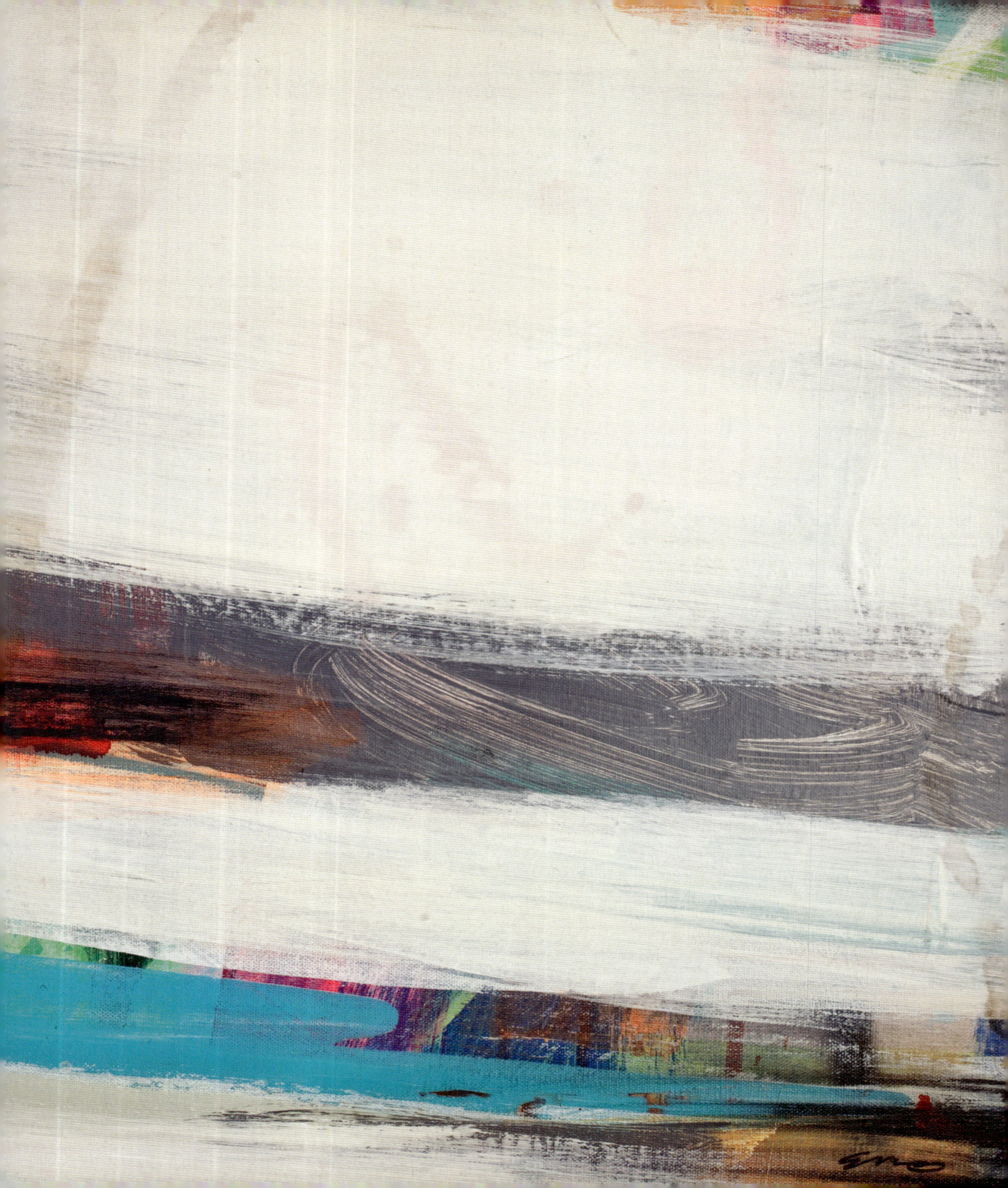

PAINT ALCHEMY

EXPLORING PROCESS-DRIVEN TECHNIQUES THROUGH DESIGN, PATTERN, COLOR, ABSTRACTION, ACRYLIC, AND MIXED MEDIA

EVA MAGILL-OLIVER

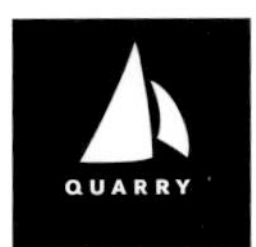

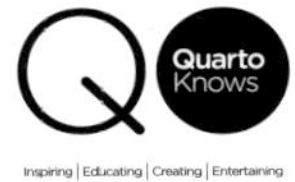

First Published in 2018 by Quarry Books, an imprint of The Quarto Group,
100 Cummings Center, Suite 265-D, Beverly, MA 01915, USA.
T (978) 282-9590 F (978) 283-2742 QuartoKnows.com

10 9 8 7 6 5 4 3 2 1

ISBN: 978-1-63159-596-7

Digital edition published in 2018
eISBN: 978-1-63159-597-4

Library of Congress Cataloging-in-Publication Data

Magill-Oliver, Eva Marie, author.
Paint alchemy : exploring process-driven techniques through design, pattern, color, abstraction, acrylic, and mixed media / Eva Marie Magill-Oliver.
ISBN 9781631595967 (trade pbk.)
Painting--Technique.
LCC ND1473 .M334 2018
750.28--dc23
LCCN 2018027957

Cover Design: Kelley Galbreath
Cover Image: Christina Wedge Photography
Interior Design and Page Layout: Stacy Wakefield Forte
Photography: Christina Wedge Photography, except images on pages 30–31, 66–67, 96–97 by Eva Magill-Oliver and page 44 via Shutterstock.

Printed in China

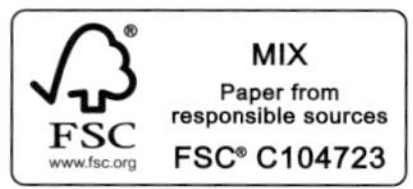

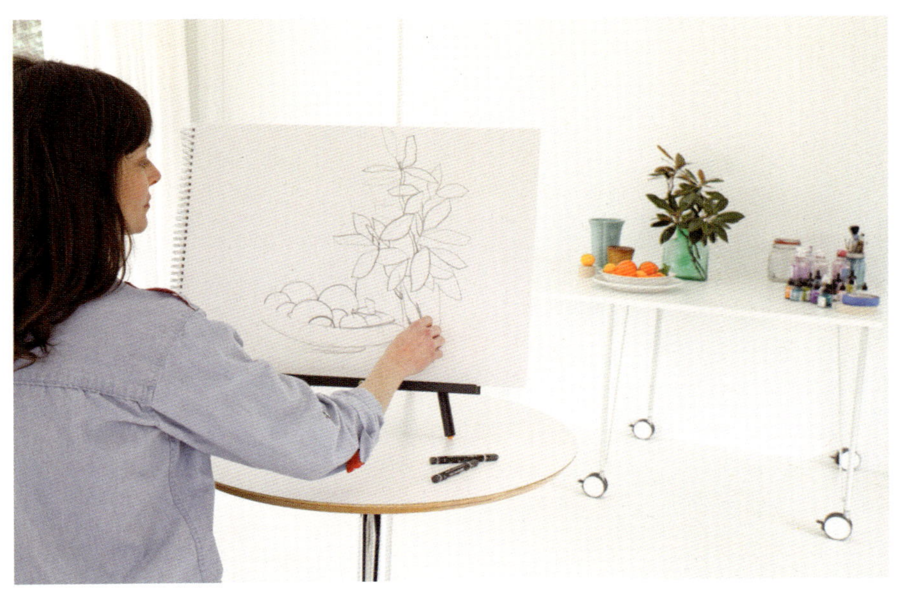

for my family

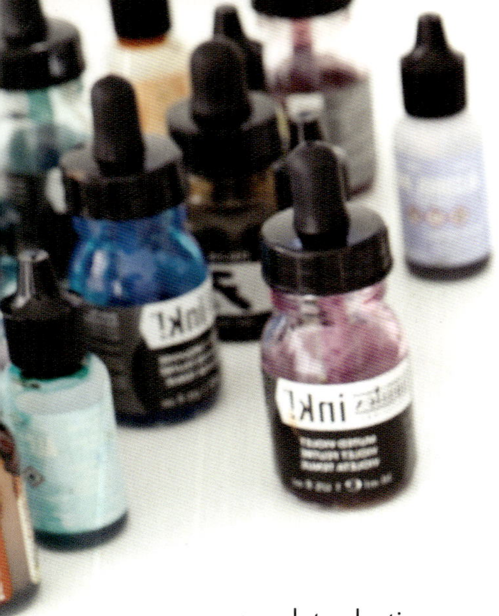

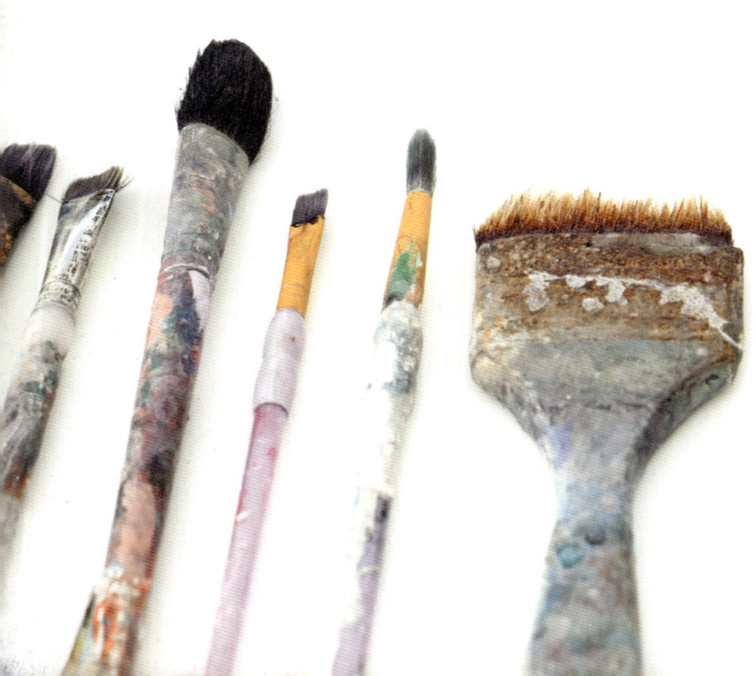

contents

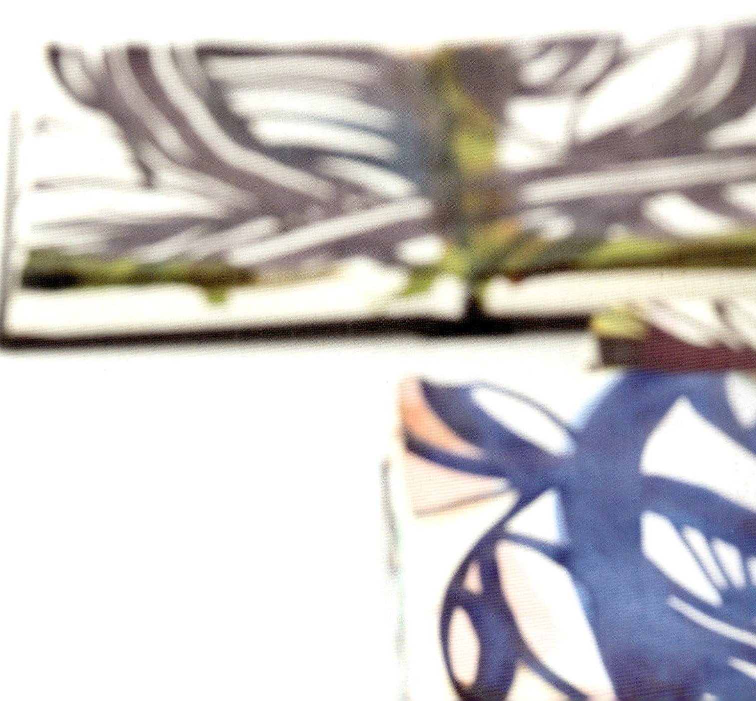

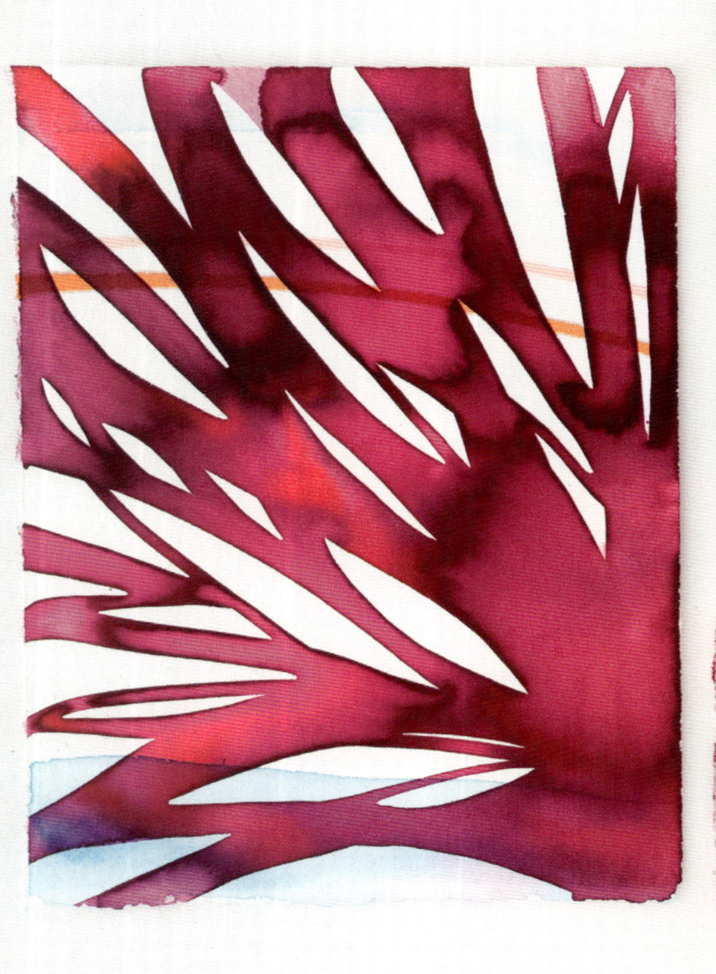

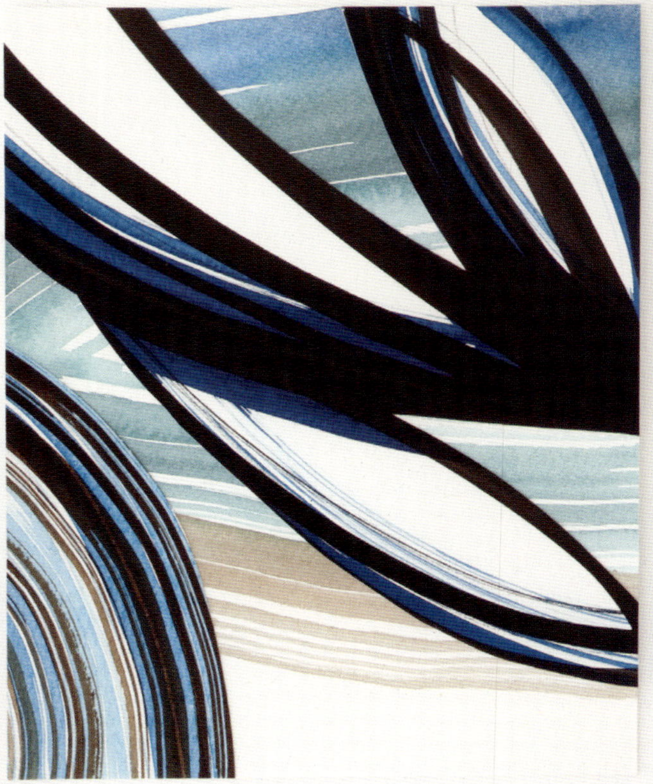

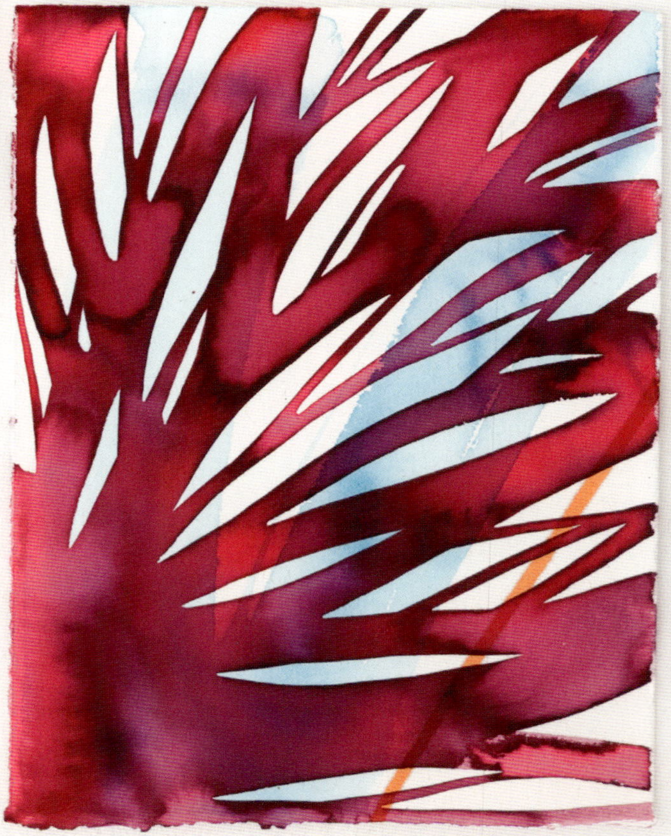

introduction

*"When I think of art I think of beauty.
Beauty is the mystery of life. It is not
in the eye, it is in the mind. In our minds,
there is awareness of perfection."*

—AGNES MARTIN

After I graduated college with a B.F.A., I started a job as an in-house artist with a fine arts publishing company in Atlanta. At the time, I was not thrilled with the position. I worked each day creating art I often did not like or choose to do, and on top of it, I did not own the rights to anything I created there. I had dreams after college of becoming a serious gallery artist and working in what seemed like a glorified art factory was not part of my original plan. However, looking back, I could not be more grateful for the years I spent there.

Every day that I was with the company, I was able to paint and innovate while working alongside truly talented and remarkable creative people. I now see how valuable that time was for me, and how much it educated me on materials, subject matter, design, and the overall art process. While I was there, I did not paint in my comfort zone. Each order and commission I received was a new challenge and pushed me to figure out how a given concept might work. I also had the added benefit of working with peers who inspired and taught me daily and who became my partners in experimentation with materials. I think of that time in my life as an

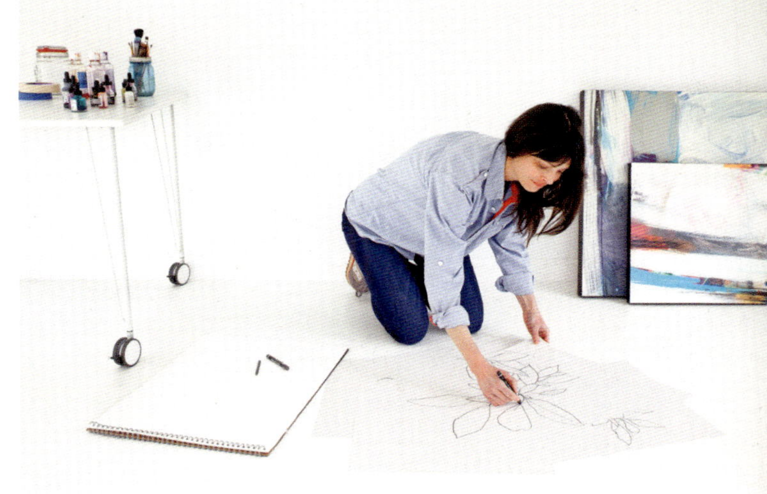

extension of my education. I mention this because a lot of the exercises in this book were developed and inspired from my time there—a time when I was gifted the freedom to experiment and learn while working and then take that knowledge and apply it to my personal work.

I became an artist for the same reasons a lot of people do: Because it gives you a voice you might not otherwise have. It is a form of self-expression that is constantly and organically changing as you are. Also, as an artist, you have the power to create something from nothing. What a gift this is! The ability to express yourself to others regardless of language, culture, or demographic differences is a constant motivation for me to continue to stay focused, stay passionate, and create art.

The wisdom and knowledge gained from your process will help sustain and support you whether you are just beginning to make art or have done so your entire life. My goal in this book is to help highlight this simple fact and to pass on some of the art process knowledge I have gained through the years.

I also hope to demonstrate how the creation of a piece of art can be viewed and thought of in countless ways. One of my favorite quotes from Richard Olsen, a wonderful professor I had in school, is that "In art, 1 + 1 = 3."

the five principles of design

My desire to achieve good design drives and challenges me and makes the art process itself as fascinating and rewarding as the final outcome. I like Alice Rawsthorn's simple definition of good design from the *New York Times*: "Even today, it's possible for something to qualify as good design simply by fulfilling its function efficiently." I think this can be applied to all areas of design, including as it relates to painting and the arts. To achieve good design, there are five areas of focus: balance, proportion, rhythm, emphasis, and unity. Yet in the end, if the painting has fulfilled its duty to the viewer as well as the artist, then I feel a successful design has been achieved.

My passion has always been figuring out how to best express myself, realistically render an object from life, or evoke energy, movement, and emotion in my art. Once I complete a design or painting, I am onto the next one because each piece is like a mystery or puzzle to solve. There is always something new to say or express that ignites a continued desire to paint, create, and innovate.

In this book, I share a number of techniques and design strategies that will be helpful whether you are a seasoned painter or at the beginning of your artistic journey. In either case, it is important to regularly reconsider and refocus your intentions and approach to techniques and design. Investing time in the mastery of certain design techniques can provide a more rewarding artistic and personal experience. This book will delve into abstract techniques that will help you compose representational art as well.

A professor once told me that you have never truly painted until you have created at least one hundred paintings. What he was trying to convey is that you develop as an artist through the process of creating art. The final product is what is offered to the viewer. It is our obligation as artists to imagine a way to create and transmit a vision, while developing our techniques and building our creative inventory along the way.

This book will help you do just that. Each chapter explores a different subject, with art process and design being the overall theme. Dip in and out of this book, using the exercises as visual and instructional references as you create, allowing them to guide, inspire, and motivate you as you focus on art. I hope it will spur new ideas and creative thoughts and that it will help in understanding and celebrating your own unique artistic process.

I wish you great success and enjoyment as you continue on your path of creating art!

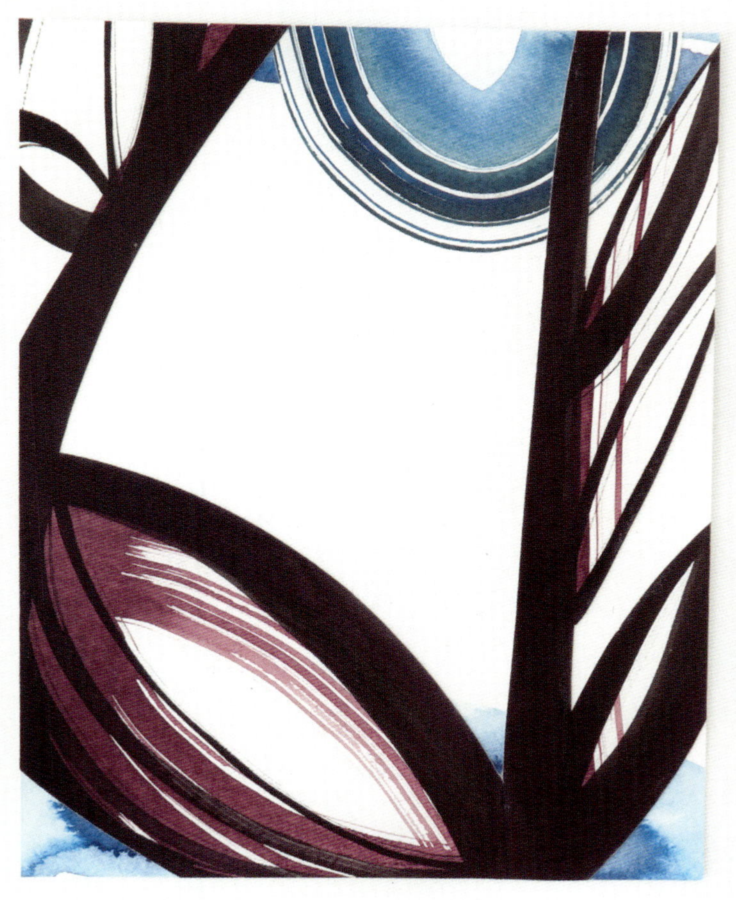
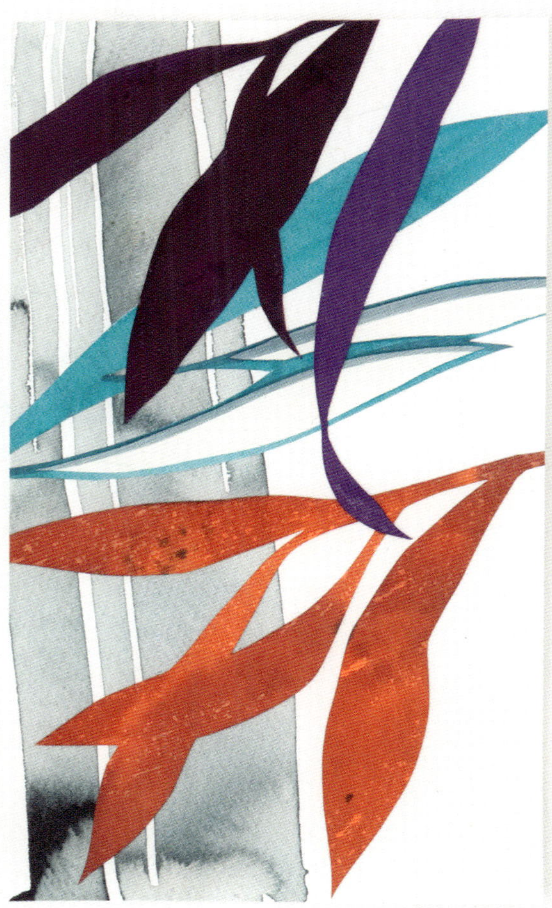
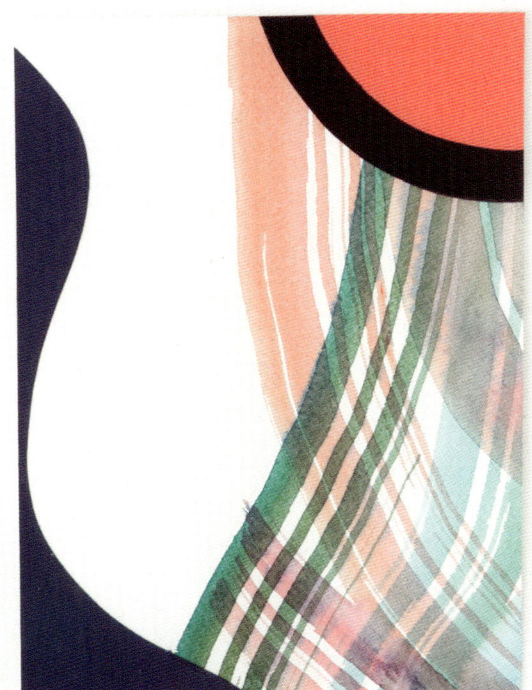

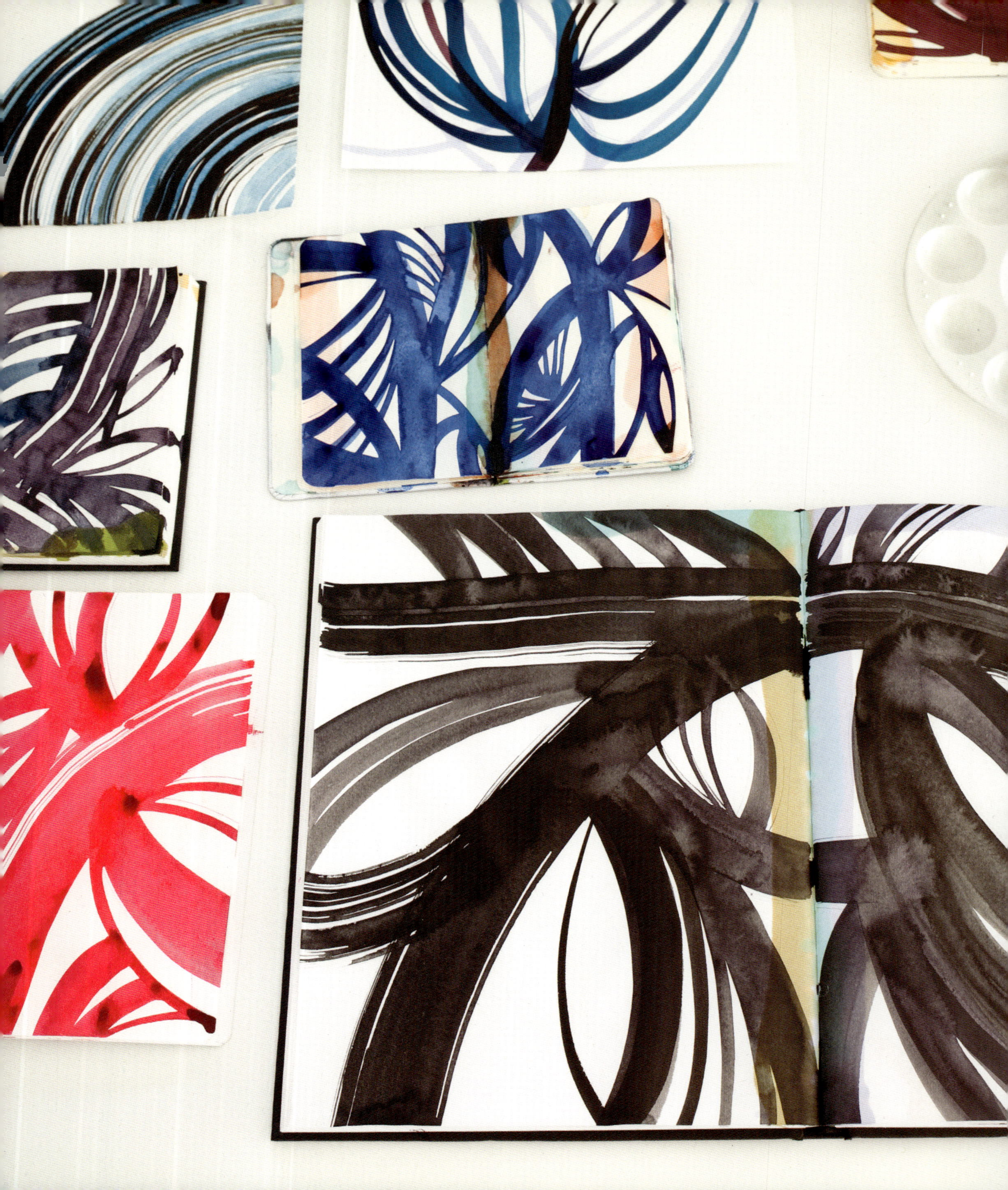

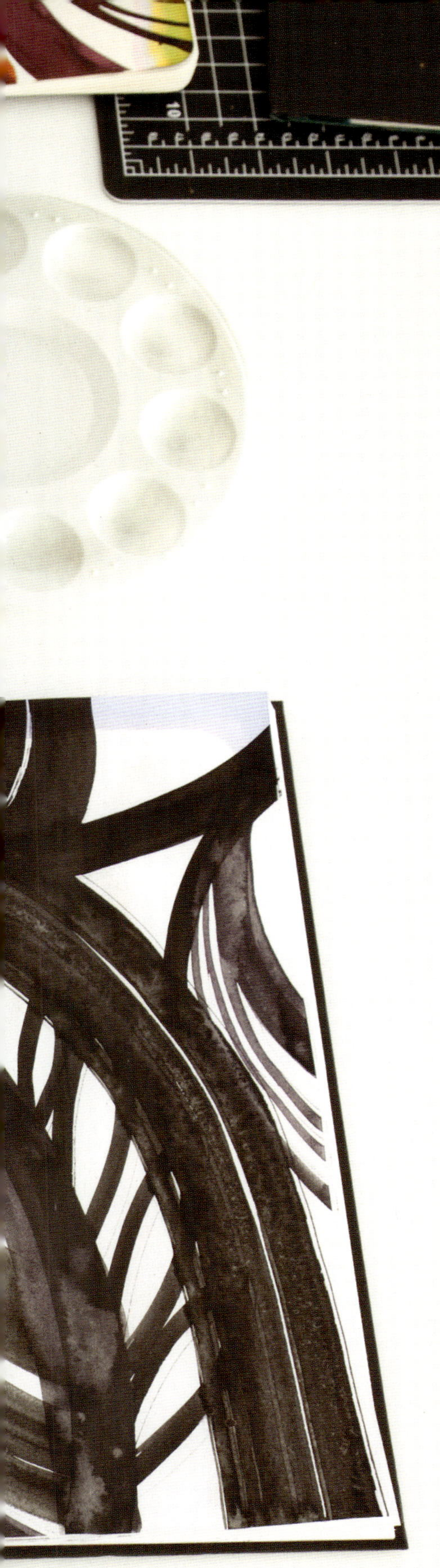

CHAPTER ONE

BUILDING A PRACTICE

"Inspiration is for amateurs. The rest of us just show up and get to work. If you wait around for the clouds to part and a bolt of lightning to strike you in the brain, you are not going to make an awful lot of work. All the best ideas come out of the process; they come out of the work itself. Things occur to you."

—CHUCK CLOSE

I have been working as a professional artist for sixteen years. Ever since I was a little girl, I have been interested in art, taking classes in oil, watercolor, and acrylic mediums. I have tested and worked with various brands and products.

On the following pages, I share how I set up my workspace and which basic studio materials and tools that I always keep handy. Most, if not all, are affordable and easy to find, either locally or online. Supplies and brands can vary greatly in price, yet less expensive brands can be of similar quality to more expensive alternatives. For example, I normally find little difference among paint brands, especially acrylics and watercolors. Oils, on the other hand, are made with pigments that can be rare, such as cadmium, which can increase their cost significantly. If you limit your paint choices to just the water-basec varieties, you can keep the cost of your materials at an affordable level.

preparing your **workspace**

I prefer to stand rather than sit when I paint and create. I enjoy the freedom of movement it permits. Acrylics, watercolors, and inks all dry fairly rapidly, so it is helpful to be able to move quickly and easily around a piece as you work.

While standing, I can easily step back and observe my progress from a distance. I can walk around a piece and view it from different angles and perspectives. It is important to consider your work in its entirety and not to focus solely on one area. Overall balance should be a priority as you create.

I work on the floor and use a waist-high work table, which allows me to stand as I draw. On the table, I keep drawing supplies within reach as I work. These include, but are not limited to, pencils, erasers, markers, and some inks. I keep the majority of my paint supplies separate in an effort to keep one area of the studio clean and paint-free.

Drop cloths are an inexpensive way to protect your floor and table and are found at most home improvement stores. I often stand on cut-up cardboard boxes. A bonus is that after they have become messy and covered in paint, they can be folded up and recycled.

Always work in a well-ventilated area or move your process outdoors, if possible. Not only does working outdoors cut down on paint fumes, it also provides natural light, which is the best lighting for painting. Lamps or fluorescent lighting can visually alter the colors in a painting, making them seem yellow, flat, or as if they have a blueish hue. If you have to work under artificial light, periodically view your progress in natural sunlight before making any big changes or decisions in terms of color.

materials

This is a basic overview of all the materials I use in my studio. Standard Materials (see at right) are the ones you will need to create the exercises in this book. The items in Specialty and Unconventional Materials (see page 17) are those I generally use and recommend, but are not necessary to complete any of the exercises. All of the materials can be found at most art supply stores, home improvement stores, online, and at your local grocery store (e.g., coffee, salt, tea, straws, and so on).

standard paints and inks

Acrylic paints and inks are the mediums I use most often in my work because they are versatile, fairly inexpensive, and less toxic than oils. They also come in many different shades and colors. As they are both water-based, they can technically be used together, but because of the difference in their viscosity, they are not interchangeable. I normally use one or the other, or if using both, I layer them as opposed to mixing them. Because inks dry faster than acrylics, they soak into paper more quickly. Acrylic paints allow for more time to be manipulated before the water begins to evaporate from them, leaving just the pigment behind.

→ **INDIA INKS** provide a strong, vibrant color and can be diluted and softened with water. They are permanent and adhere to nearly all surfaces. The colored inks are transparent, similar to watercolors, but the black is opaque and useful for drawing.

→ **WATERCOLORS** are water soluble and come in tubes or pans. Similar to inks, most watercolors are transparent, but less concentrated in pigment. There are some subtle differences between tubes and pans, but ultimately, it comes down to personal preference. The tube paints can be slightly more vibrant, but they also generally cost more. Pan paints are also more portable.

→ **ACRYLIC PAINTS** are also water soluble and come in a large variety of shades and colors. They can be purchased in tubes or bottles. The brands range from craft paints, typically found in bottles, to more art-specific brands normally found in tubes. I use both in my work, which allows for a larger variety of color choices. Also, I have noticed that there is no issue combining the two. The tube paints have a thicker, creamier consistency, which is something to consider if adding texture is one of your goals.

→ **CONCENTRATED LIQUID WATERCOLORS** are tinted, concentrated paints with rich color. I use these often because I love how the colors stay so vibrant and saturated when painting. Watercolors in general tend to soften into more pastel-like hues when water is added to them. (The concentrated liquid variety can be found online at discount school supply companies.)

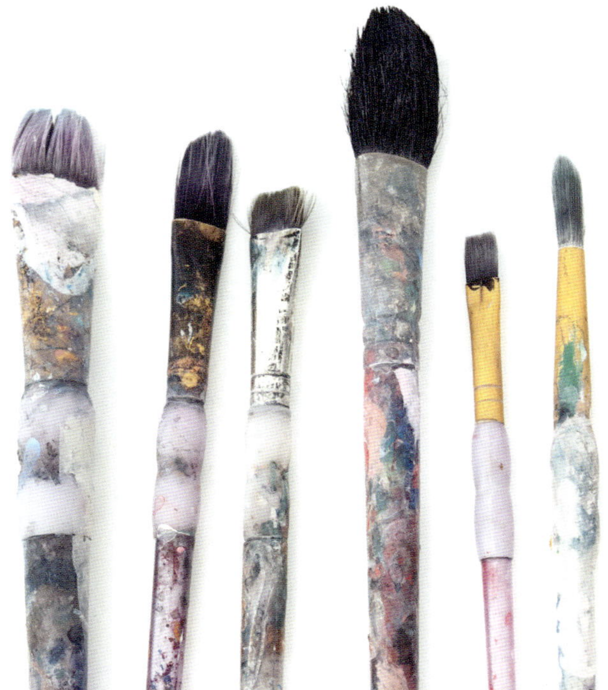

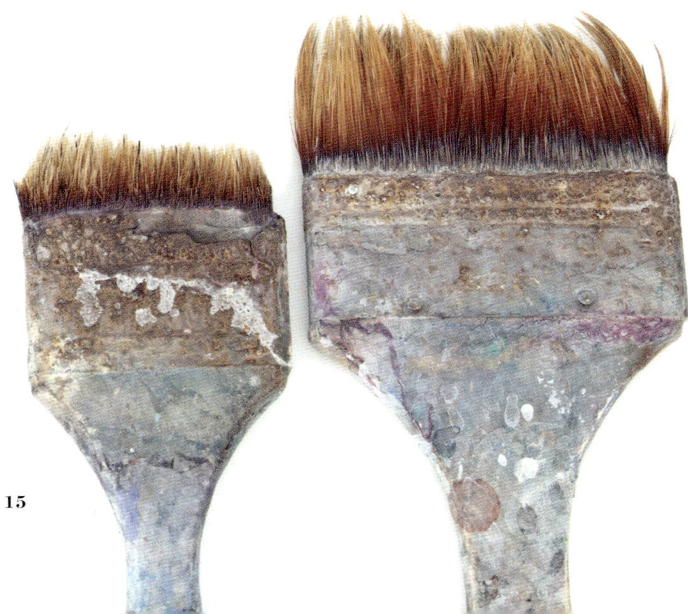

standard paintbrushes

Artist paintbrushes come in various sizes and shapes. I prefer to use synthetic hair brushes, which are softer than natural hair brushes and much less expensive. They can be used easily with watercolor, inks, and acrylics so that it is not necessary to purchase separate sets of brushes for each medium. I paint most often with either round or flat brushes.

- **FLAT, SOFT-HAIR SYNTHETIC BRUSHES**, 1" to 4" (2.5 to 10 cm) in size. Flat brushes are suitable for filling large areas with color and making bold strokes. The edges are great for straight lines.
- **ROUND, SOFT-HAIR SYNTHETIC BRUSHES**, sizes 6, 10, and 12. Round brushes have pointed ends and can be used for more detailed work, filling in smaller areas, and making lines that vary in thickness and curved lines.
- **FILBERT BRUSH**, size 6. This brush is a combination of both round and flat. The hairs curve in on the side, forming an oval shape. This brush is perfect for blending and is what I use to make soft organic lines and shapes.
- **FLAT BRISTLE BRUSHES (ALSO CALLED "CHIP" BRUSHES)**, 2" and 3" (5 and 7.5 cm) in size. These brushes are inexpensive and can be found at most home improvement stores in the paint section. A downside to these is the hairs often fall out, so before use, make sure to pull out what you can first using your hands. Then, run the brush across sandpaper several times to release any loose hairs.

TIP ▸ I have always obtained my palettes for both oils and acrylics by buying precut acrylic glass from home improvement stores. They usually have them in the glass section and they come in a large variety of precut sizes you can choose from. One type, Plexiglas, has the added benefit of being easily washed and scraped (i.e., scraping off paint), and it is ultimately recyclable.

standard tools

Many of the tools below can be found around the house or purchased at art supply stores or online. (See Resources on page 117.)

- Craft knife, such as X-ACTO, with extra blades
- Scissors
- Self-healing cutting mat
- Regular pencils, numbers 2B, 5B, 8B, and no. 2 mechanical pencils
- 1" (2.5 cm) painter's tape or masking tape
- Permanent markers
- Ruler
- Printmaker's brayer
- Water containers, such as glass jars (Used is fine.)
- Sketchbooks, book-bound, as opposed to spiral-bound. This type of sketchbook helps to keep your composition fluid and not disjointed with two distinct sides. My preferred sizes are 4" × 6" (10 × 15 cm) (A6), 6" × 8" (15 × 20 cm) (A5), and 8.5" × 11" (21.5 × 28 cm) (A4). Always buy ones with multimedia or 140 lb (300 gsm) cold-press paper. This paper works well with water-based paints because it has

increased amount of sizing, which is the protective layer of glue that's added to paper when it's made.

- Sheets of watercolor paper, 140 lb (300 gsm) cold press. This thick paper has texture to its surface and can stand up to repeated uses.
- Primed canvases, sizes 10" × 10" (25.5 × 25.5 cm), 11" × 14" (28 × 35.5 cm), 18" × 24" (46 × 61 cm), and any additional sizes of your choosing.
- Acrylic glass, such as Plexiglas, for use as a palette. (See tip opposite.)
- Dry rags or paper towels
- Heavy matte gel or gel medium

specialty items

These are all items I use frequently, but are not required to complete the exercises in this book. If you are considering extending your art practice, I would recommend investing in some or all of these useful items.

- Workable fixative. This spray helps to prevent pencil smudging and allows you to easily rework a piece.
- Palette knife
- T-square ruler
- Kneaded rubber eraser
- Pencil sharpener
- Spray or squeeze bottles
- Joint knife (housepainter's tool). It can be used to apply paint, create texture, and scrape off old paint from your palette to create a smooth surface.

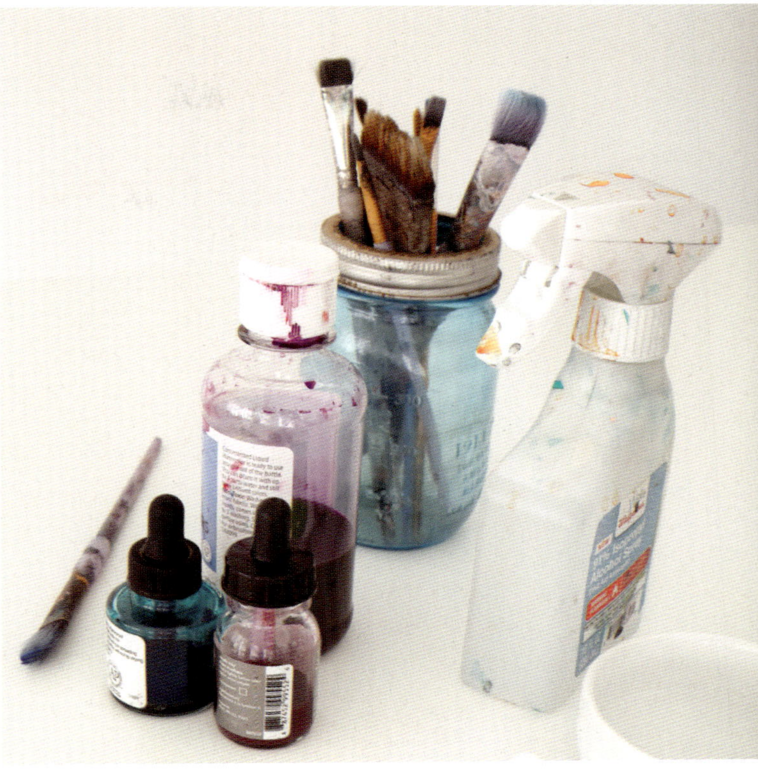

unconventional materials

Many of the following items can be found at home. Use this list as a starting point from which to develop your own set of materials.

- Sponges
- Scrub brushes
- Yarn
- Rubbing alcohol
- Spray paint
- Salt
- Straws
- Coffee/tea
- Wood stain

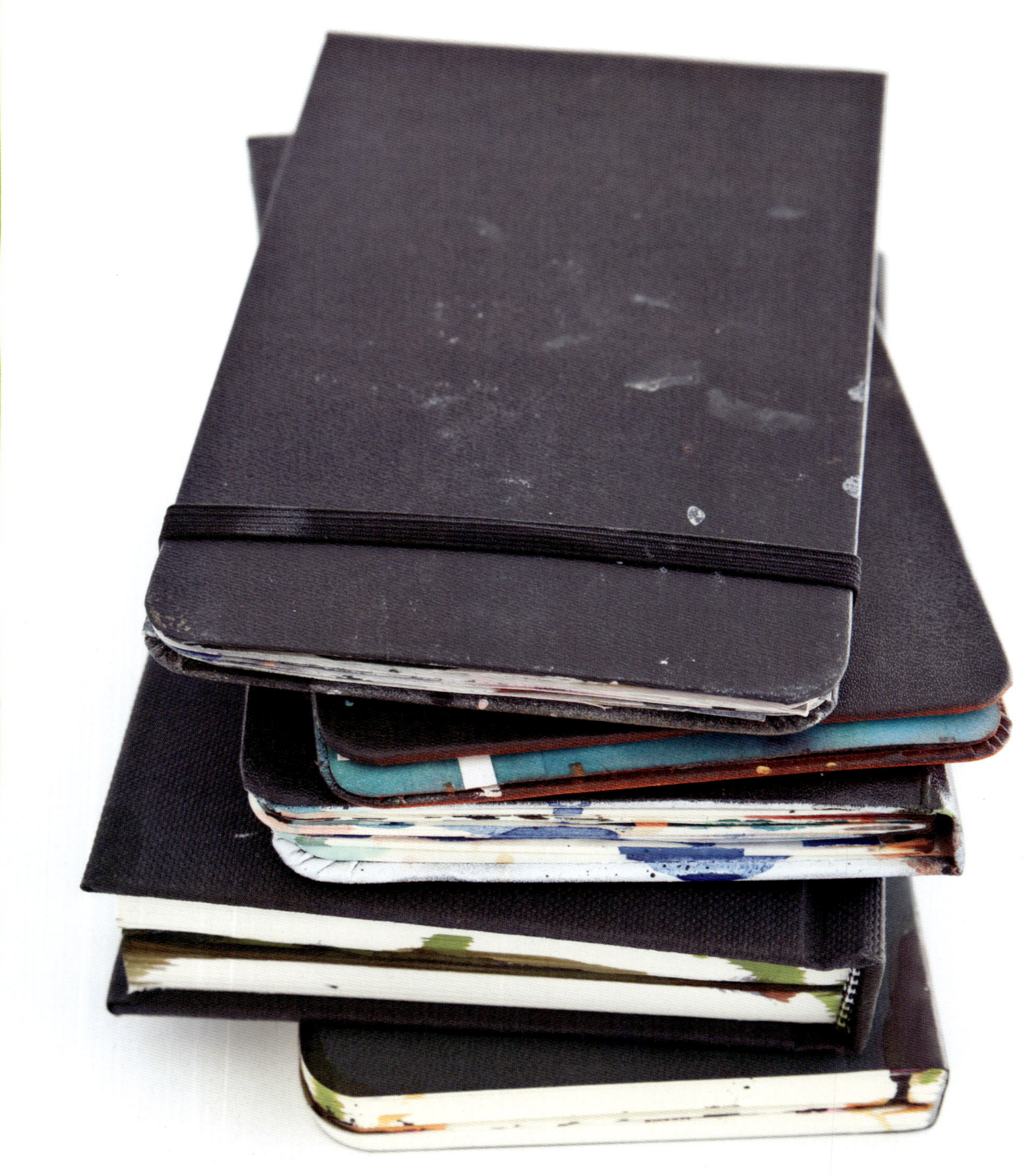

using a sketchbook

to develop your practice

The practice of keeping journals and sketchbooks is one of the main foundations on which to build your artistic life. Keeping a sketchbook centers you, focuses you, and allows you to explore your ultimate, true self, free from outside criticism and judgment. It is an essential artistic tool, whether you have just started to create or you have woven creativity into your life for many years.

Sketchbooks also provide the opportunity to be creative, even when circumstances make it challenging or prohibitive to work in a studio. My husband and I lived in Paris for a few years when we were first married. It was ironic to live in such an inspiring city with its rich artistic history and status and not have any time or even physical space to paint or create art. I was in mental overdrive to soak up as much of the culture as I could, learn the language, and essentially start a new life. Every place we traveled in France and across Europe was breathtaking. During this time, I couldn't physically paint, but I sketched all the time, constantly collecting ideas and inspiration.

I have had other times in my life when painting was simply not an option—for example, immediately after the birth of my son. As any mother knows, during those first few months to a year, you have only one all-consuming job: to be a mother. Yet, when I did have a few moments of reflective thought, I used my sketchbook as an outlet. Sketchbooks are a meaningful thread that keeps you connected to your artistic life no matter what your circumstances.

Sketchbooks are also private. Art, by definition, is to be seen, studied, and displayed—made available for all to view and have opinions and assumptions about. Yet, your sketchbook is a sanctuary—a safe place to find ideas, experiment, and reflect. A critical facet of becoming an artist is to continue to search and discover new ideas. It is important to have a concrete way to record, examine, and develop these changes.

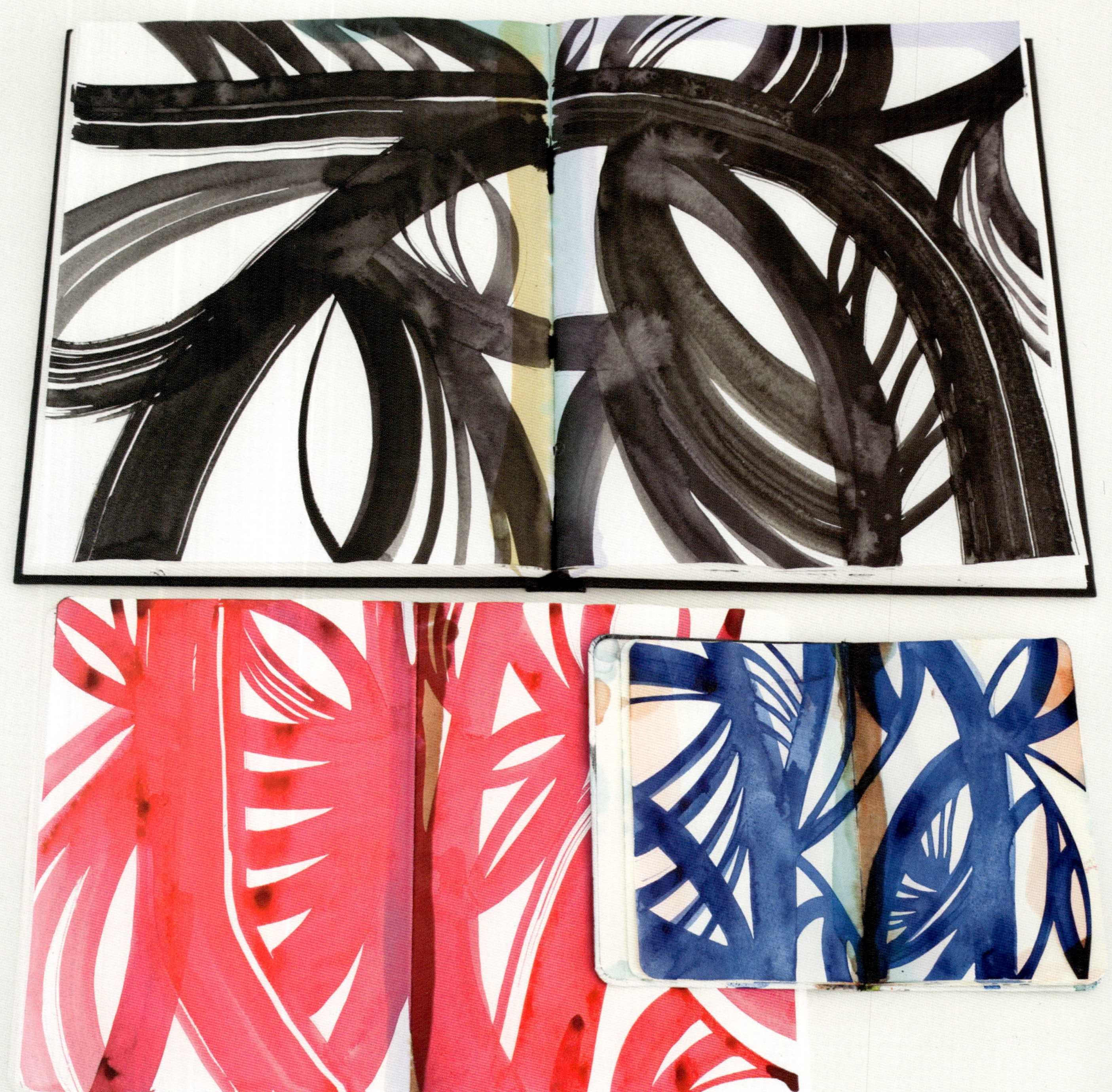

EXERCISE ONE

creative mental warmups

flex your artistic muscles with personal mark making

MATERIALS

- sketchbooks, either made of 140 lb (300 gsm) cold-press watercolor paper or mixed-media paper, in a variety of sizes
- paintbrushes, in an assortment of sizes and shapes
- ink, in two or three different colors

Some artists reserve their sketchbooks for writing and drawing. I love creating mixed-media artwork, which naturally extends to my sketchbook. For these exercises, I recommend buying a few sketchbooks of varying sizes—make sure they are made with either watercolor paper or are intended for mixed media. Make it a routine practice to do some mental, creative warm-ups using your sketchbook when you first walk into the studio or sit down to create.

prepare

→ Working in multiple sketchbooks gives you the freedom to move among ideas and execute your thoughts while they are fresh in your mind.

→ I prefer to use a book-style sketchbook, wherein the pages are sewn in signatures, as opposed to a connected by spiral binding. The connection at the binding allows you to use the entire work area as one large page rather than having a gap in the middle that clearly separates the composition.

→ Use at least three to four paintbrushes in various shapes and sizes to vary your mark making.

→ When learning more about paintbrush application and mark making, vary not only your brush sizes, but also your brush angles and the pressure that you apply. For example, flat brushes are great for making bold lines, but by just turning your wrist slightly, you can create a totally new and more delicate line.

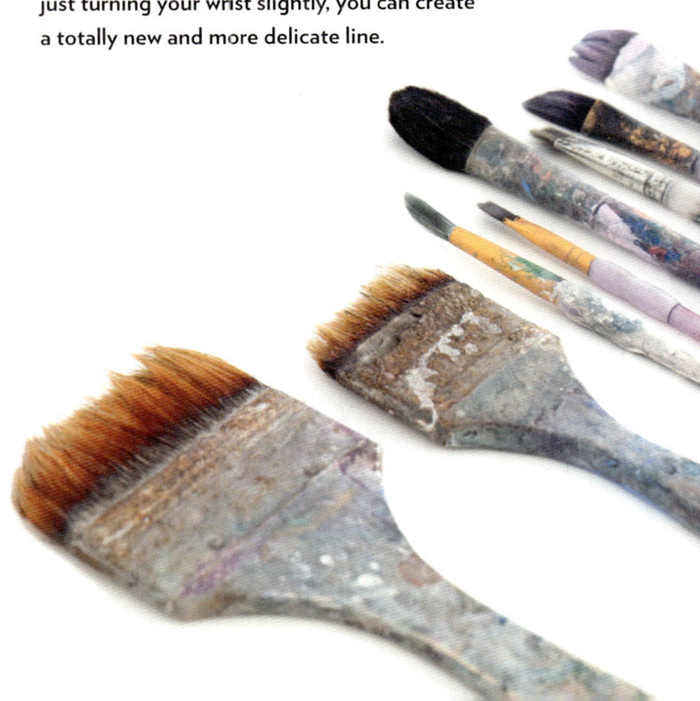

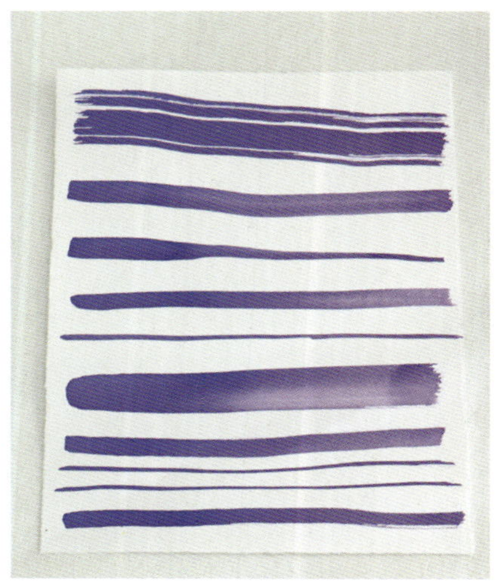

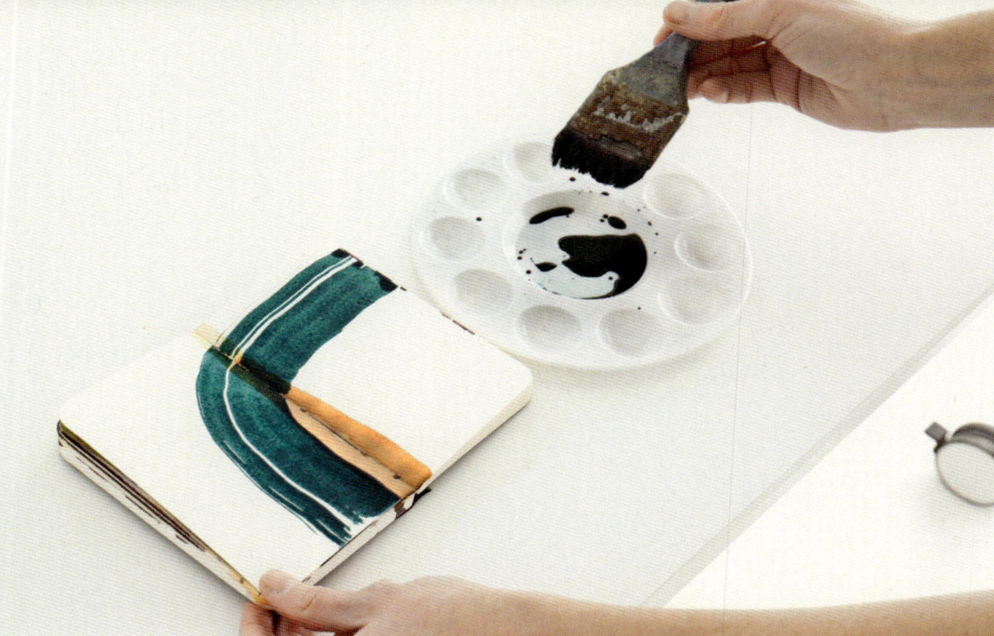

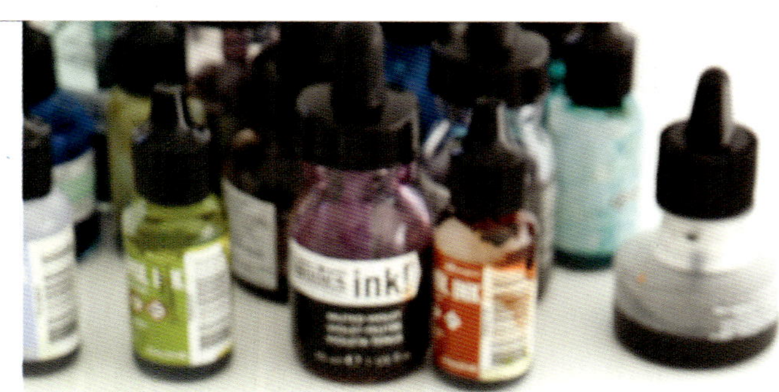

- For making a clean, saturated line, load up your brush with plenty of ink. This practice is called having "a loaded brush."
- For this first exercise, I recommend using just one or two colors to avoid getting bogged down and visually stumped on color, texture, and contrast.

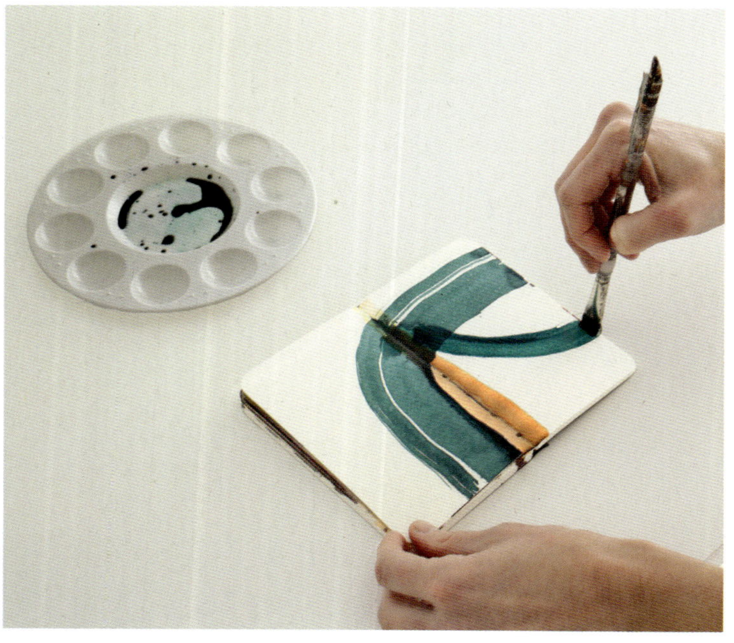

create

Start with one ink, creating lines, shapes, and marks. Ink is enjoyable to work with because it is so fluid, which makes forming different lines and forms fast and easy.

This is a no-judgment exercise. All you have to do is make the first mark to get started. Use the first mark to decide how to make the second and so on. Vary your lines using different paintbrushes and changing your directions of movement. I tend to mimic shapes and marks found in nature, but you will find your own sources of inspiration. Do this exercise multiple times using different themes for inspiration, such as architecture, the human figure, patterns, interiors, and so on.

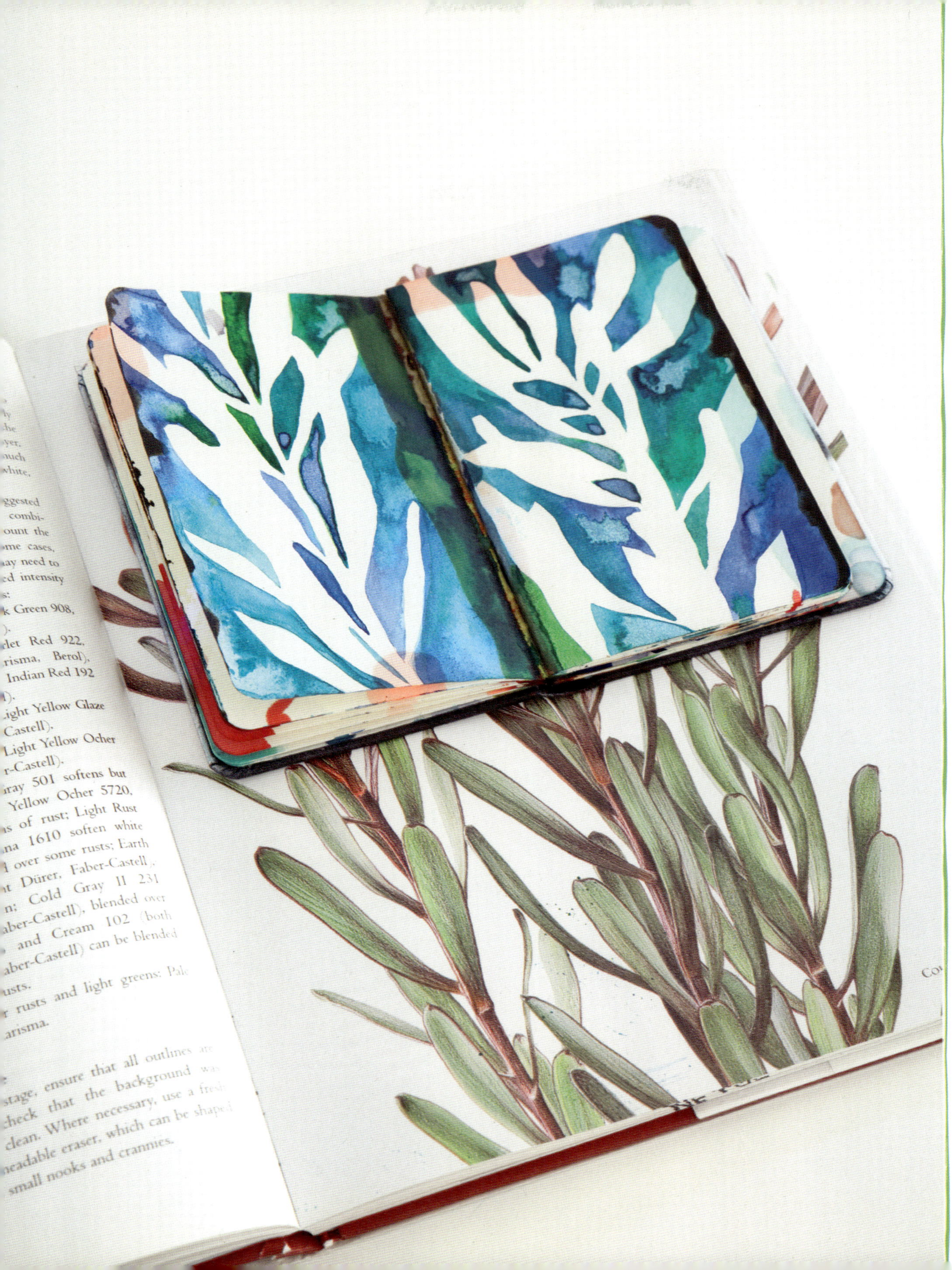

ly
the
oyer,
such
white,

ggested
combi-
ount the
me cases,
ay need to
ed intensity
s:
k Green 908,
).
rlet Red 922,
risma, Berol),
Indian Red 192
).
Light Yellow Glaze
Castell).
Light Yellow Ocher
r-Castell).
ray 501 softens but
Yellow Ocher 5720,
s of rust; Light Rust
na 1610 soften white
l over some rusts; Earth
t Dürer, Faber-Castell),
n; Cold Gray II 231
aber-Castell), blended over
and Cream 102 (both
aber-Castell) can be blended
usts.
r rusts and light greens: Pale
arisma.

stage, ensure that all outlines are
check that the background was
clean. Where necessary, use a fresh
neadable eraser, which can be shaped
small nooks and crannies.

EXERCISE TWO

using the sketchbook to achieve focus

collecting, arranging, and reflecting on inspirational images

A sketchbook is also a great place to save pictures, words, colors, and ideas that you find inspirational. During the course of the day or week, you hear, encounter, and experience things that you find exciting or noteworthy, yet you may not be able to fully reflect on or digest them at the time. A sketchbook is a perfect and safe place to store all these words, images, colors, and thoughts for future examination.

Even though art is primarily visual, words are an enormous influence in one's work. Whether you jot down a dream or a song lyric or simply write in a stream of consciousness, you can start to piece together and find cohesion across your interests. Magazines are another great source of inspiration, as they typically stay current with ever-changing trends that you can use to inspire or experiment with in your own work. And you can cut up images in them for your sketchbook.

MATERIALS

medium or large sketchbook

magazine clippings, color samples, old photos, or similar items

paintbrushes, in a variety of sizes and shapes

prepare

→ For this exercise, collect several items of paper ephemera such as magazine clippings, color samples, old photos, or simply an assortment of words and thoughts.

→ Dedicate one side of an open sketchbook and arrange them in a way that makes sense to you. In doing this, you can start to mentally and visually organize yourself in preparation for creating a larger piece of work.

→ Use the facing page to organize and decipher what these images mean to you. You can create color palettes or make marks, simple contour shapes, and other gestures that are your interpretations of these items.

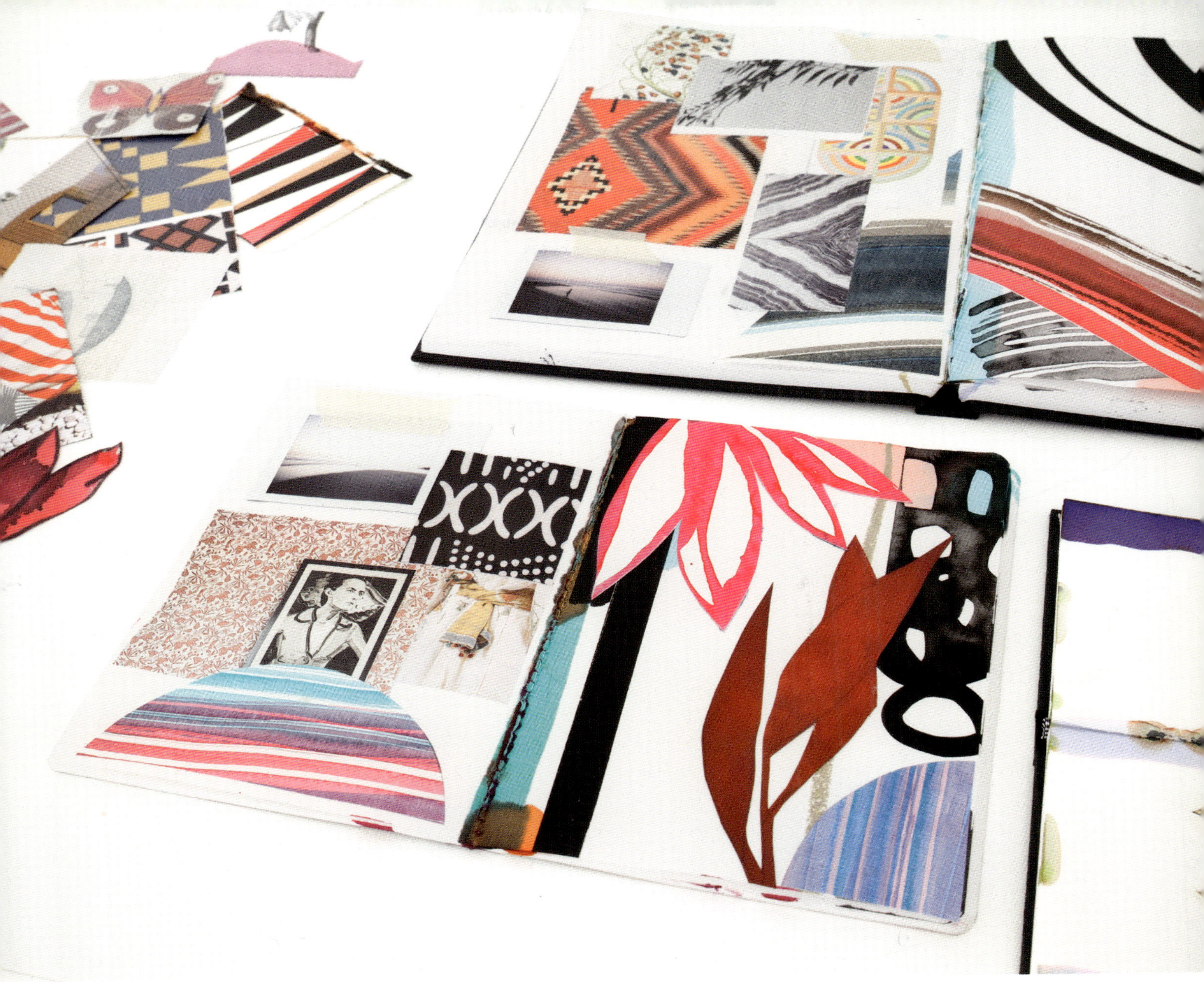

→ **Make notes and jot down words and/or phrases that accompany the images you are creating and that you would like to reflect upon further.**

This practice is a great way to keep ideas fresh, evolving, and personal. It gives you the power to generate your own inspiration, rather than relying on an outside source to create that spark. It can be reassuring to know that your ideas have been inside you the whole time.

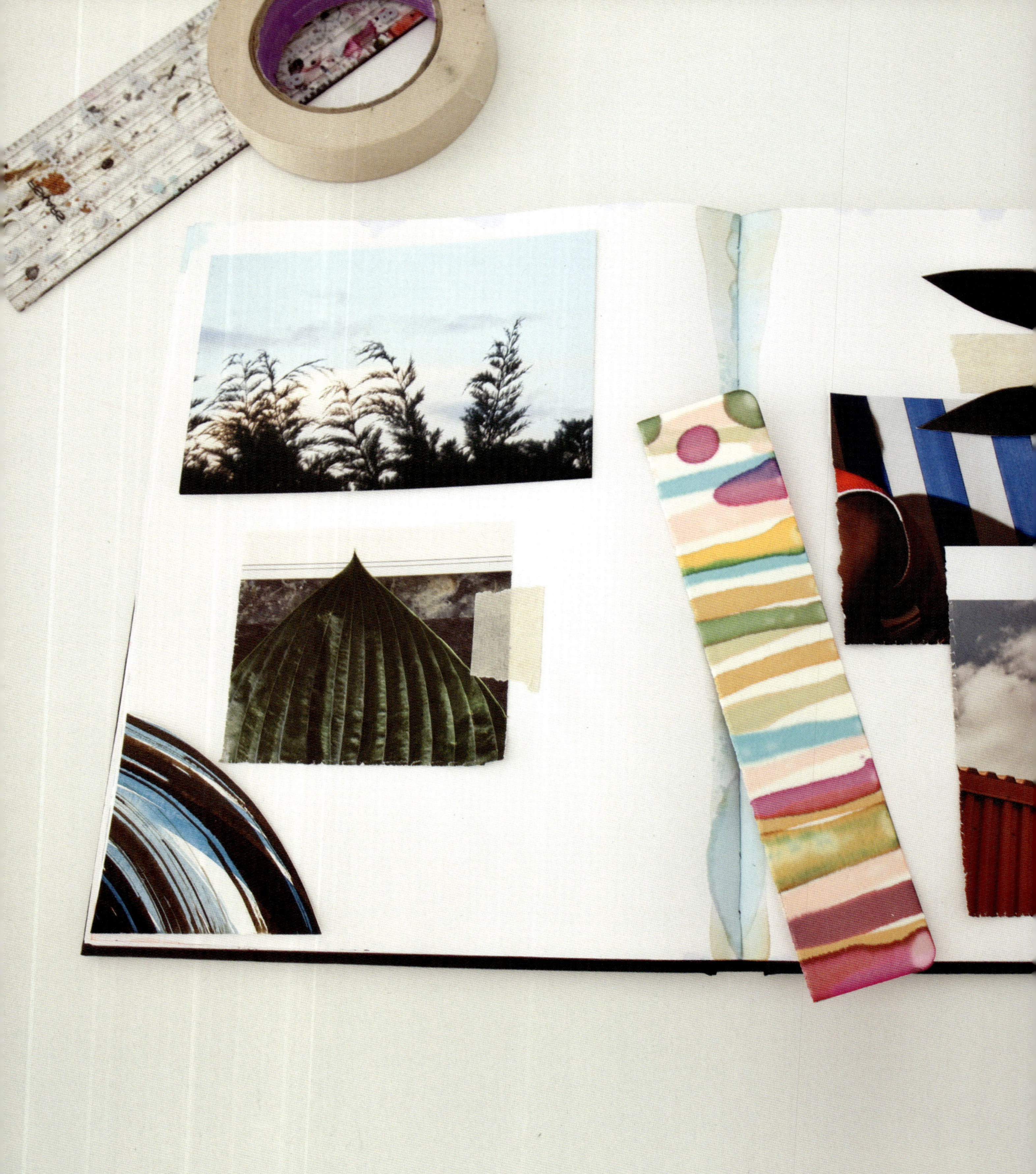

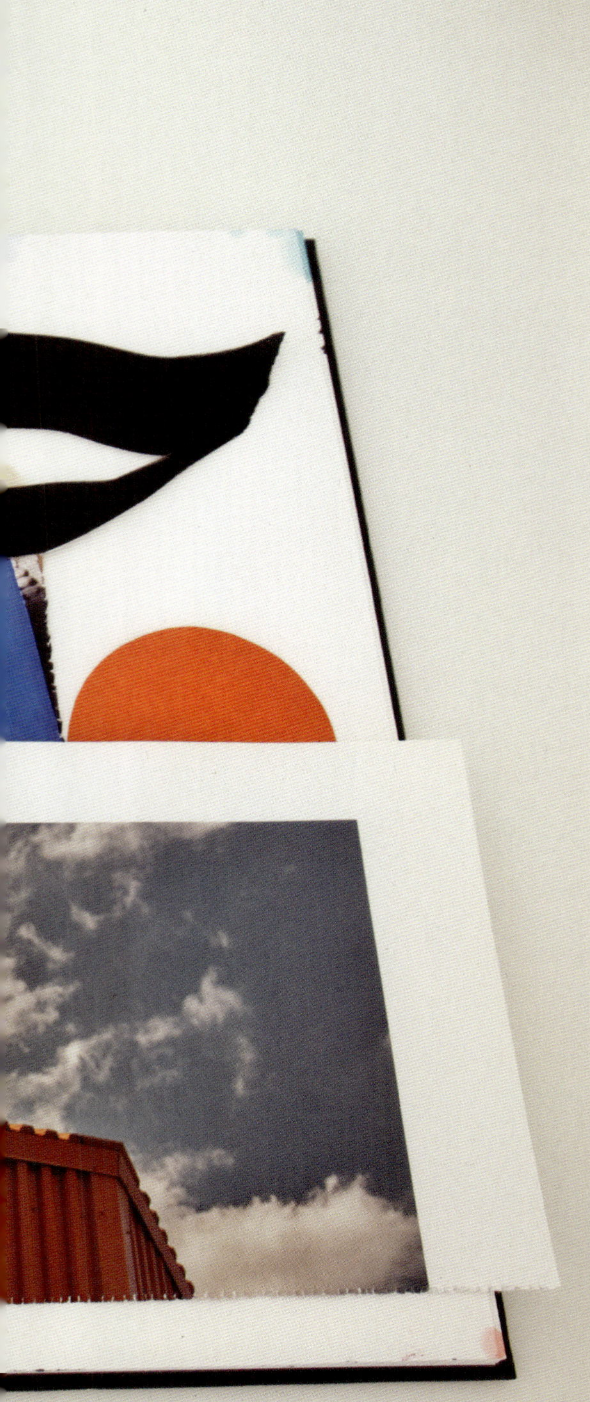

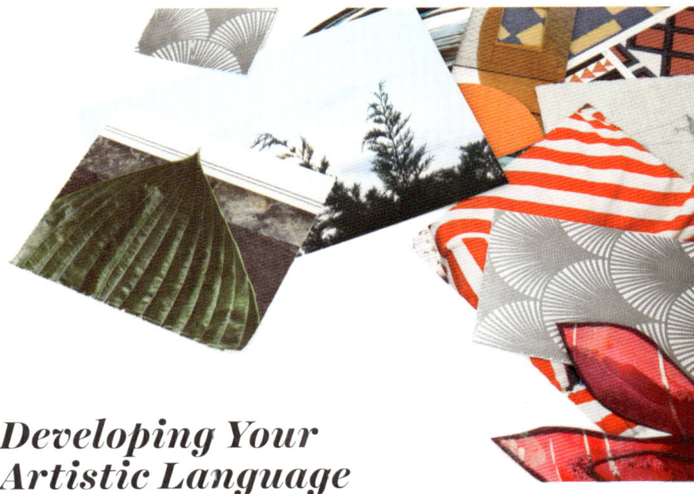

Developing Your Artistic Language

A significant, artistic developmental stage in my life was my move to France in 2007 with my then fiancé (now husband). During this time, I studied the French language and absorbed as much of the beauty and culture of the country as I could. I was overwhelmed with how much inspiration was around me. From the people, countryside, and architecture to the food and museums, everything was fascinating.

I paused from painting during this time and instead resorted to my sketchbook as my place for quiet, artistic reflection. It was the sketchbook in which I was able to sort through new ideas, colors, and concepts. This is why a journal or sketchbook should be an important tool for an artist. You never know where you're going to be when inspiration strikes. Ideas and images can be jotted down and captured in the moment and referred to later.

Even though at the time I was not making larger, more substantial pieces of art, I was gathering ideas and inspiration from the routine of daily life to incorporate into art later. I was organizing and recording all that was happening externally to be understood and evaluated internally. I was cultivating the practice of creating a personal artistic language. What is most important about finding your own artistic language is to make sure it comes from your own self. Outside voices, experience, and visuals influence you constantly, but it is how you internalize and decipher them that allows your own artistic voice to develop.

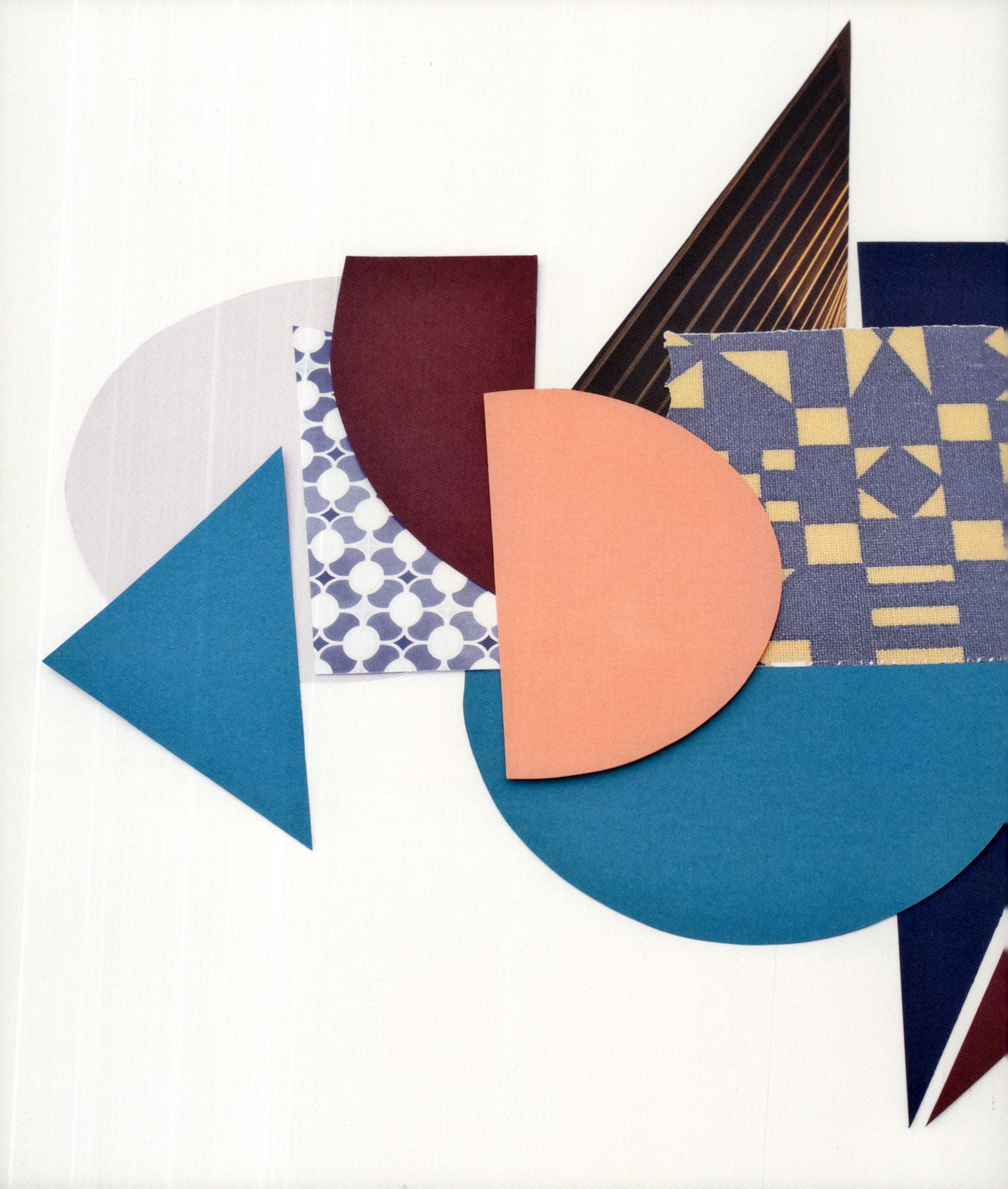

CHAPTER TWO

FOUNDATIONS OF DESIGN

"The negative is just as important as the positive."

—ELLSWORTH KELLY

Fine artists should always be aware of the foundation of good design. The five core principles of design are balance, proportion, rhythm, emphasis, and unity. Certain art disciplines, such as graphic design, require a more literal approach to these principles in order to convey their message. However, artists working with abstract work often attempt to do much more than just relay certain information.

Sometimes we wish to evoke emotion, trigger memories, tell a story, or even raise questions and express opinions. It is important to respect the five principles of design; however, it is more important to respect your own artistic aims. With this in mind, the five elements should serve more as a basic guide, but should in no way hinder or constrict your vision.

the five principles **of design**

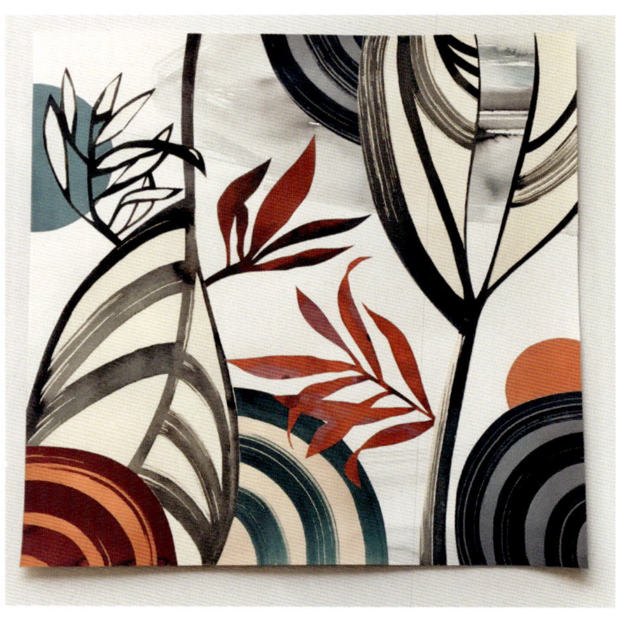

1. BALANCE

Balance in art refers to using symmetrical elements (forms of equal weight on either side of a central point) or asymmetrical elements (shapes and forms are uneven, but still balanced in terms of their visual weight). Finding this balance can be a challenge when painting, but the more you experiment and practice, the easier it will be to get the "feel" of what balance means.

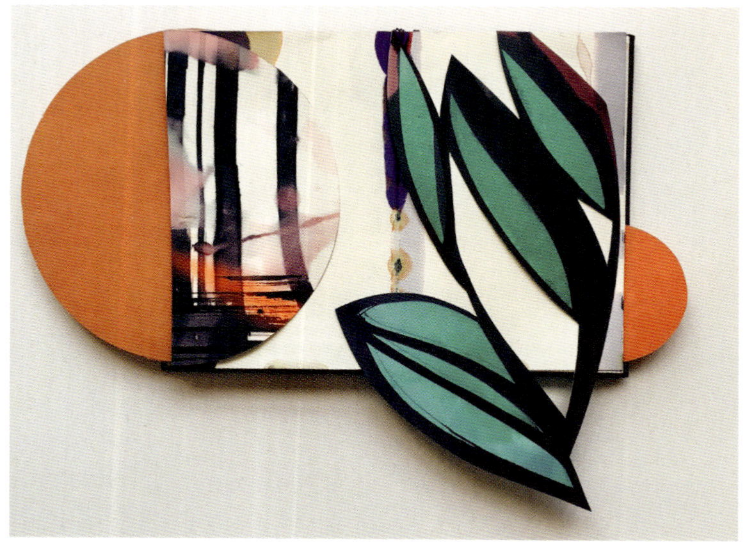

2. PROPORTION

Proportion has to do with the size and scale of the various elements in a painting. Each element is in relation to the other and also with the whole. These different elements should not fight each other for importance. If they are, the overall message and composition of a piece will be confusing and unclear.

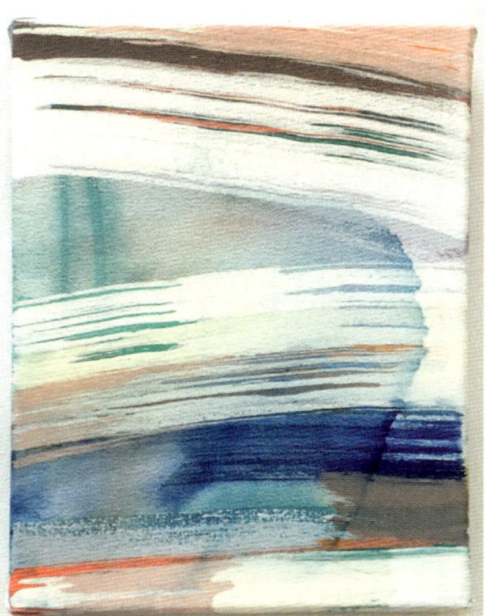

3. RHYTHM

Rhythm in a painting is defined as creating certain marks, colors, lines, or shapes in a continuous and repeating manner—in other words, a pattern. Repetition and pattern help to move the viewer's eye around a painting in an easy and fluid fashion. They act as facilitators to guide the eye to components you want to emphasize and to encourage movement, interest, flow, and overall unity.

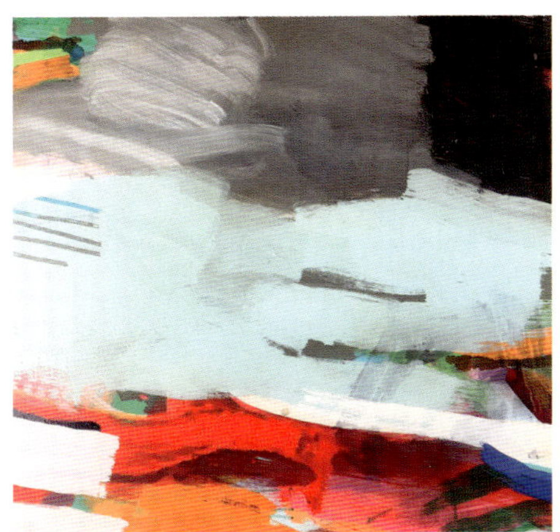

4. EMPHASIS

Emphasis has to do with finding your focal point or what you wish to have the viewer most drawn to (see Exercise 14 on page 89). It is about what element you choose to be dominant. You can create emphasis in a variety of ways: increasing an object's color intensity, darkening or lightening contrast, through the use of converging lines, or even isolating the object you would like to carry the most weight.

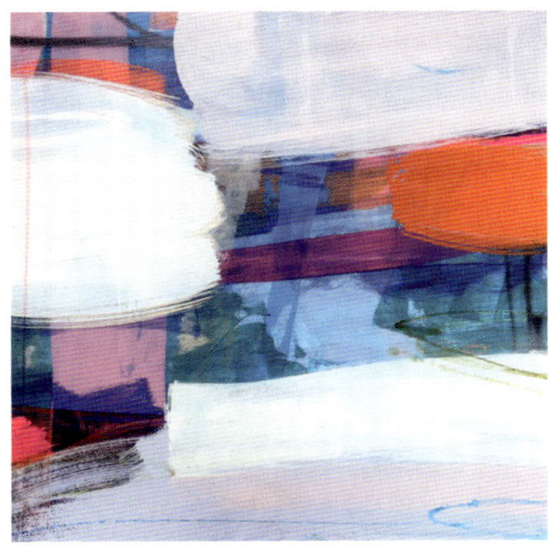

5. UNITY

Creating unity in art is often based more on a sense than a strict set of rules. It has to do with resolving any conflicting elements and making the overall work come together in harmony. Unity happens when the work has a sense of completion and every element serves its purpose in relation to all the others.

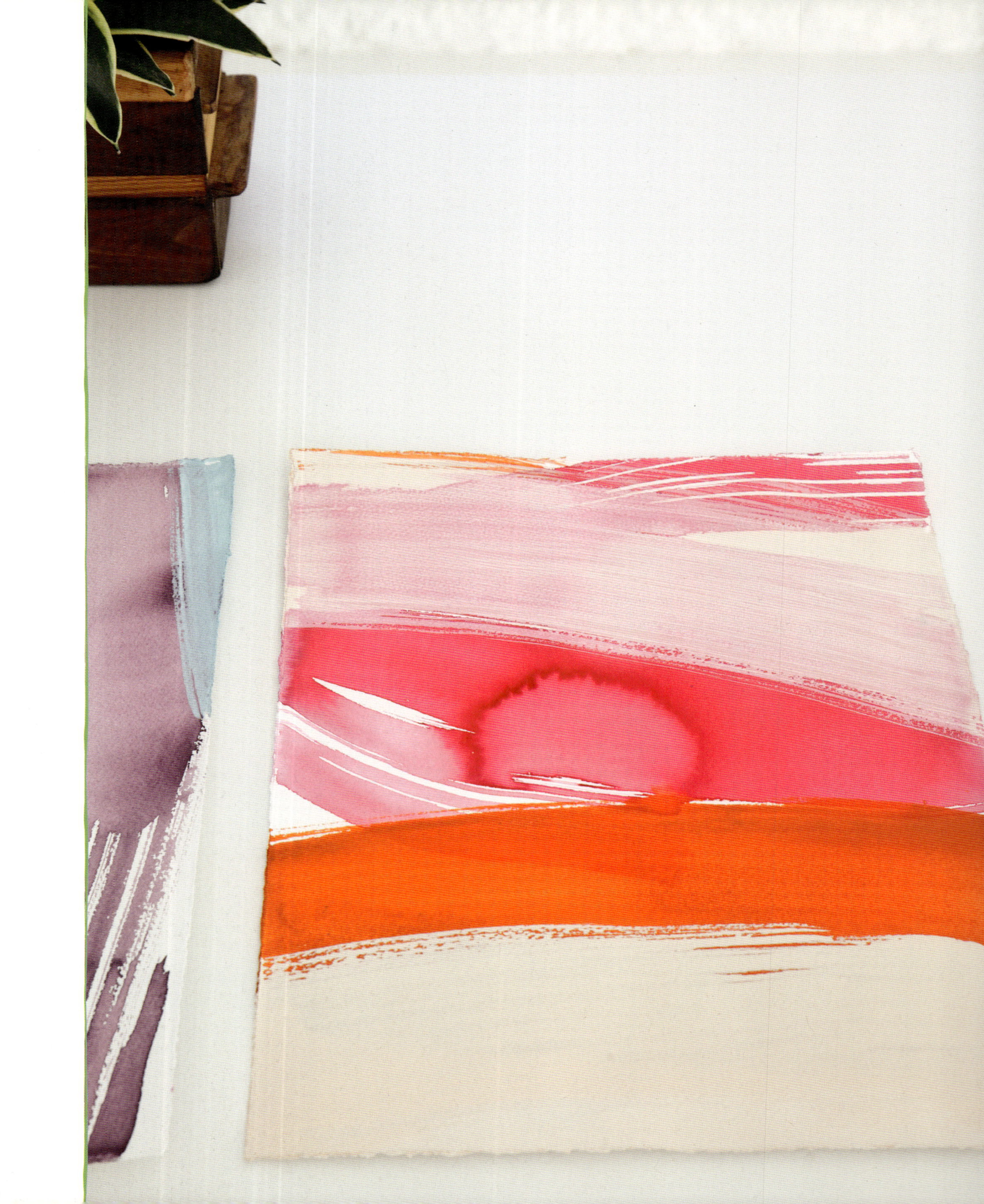

EXERCISE THREE

color wash paintings

understanding size, shape, and color

MATERIALS

- mixed-media paper or canvas (up to 11" × 14" [28 × 35.5 cm])
- three colors of acrylic paint or ink with varying chroma (See sidebar on page 34.)
- round and flat paintbrushes, in a variety of sizes
- 1"–4" (2.5–10 cm) chip brushes

Size, shape, and color are key components of design and play a major role when creating an abstract painting. They each effect the others, and although they are important individually, they need to work as a cohesive whole.

When first starting, it can be a bit overwhelming to create a painting while trying to manage these three elements. Therefore, in this exercise, we will break this process down into steps and set limitations on the color palette. Having fewer options helps us start to understand how these principles work together. As the process becomes more intuitive, you can begin to add more and more color.

prepare

→ **Start with either mixed-media paper or a primed canvas. Keep your working surface small—between 10" × 10" (25.5 × 25.5 cm) and 11" × 14" (28 × 35.5 cm) is perfect.**

→ **Before you begin, create a few color samples using only your three color choices on small scraps of paper. This will allow you to see how the colors work together. Also, make sure the color tests dry completely before you make your choices, as paint colors can look quite different when wet.**

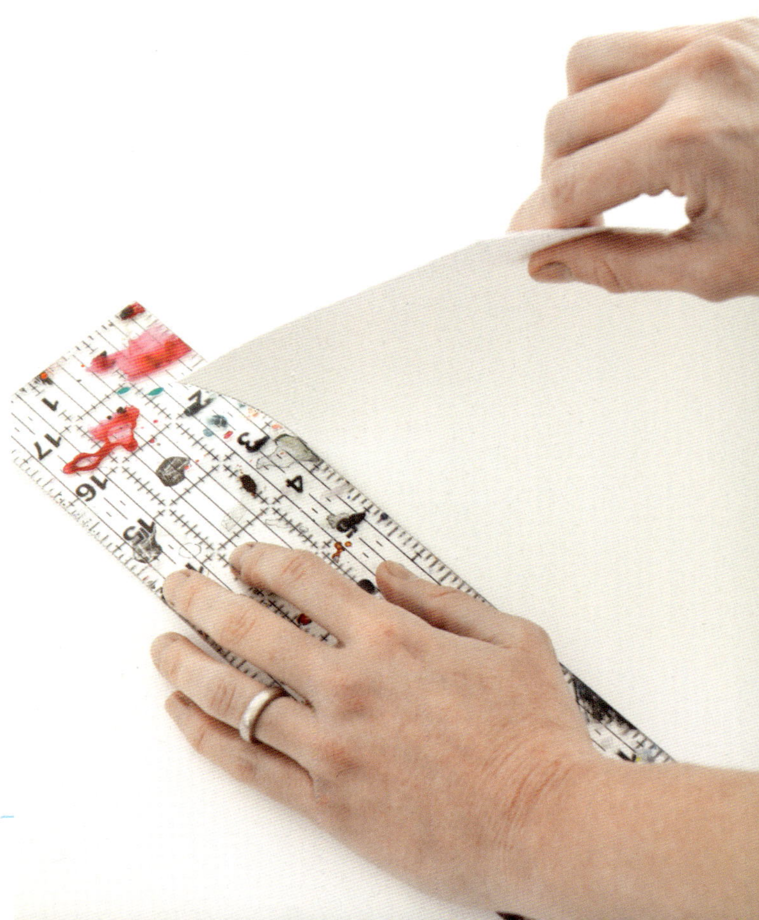

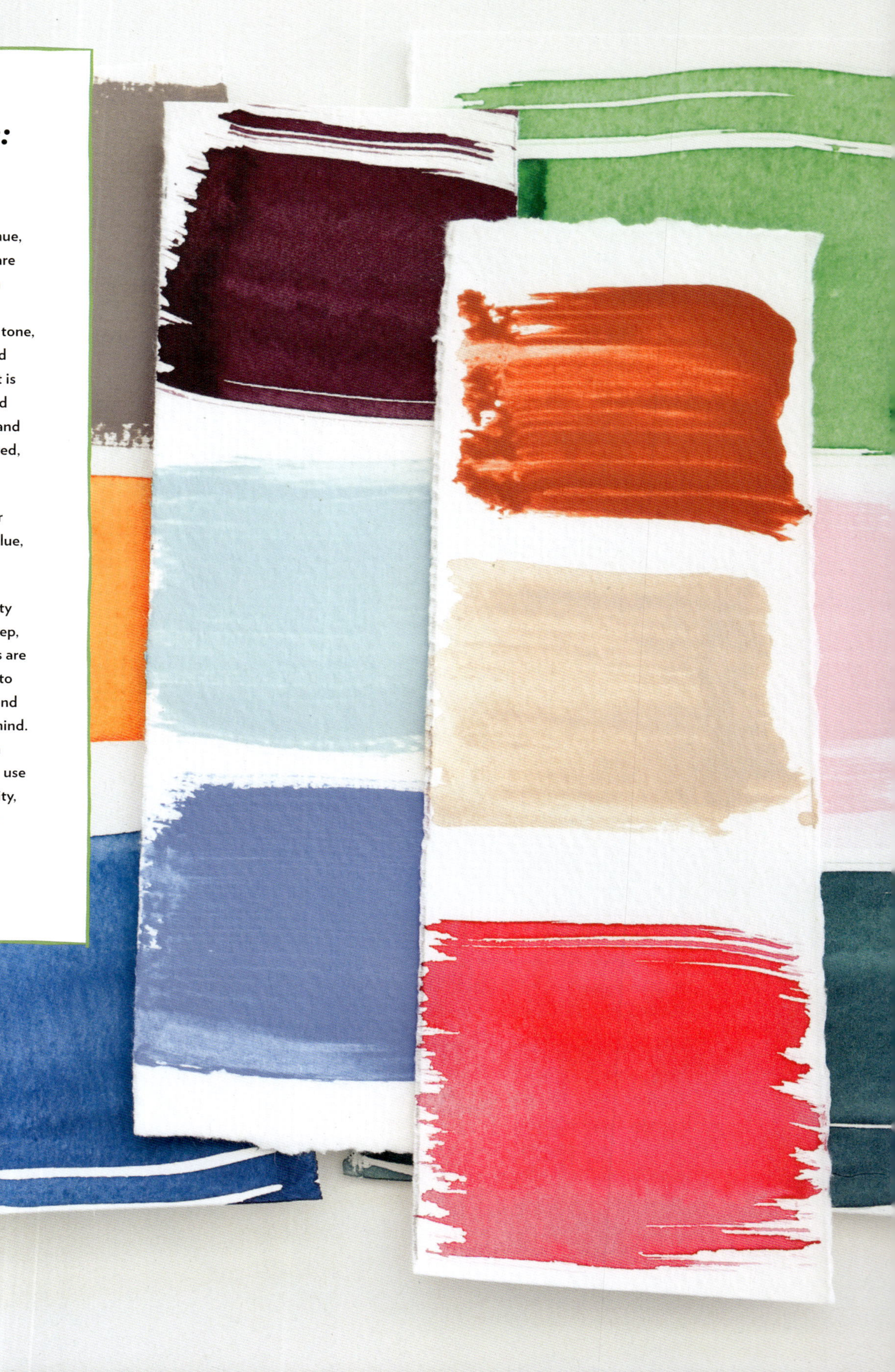

Material Considerations: What Is Color Chroma?

Colors have three characteristics: hue, value, and chroma. Hue and color are often used interchangeably among artists and designers. Yet color is a general term used to describe tint, tone, and shade. Hue is more specific and refers to a dominant color family. It is connected to the origin of color and stems from one of the six primary and secondary colors—yellow, orange, red, violet, blue, and green.

Value refers to a color's lightness or darkness. White has the lightest value, and black has the darkest.

Chroma is the saturation or intensity of the color. Some colors have a deep, rich pigment saturation, and others are brighter and appear less saturated to the eye. When considering colors and how to use them, keep chroma in mind. You will want to select colors with a range of chroma. If every color you use has the same saturation and intensity, your painting can look flat and lose visual interest.

- Gather round and flat brushes in an assortment of shapes and sizes. My go-to brushes are a size 10 pointed round, a size 8 or 10 flat, and a 6 or 8 filbert. Having several sizes and shapes will allow for more variation in your forms and mark making.

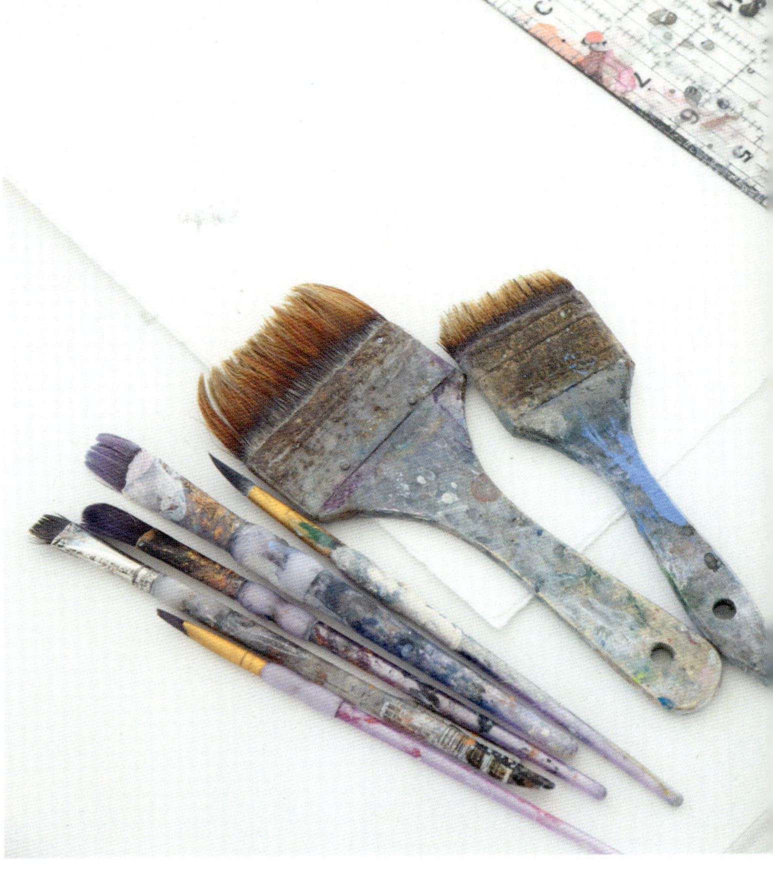

create

Paint the largest shape first with your largest brush. This works as an anchor for the piece and provides an initial base element that you can work from as the painting evolves.

Change brush size and begin to add the second color and shape. Vary the way in which you create this shape and apply the paint. You can use many methods to apply paint to the surface. This exercise will illustrate two different approaches.

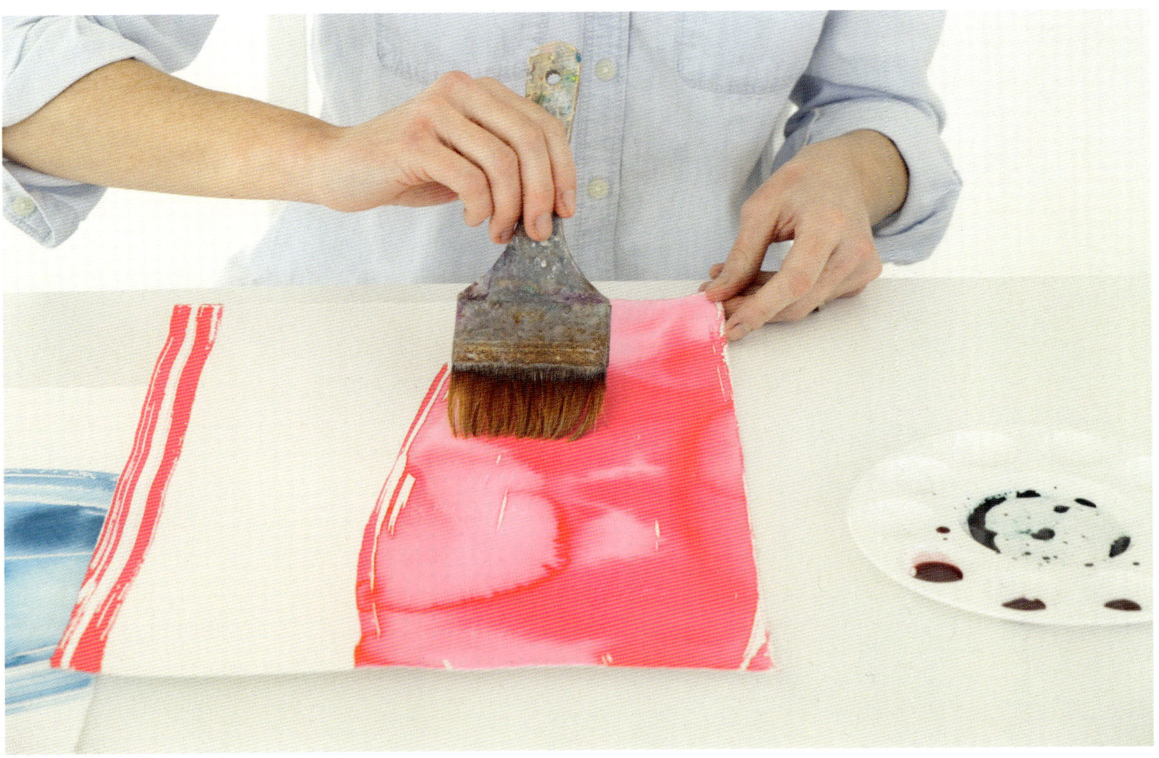

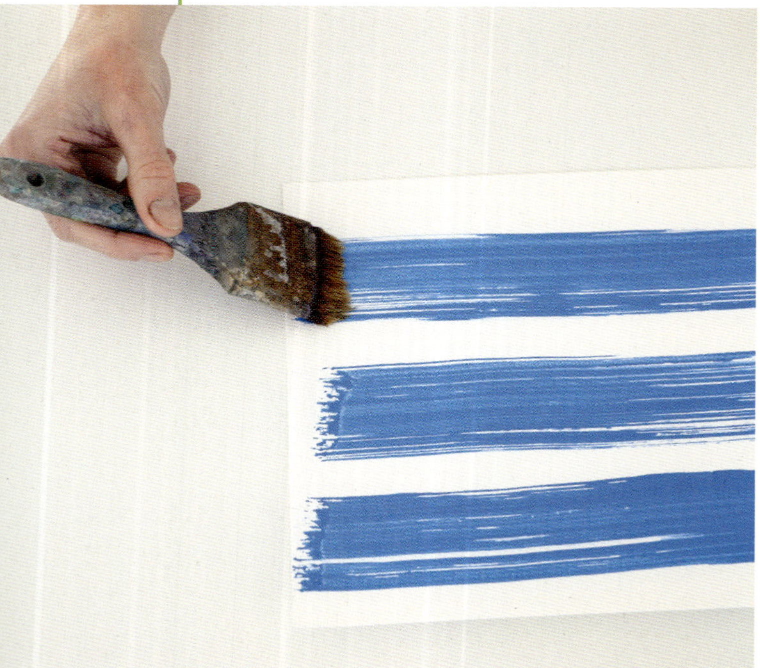

TIP ▸ When painting, keep more than one clean water container for your brushes. This helps keep your process smoother by not having to stop to clean water and brushes.

1. **CREATE A WASH.** Watering down the paint can help you to create more free-flowing, organic shapes and forms. It's easier to move your paintbrush more fluidly across the surface when paint is thinner. Using this method, you can also build up layers and a feeling of movement in your work.
2. **PULL THE PAINT.** Using your first color, drag the brush across the surface while holding it at a 45-degree angle to make a stronger, architectural-type mark. Both of these methods also change the texture of the painting. Varying textures create visual interest.
3. **SWITCH TO A DIFFERENT SIZE PAINTBRUSH.** Apply your next color selection. Once again, be sure to adjust the size and method in which you apply the paint. As you add shapes and color, it is important to stay sensitive to the negative space. (See sidebar opposite.)
4. **ONCE YOUR PAINT IS DRY, REPEAT THESE STEPS.** Layer and adjust your shape and its size using the third color. By repeating the steps, you can build from your previous marks and begin to see how these three elements work together.

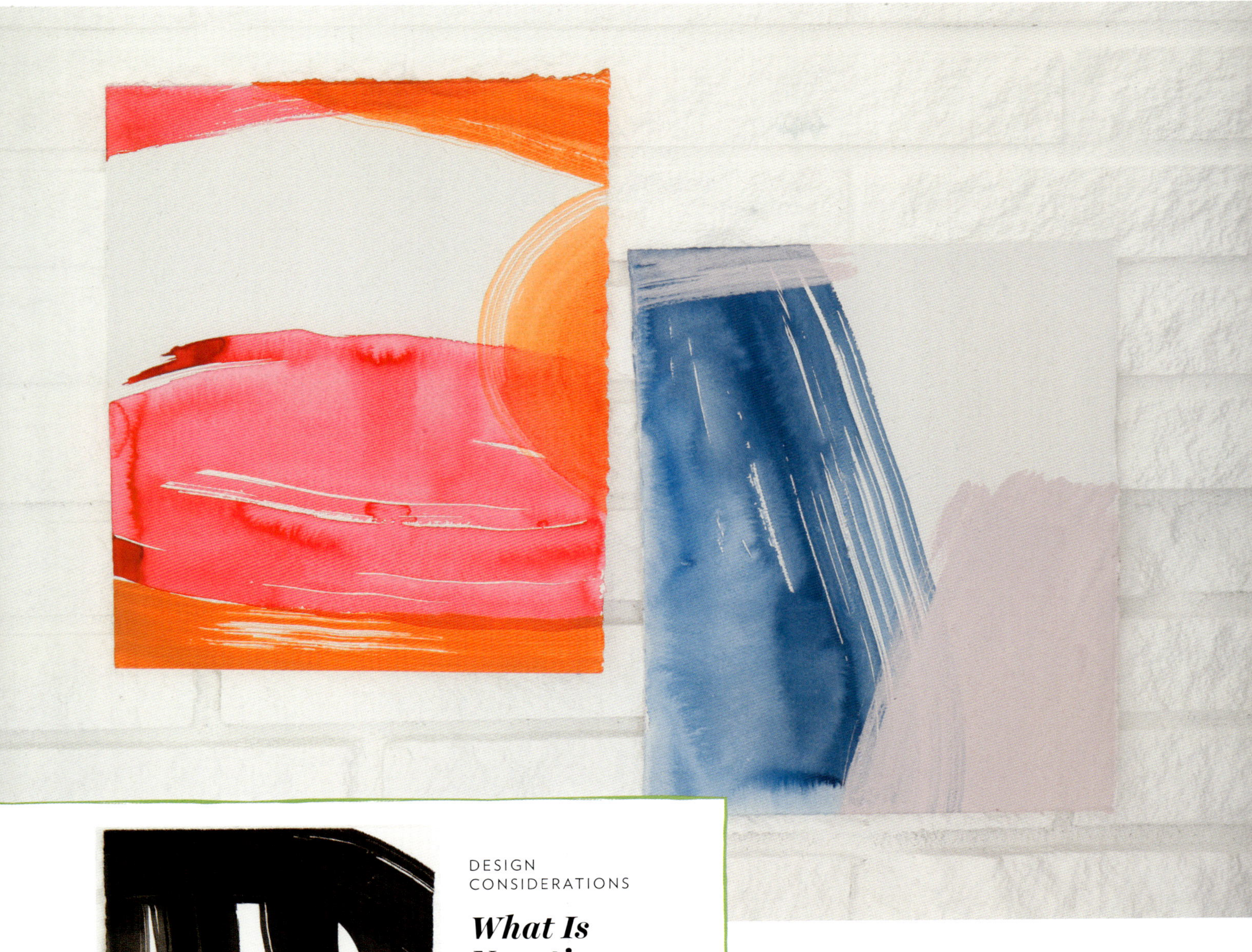

DESIGN CONSIDERATIONS

What Is Negative Space?

Negative space is the area around and between the elements of an image. These spaces can also form interesting and relevant shapes as your work progresses.

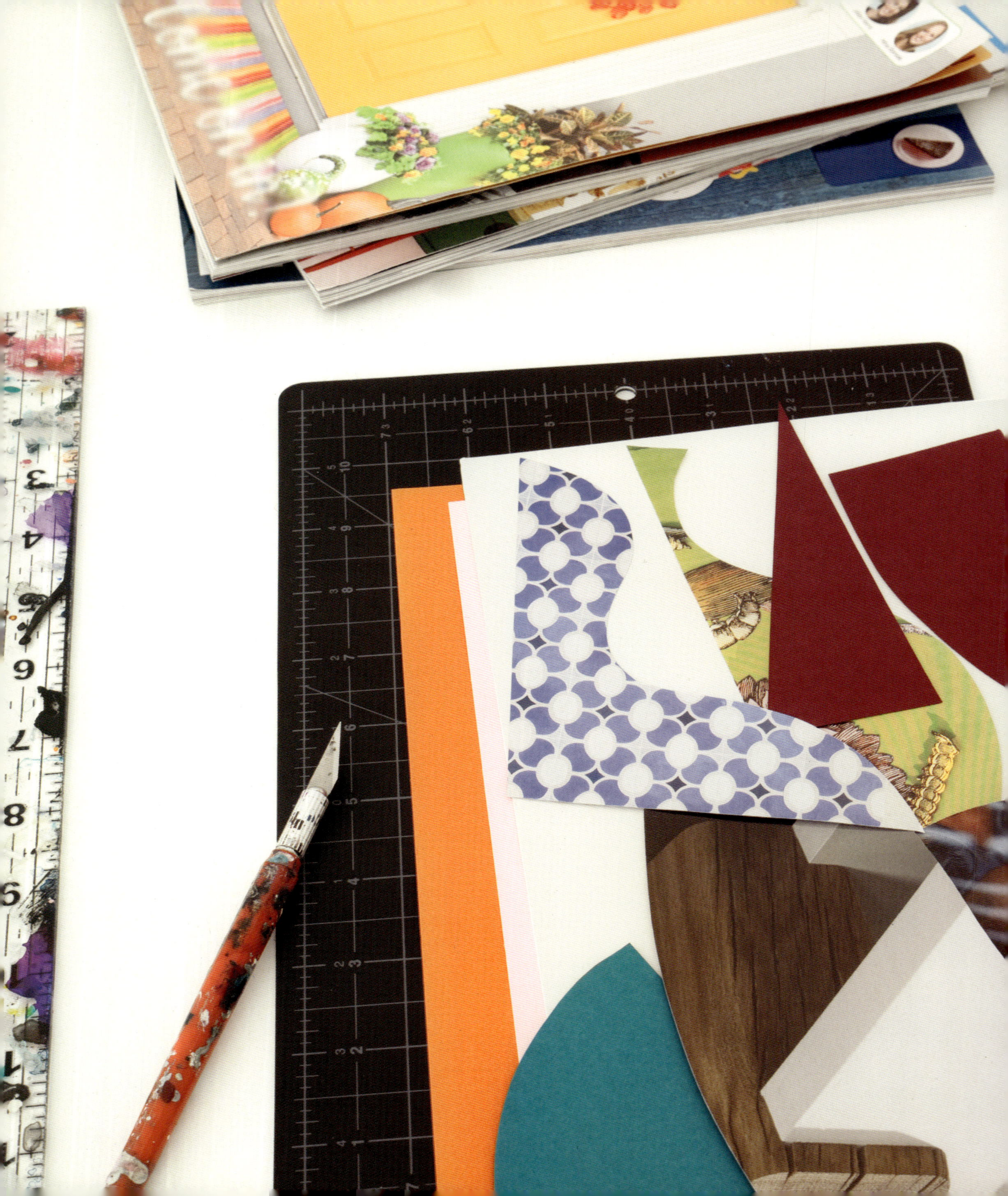

EXERCISE FOUR

the five key elements to good design

putting principles into practice with paper

MATERIALS

- six to eight different pieces of colored paper
- several old magazines that will be the source of images, patterns, and colors
- craft knife or scissors

It can be intimidating to incorporate all five principles of design (see page 30) at once in a painting. As a starting point, you'll work with colored paper and magazine cutouts to organize your thoughts and composition. Using paper will eliminate some of the pressure that can be associated with painting. This practice will allow you to focus on the overall design quality without being distracted by the physicality of paint.

prepare

→ Cut your colored paper pieces into different shapes and sizes. Be sure to make some more curved and organic and others straighter and more geometric.

→ Look through the magazines and tear out several different patterns, angles, colors, and items that you find interesting. Cut these into different shapes and sizes as you did with the paper.

→ I often write and use words in my journals and sketchbooks, but feel words can be distracting and too literal in a piece of artwork. However, feel free to consider whether using text will work for you.

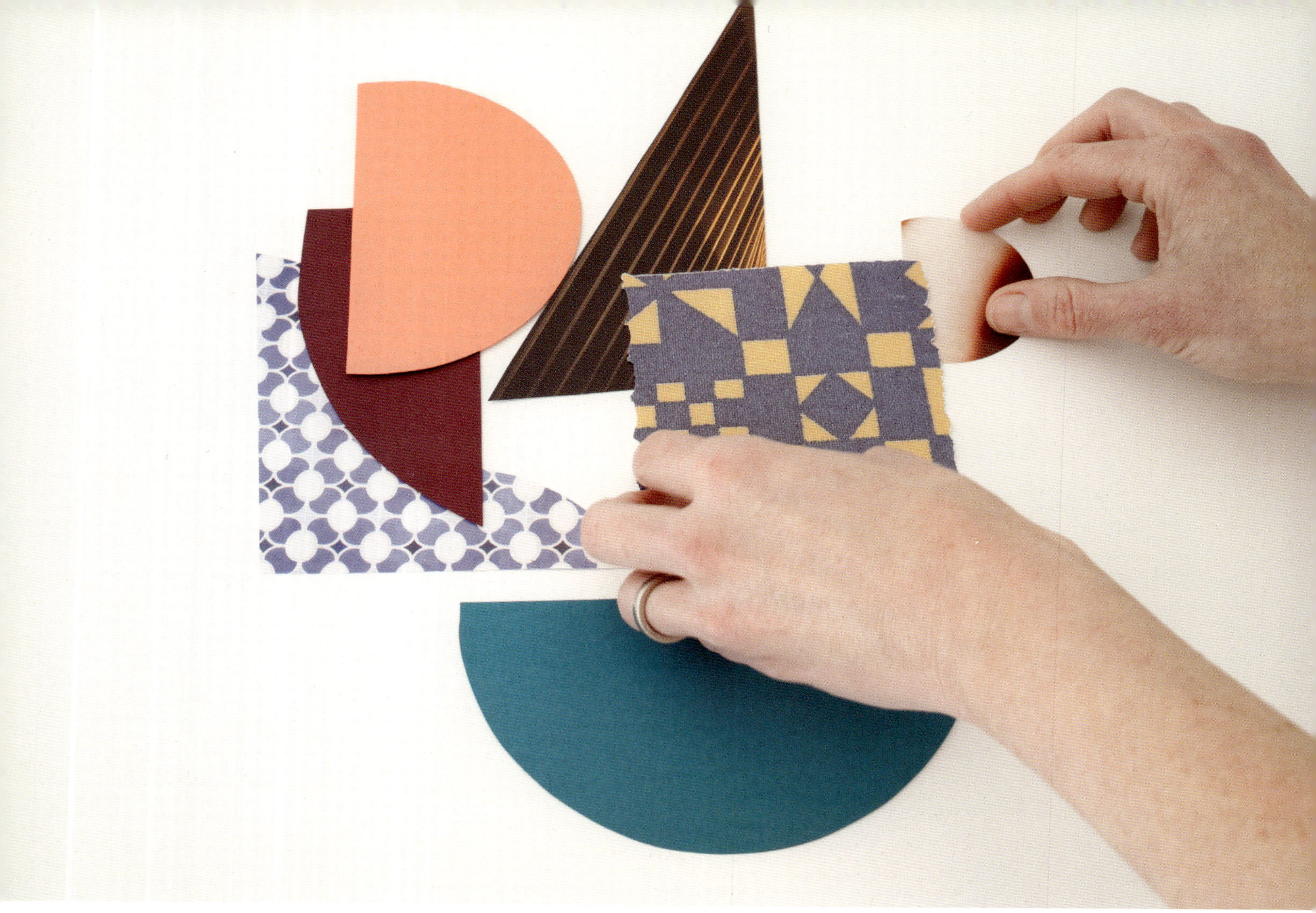

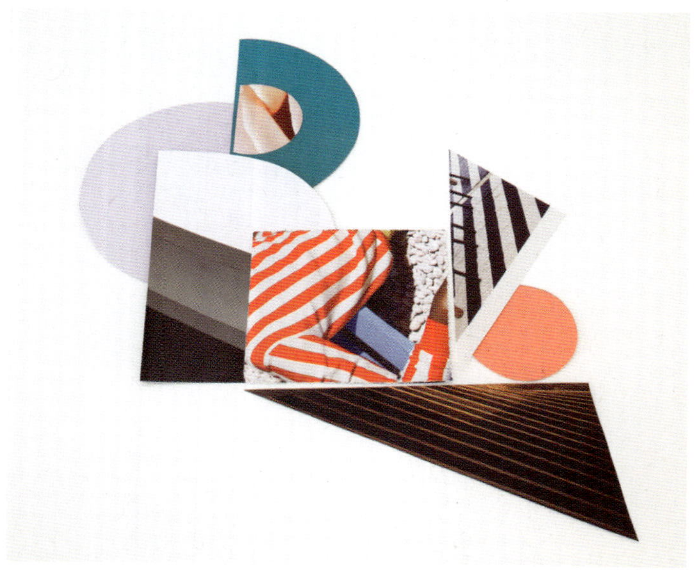

create

→ On a clear surface, arrange your papers to develop your composition. Feel free to overlap them or continue to cut or manipulate them further as your composition develops.

→ As you work, keep in mind the five design principles discussed earlier.

As the final design begins to take shape, ask yourself these questions:

1. **Is it balanced?**
2. **Can you focus on the entire work easily, or does the eye begin to slide off to one side or the other?**
3. **Do the proportions make sense? Are objects varied in size and shape while still relating clearly to one another?**
4. **Could you create some interesting patterns and repeating shapes with the magazine images?**
5. **Were you able to create a focal point, and is your eye drawn to one area in particular?**
6. **Last, does the piece have a sense of overall unity?**

As you ask yourself these questions, continue to move and adjust the papers until you feel you have achieved these goals.

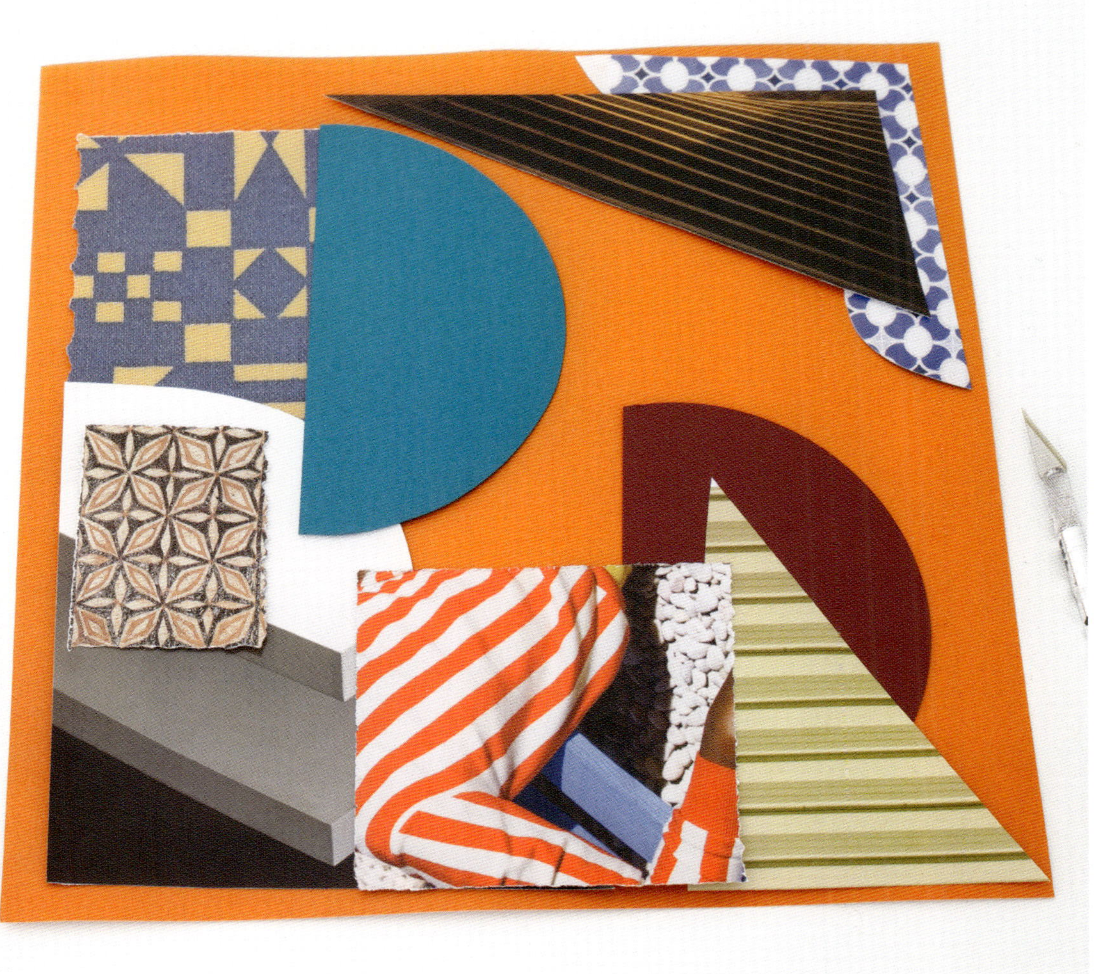

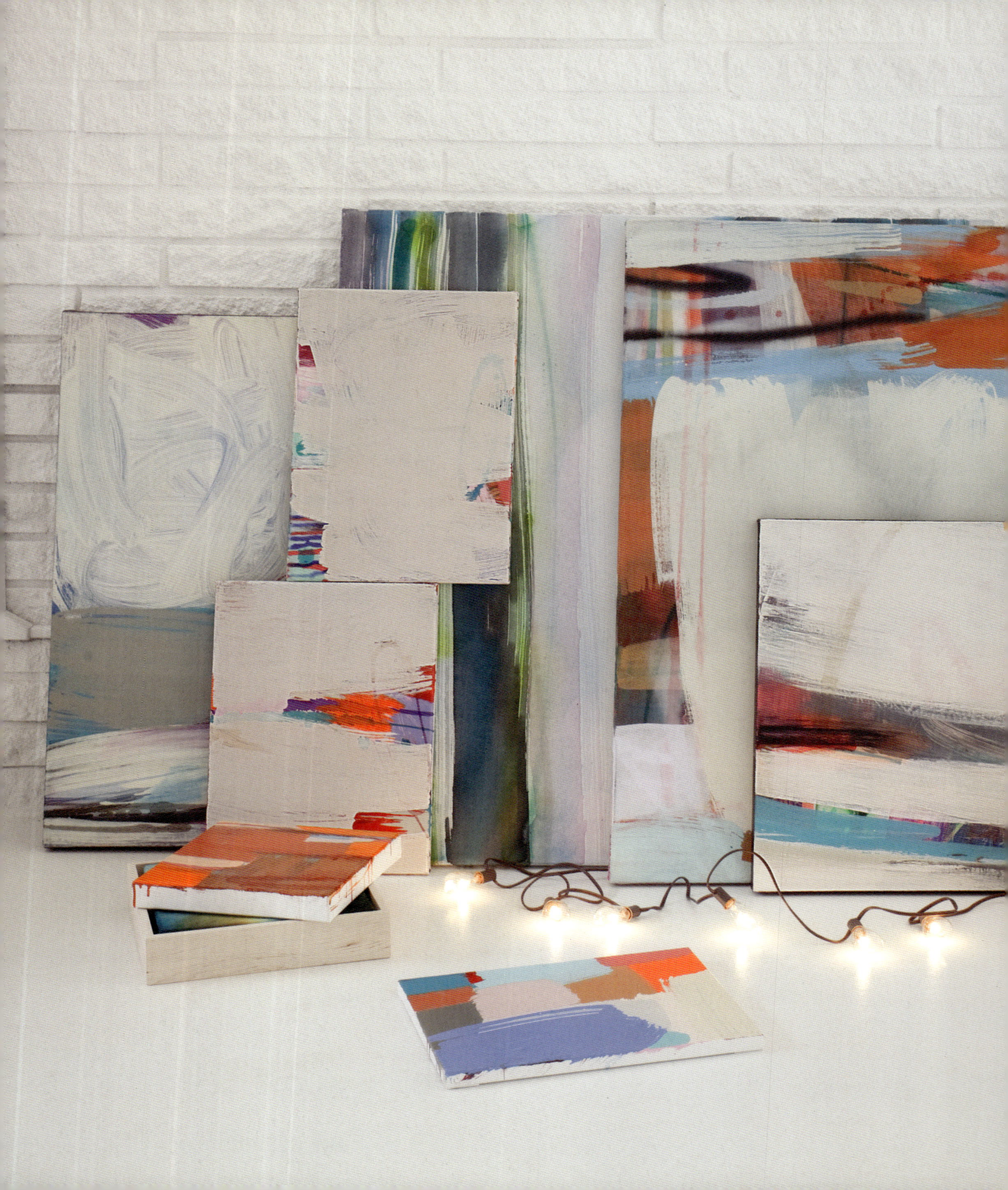

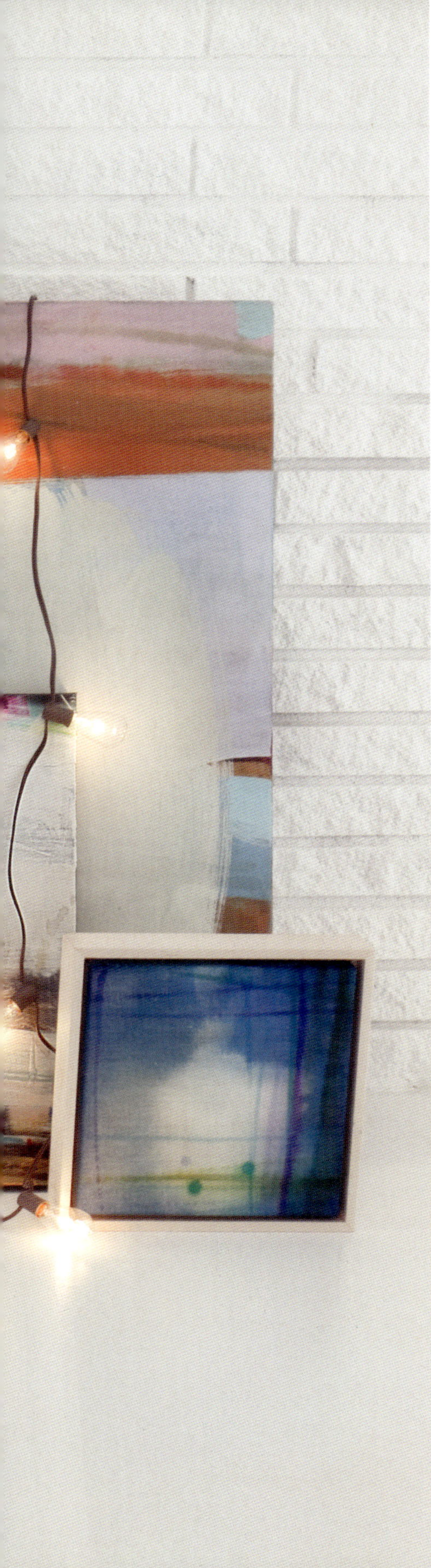

CHAPTER THREE

SEEKING BALANCE

"A form gives me an idea, this idea evokes another form, and everything culminates in figures, animals, and things I had no way of foreseeing in advance."

—JOAN MIRÓ

Finding and creating balance in your art is essential not only for the art itself, but also for the viewer. An unbalanced piece of art contains tension and confusion. The viewer's eye is forcefully drawn to the more weighted areas, which ruins the flow and overall composition of the piece. A well-balanced piece of art has a clean, open, and well-constructed composition. The viewer's eye moves effortlessly from one area to the next, allowing them to pause on certain areas of interest as they wish, without being inadvertently forced to a particular focus by an unstable or disproportionate composition.

When considering balance in a piece of art, keep in mind that you can't alter one area without a cascade effect into another. Each stroke, pencil line, and mark making will be in a relationship with all the others. The beauty of achieving good balance is that once the elements are working together and complimenting one another, the result can be impressive. The key part of learning how to create and maintain balance is learning to recognize the moment when every section can stand alone as well as form a cohesive whole.

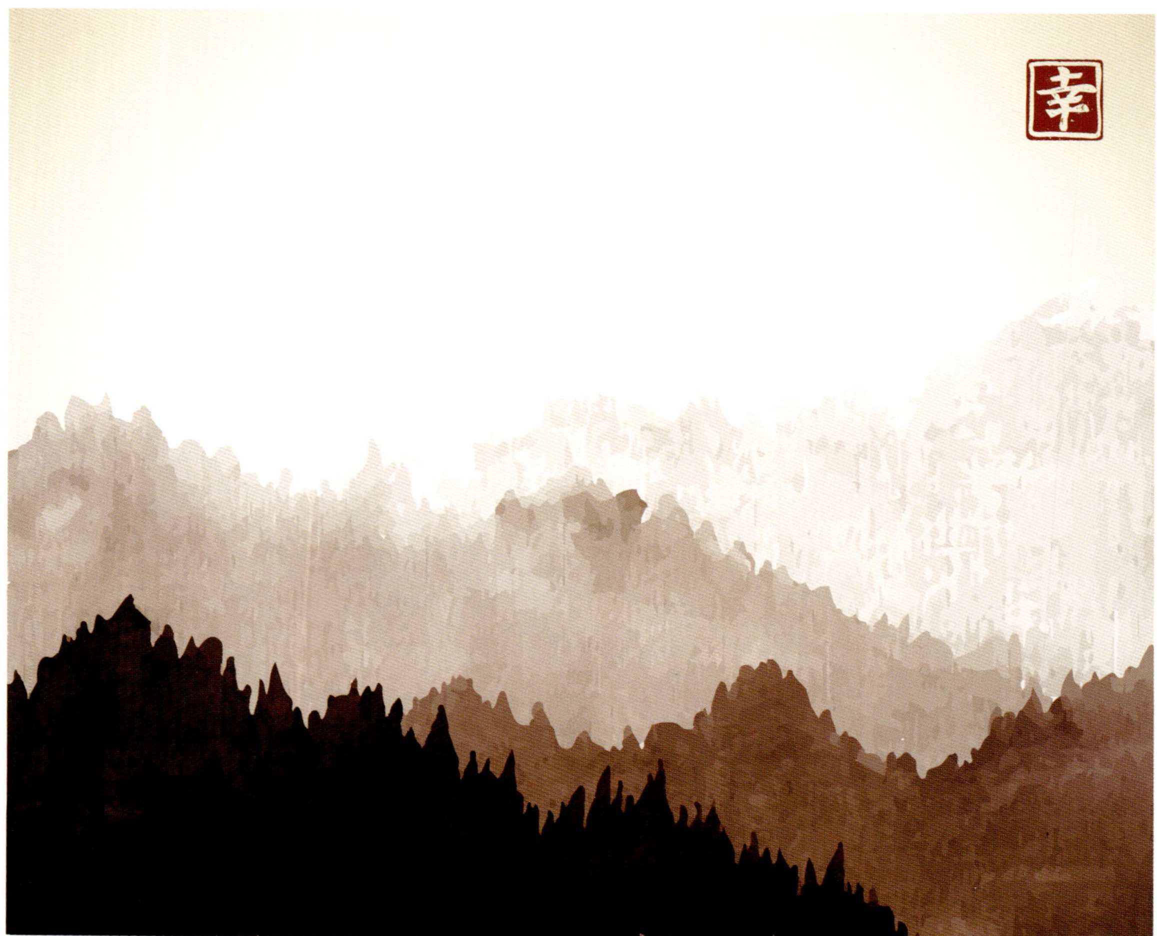

BY ELINA LI

When exploring balance in your work, keep in mind two fundamental design principles: contrast and space. These two variables play an indispensable role in the creative process. Contrast is the arrangement of elements in opposition to one another. Basic examples include light vs. dark, large vs. small, and so forth. Space is the distance around each area of interest in the work.

Traditional landscapes are great examples of balance in which contrast and space are particularly well demonstrated. A landscape is defined by a horizontal division of a surface plane into two distinct sections: open sky and land. In its basic form, the land is usually darker in contrast and typically takes up much less space. The eye of the viewer is drawn to the darker contrast of the land, but by enlarging the spatial area given to the sky, a harmonious balance is achieved. The darker area below is balanced not only by the lighter sky, but also by the space dedicated to it. A viewer will take this concept of balanced design for granted, yet it is up to the artist to learn and convey balance as a way to give meaning and beauty to their art.

EXERCISE FIVE

shape paintings

learning to create balance

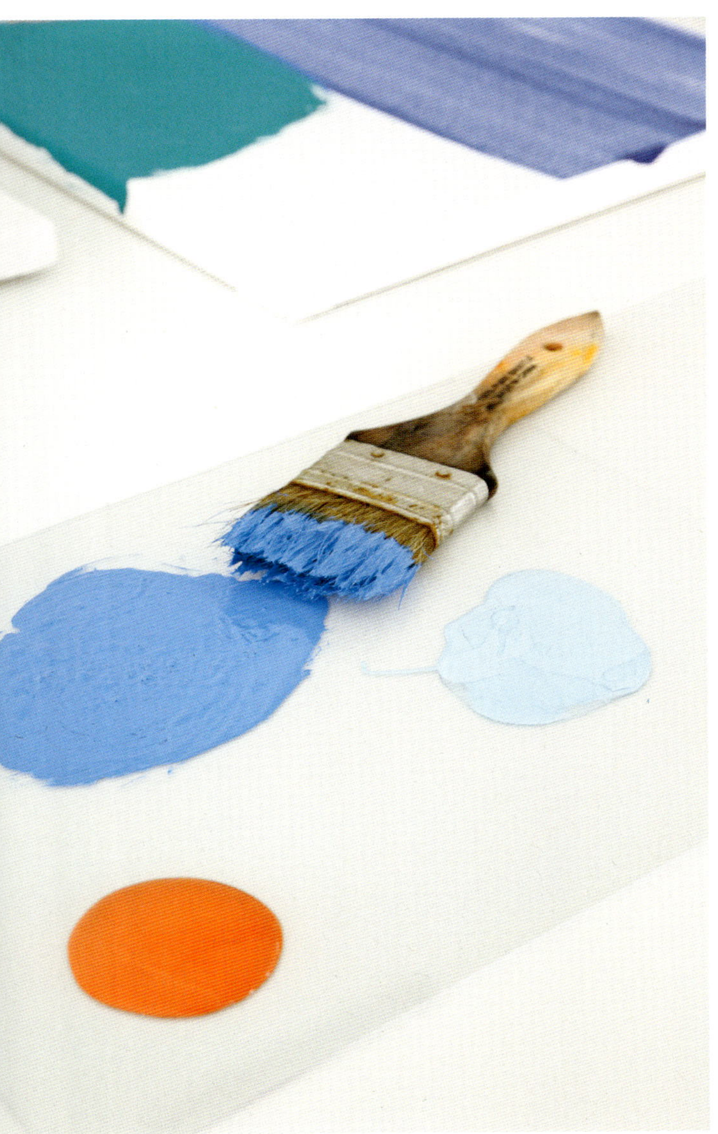

MATERIALS

small to medium primed canvases (from 11" × 18" [28 × 46 cm] to 18" × 24" [46 × 61 cm]); square formats can also be used.

an assortment of at least ten to fifteen colors of acrylic paints of your choice, plus black and white to adjust contrast

large and small paintbrushes

Balance in abstract painting has a lot to do with how you use and manipulate shapes on the surface. Also, when thinking about achieving a well-balanced piece, you must be aware of the negative space and the shapes that it creates. The moment when all the shapes and forms are resolved and balanced can be an intuitive feeling. The more you create and practice, the more easily you will recognize when this moment occurs.

prepare

→ **Make sure you have a well-protected work area. I prefer to paint standing up at a floor easel or standing up with the canvas flat against the table. Maintaining a flat canvas** prevents the paint from running or dripping and allows it to dry undisturbed.

→ I recommend having two to three clean water containers available to clean brushes quickly and keep the process continuous.

TIP ▸ Turning your canvas in different directions, or even upside down, helps you see and create balance. By viewing it at different angles, your eye will be able to make new associations that were previously hidden.

create

→ For this exercise, work in threes. In other words, you will create three shapes at a time, pausing in between to notice how they relate and interact with one another.

→ Vary your shape making each time. Create some that are large and organic, some that suggest movement, and others that are symmetrical and rigid.

→ After each cycle of three shapes, take a moment to study your work. During the pause, observe how the shapes work together and use that to plan for your next three.

→ Allow each layer to dry before moving on to the next. This will prevent unwanted mixing of colors, which can result in muddiness.

→ Continue this progression of making three shapes at a time until you feel like the work is beginning to find balance and resolution. This instinct is developed through practice.

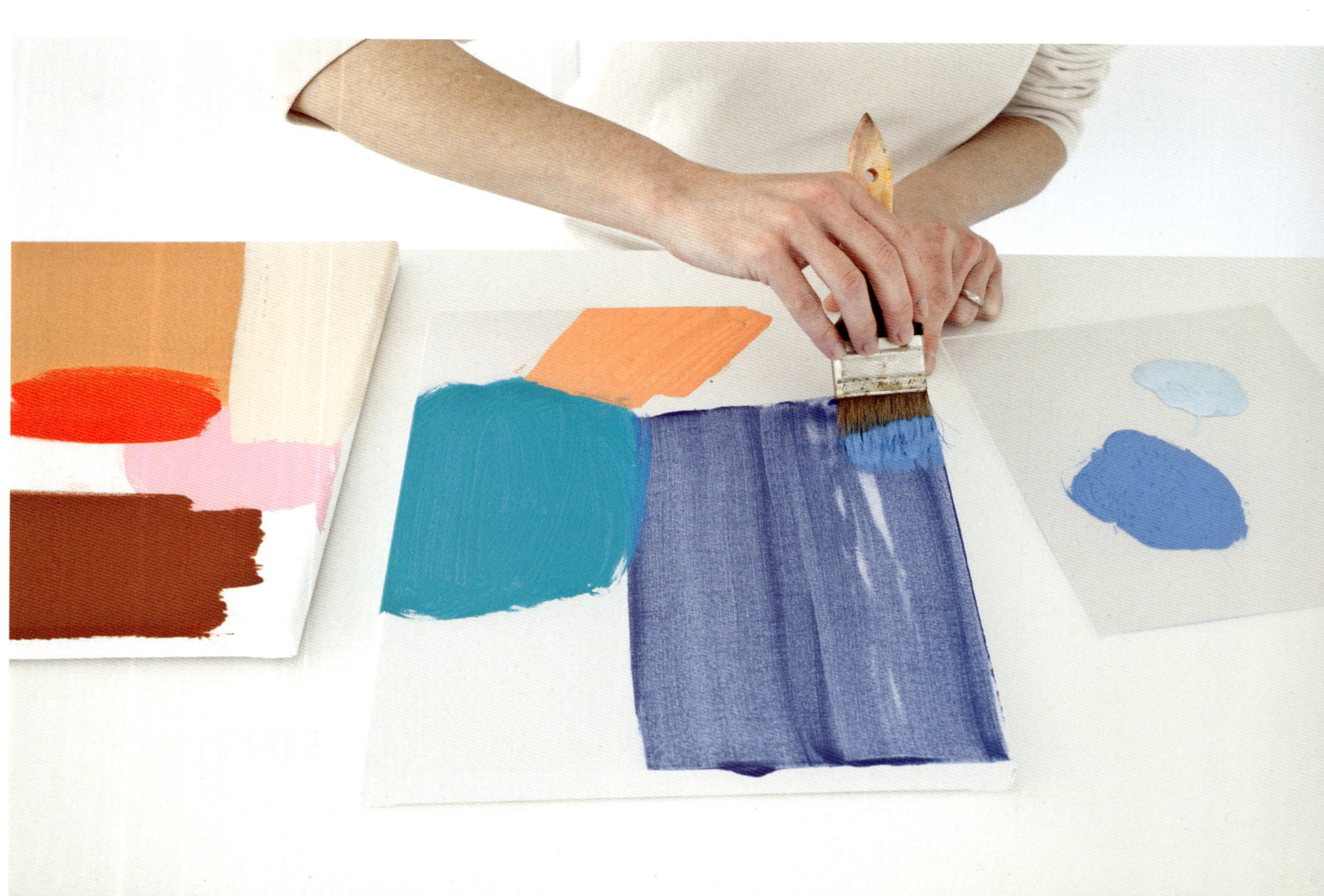

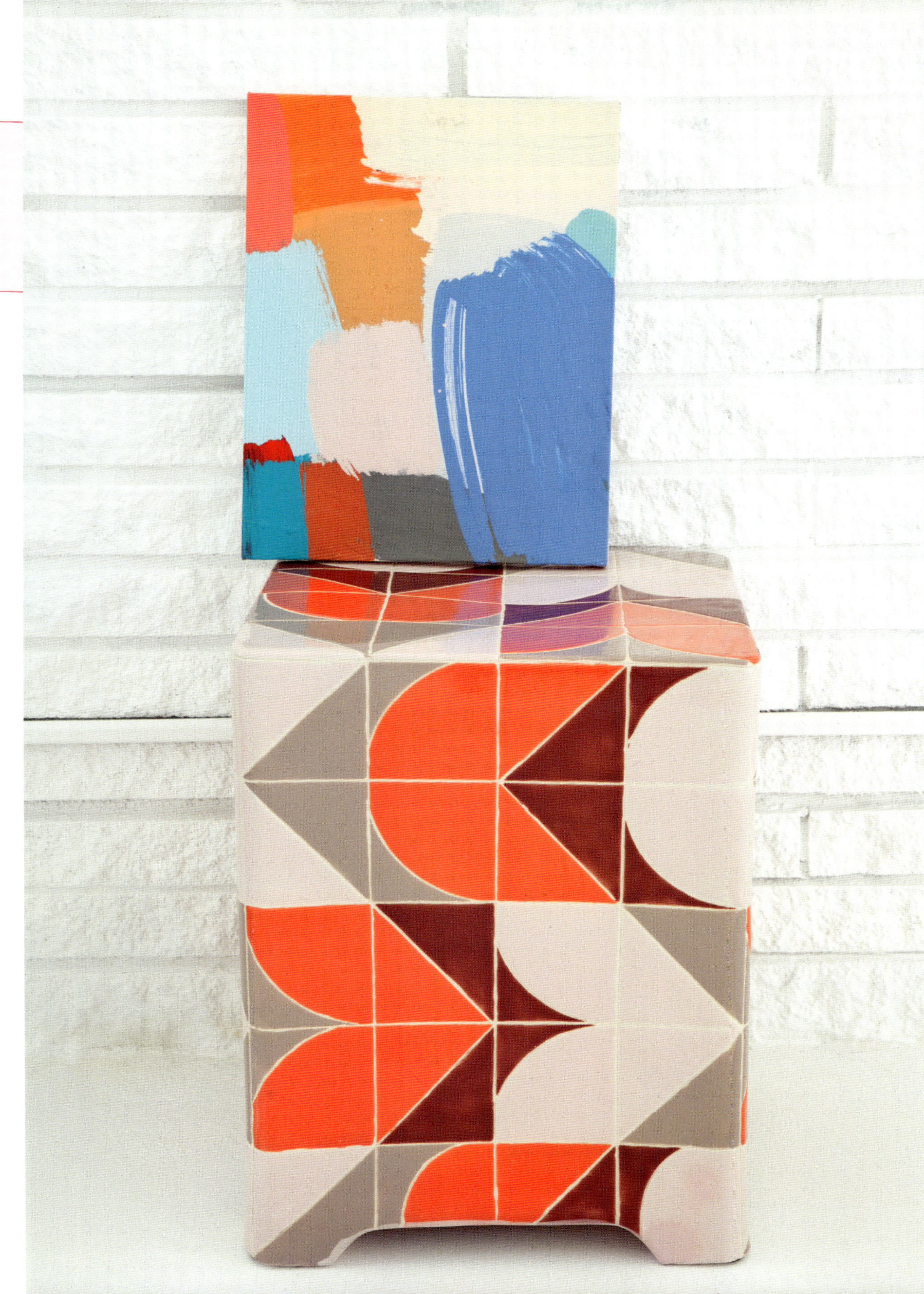

EXERCISE SIX

the ripple effect

use collage to create composition

As you develop a certain design or composition, you will notice that one section cannot be altered without the whole composition being altered as well. This is called the ripple effect. A painting must be considered in its entirety, not segmented into individual sections as you work. This is not always an easy task.

For this exercise, I wanted to work in another medium that I love, which is collage. I was steered away from collage in college when a professor mentioned he didn't view it as a true art form. Although in my head I wondered what Matisse, Picasso, and Rauschenberg would have thought of that statement, I stopped making collages for a while. However, I am glad to have found my way back to working in this medium. The simple nature of collage will help you fine-tune your skills in creating compositions. It will help you master, recognize, and balance the ripple effect.

MATERIALS

- several different colors of quality card stock
- craft knife or scissors
- self-healing cutting mat
- 8" × 10" (20 × 25.5 cm) heavyweight paper or watercolor paper
- heavy matte gel (Common brands include Golden and Liquitex and can be found online or in arts and craft stores.)
- printmaker's brayer
- standard 12" (30.5 cm) ruler

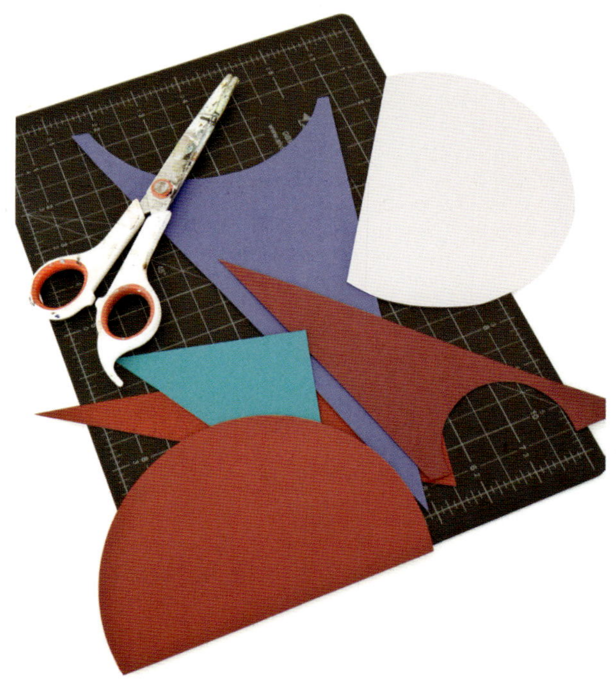

prepare

→ **Cut your papers in a variety of organic and geometric shapes and size. I usually hand-cut my collage materials, but you can also use rulers or other objects, such as plates, to become your templates for creating shapes.**

The ripple effect in action

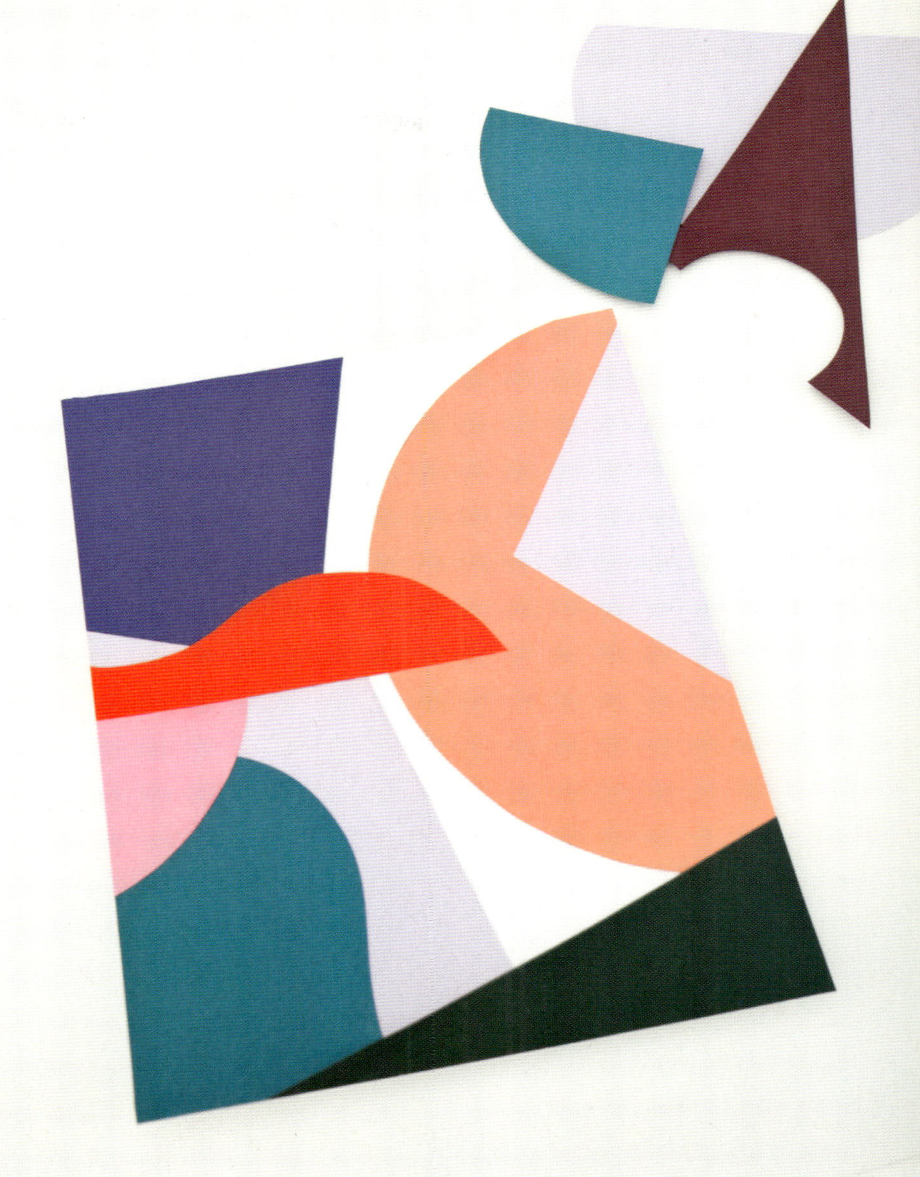

- → Organize your shapes in three piles of small, medium, and large.

create

- → Use your 8" × 10" (20 × 25.5 cm) sheet of paper as your base. It will serve as the parameter of your piece.
- → Begin to place the shapes on your paper, alternating each time between the three sizes.
- → Notice that no matter the size or color you have chosen, each time you add a new piece, the entire composition is completely transformed.

Continue to arrange and rearrange the papers until you feel the piece achieves an overall balance. You might have to continue to cut the papers and/or overlap them to reach this resolved point.

Once you have decided on your final design, take a mental or even physical photo of the work; this will help you remember their position on the paper when you collage the pieces to create your finished work.

Remove the papers and begin to apply the heavy matte gel sparingly to the back of each piece.

After one is put into position, use your brayer to smooth out and evenly disperse the matte gel. This also helps to remove any bubbles that might occur underneath the paper. Use a clean cloth or extra paper in between your work and the brayer as an added layer of protection.

Once all is in place, either use a heavy board or books to weight down the piece as it dries for at least 24 hours.

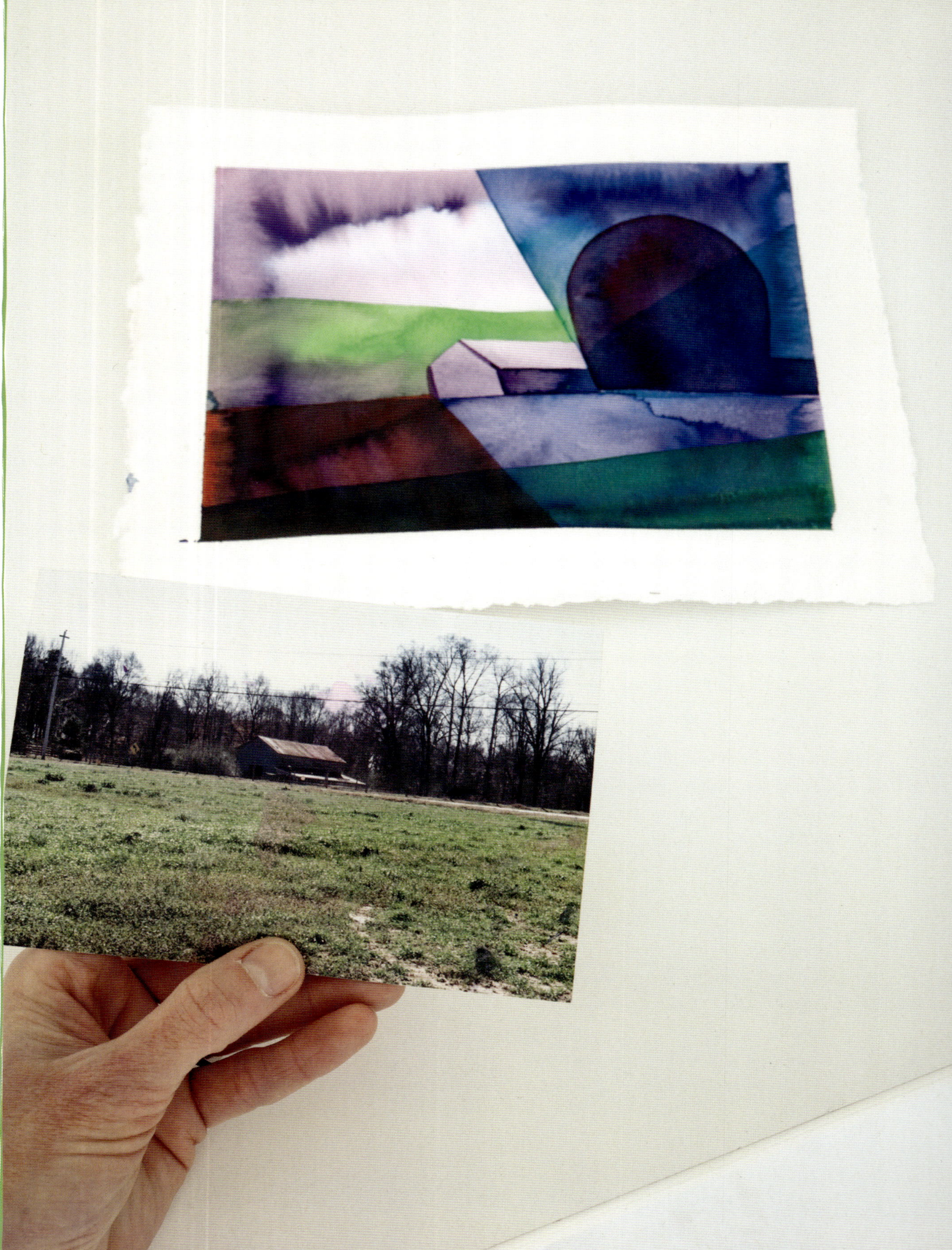

EXERCISE SEVEN

deconstructing a landscape to abstraction

three ways with watercolor

Landscapes have been a rich and significant subject of art in all cultures. A traditional landscape typically depicts natural scenery such as mountains, trees, rivers, lakes, forests, etc. The picture plane of a landscape is divided into two distinct sections where the horizon separates the earth from the sky.

Ever since I started painting, I have enjoyed studying and creating landscapes. They represent a moment in natural history and can evoke a personal connection and emotion for the viewer. It has always fascinated me that landscapes have the power to do this without the use of words or figurative elements.

In this exercise, we will deconstruct a landscape to its basic components and elevate those to be the subject of your work. We will do this exclusively with watercolors and discuss some of the basic watercolor techniques in the process.

MATERIALS

Choose three different landscapes from photos, magazines, or books. Make sure they vary quite a bit in composition. For example, one might have a lot more open sky and on another, the presence of water.

three separate cut or torn sheets of watercolor paper

- square format (8" × 8" [20 × 20 cm])
- horizontal format (8" × 10" [20 × 25.5 cm])
- vertical format (10" × 3" [25.5 × 7.5 cm])

soft synthetic hair round and flat brushes, in a variety of sizes, including a 2" (5 cm) soft-hair flat brush

watercolor paints, in a variety of colors. Be sure to have both cool colors (e.g., blues, teals, and greens) and warm colors (e.g., reds, pinks, and oranges) to add contrast and interest.

1" (2.5 cm) painter's tape or masking tape

acrylic board, such as Plexiglas, approximately 18"× 24" (46 × 61 cm)

no. 2 mechanical pencil for drawing

prepare

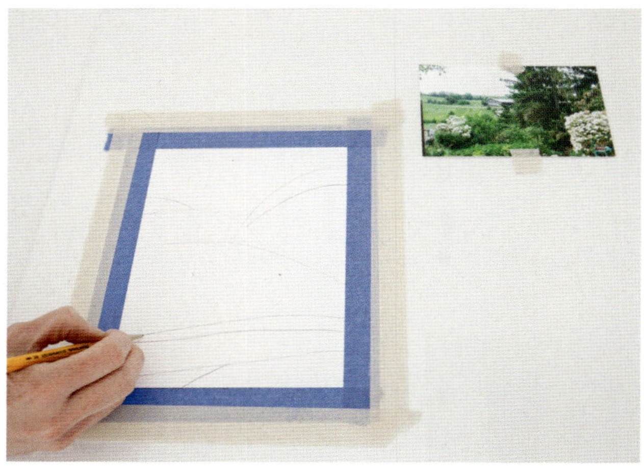

- On each of your three paper sizes, measure inward 1" (2.5 cm) and tape off to form a border.
- Then tape one of the papers onto your acrylic board. This is a necessary step to prevent the paper from curling or buckling from the water.
- Use your landscape photos as a guide and lightly draw your composition, focusing only on the shapes and forms that occur in the photo.

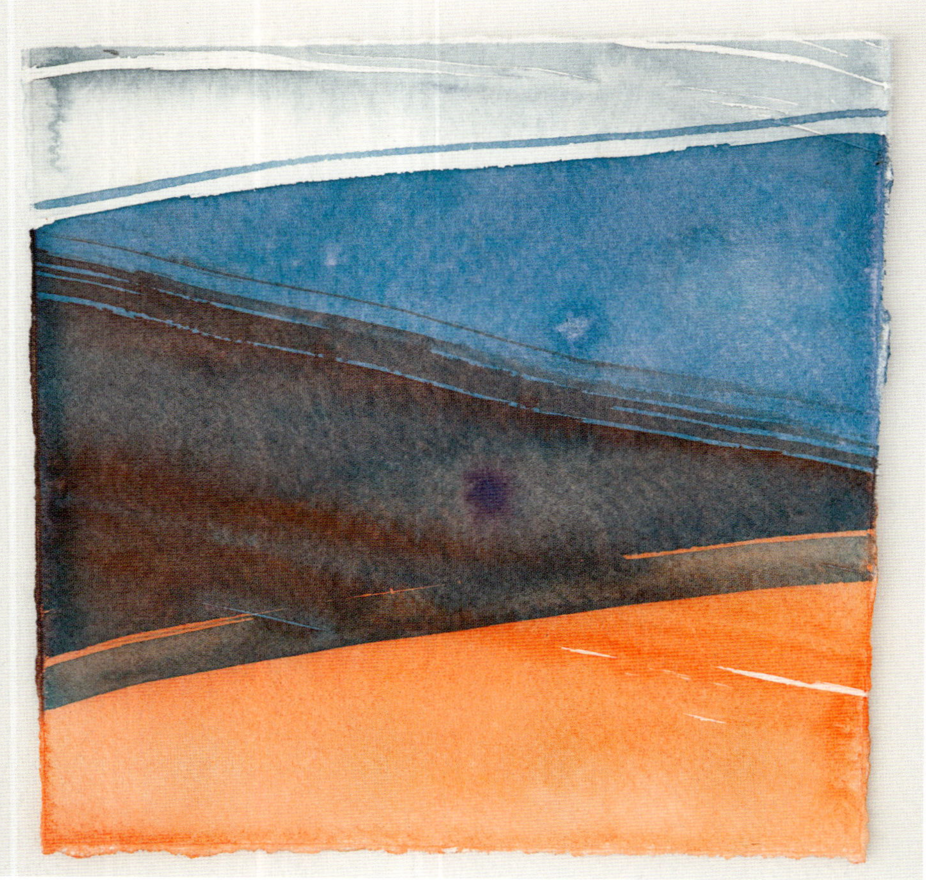

create

- Cover the entire paper with a light wash of transparent paint. This will serve as the base color as you work. Allow to dry completely.
- As you build off this initial color base, here are three watercolor techniques you can experiment with as you abstract your landscape.

1. **LAYERING AND TRANSPARENCIES.** Watercolor is transparent by nature. This transparency can be used to your benefit by layering colors to create a third, fourth, or even fifth color. To use this technique, you must allow the paint to dry completely before you add the next layer.

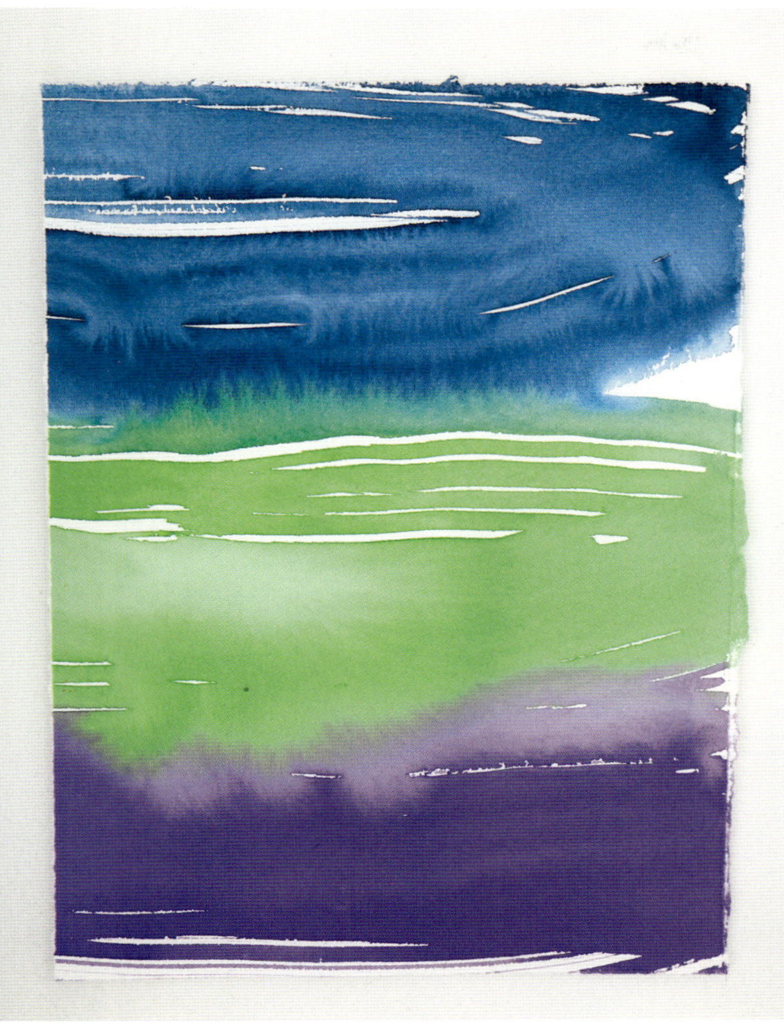

2. **A BLEED EFFECT.** If you apply two watercolors on a dry surface and allow them to touch slightly, they will create a beautiful softening and color merging. This has also been called *the cabbage effect* because the final result mimics a cabbage leaf. As it dries, don't move or agitate the paper or the effect may be altered.

3. **OMBRÉ EFFECT.** This is a great method if you want to create the illusion of water or sky. Wet the entire surface of the paper and with a loaded brush (see page 22), apply the paint to the top section only. With the help of gravity, the paint will slowly seep down the paper, but the main concentration or saturation of color will remain at the top.

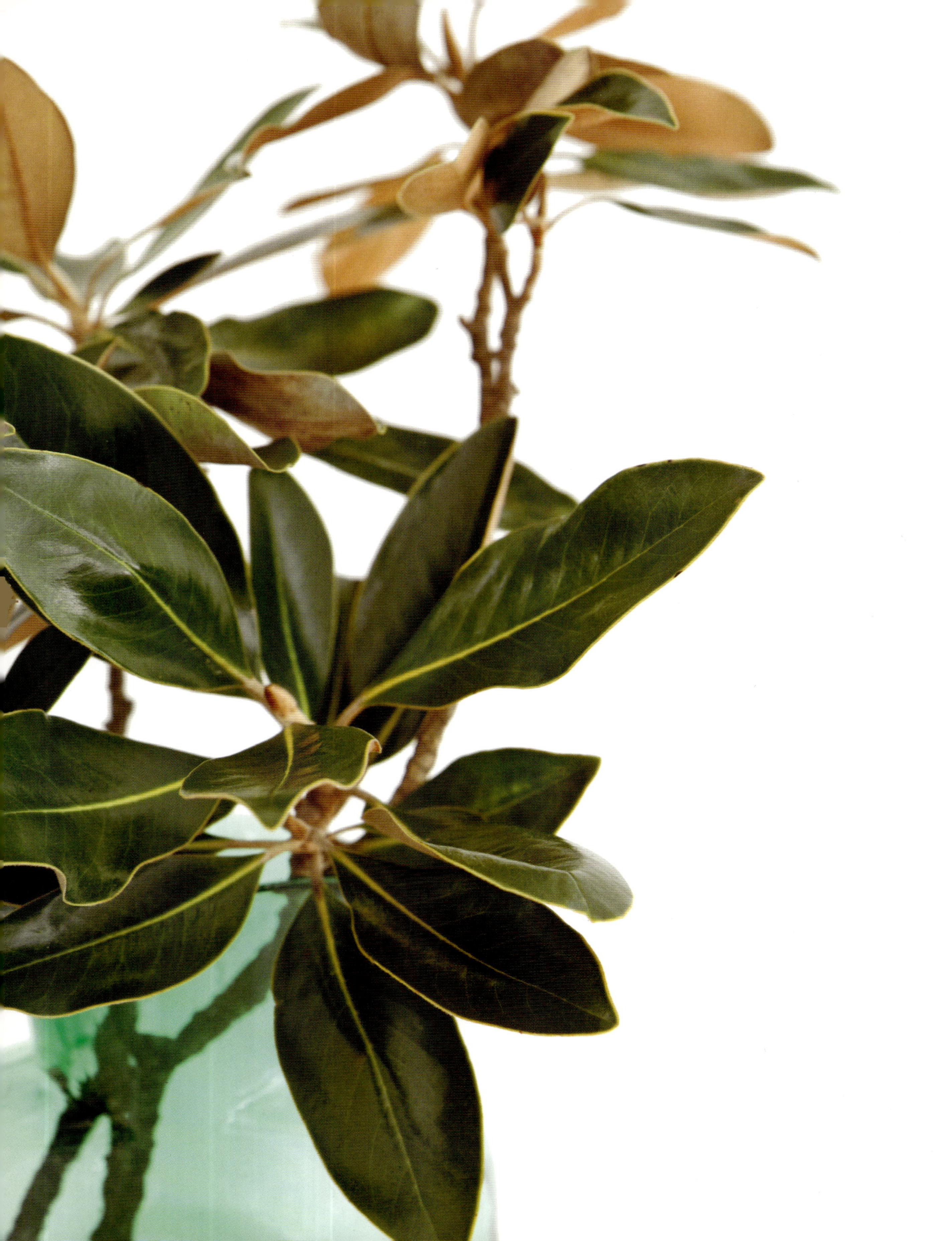

CHAPTER FOUR

WORKING WITH INTENTION

"All my work begins with drawings."

—ELLSWORTH KELLY

There tends to be two approaches to the creative process. There are artists like myself who prefer to dive into a painting, sometimes with more planning and sometimes with less. This technique can work because the development, problem solving, and ultimately, the "solution" happens somewhere along the way. There will always be time to add or edit yourself later. So there is less emphasis put on each brush stroke and less decision-making.

On the other end of the spectrum, there are artists who focus on every mark, line, and shape. Each time they touch the canvas, it is with direction, intention, and purpose. I typically do not paint in this intensely focused and self-controlled style. However, I highly appreciate and respect this technique. I wanted to discuss these two approaches because I believe it is important to create not only well-rounded art, but to strive to be well-rounded artists.

The exercises in this chapter will explore slowing down the art process, discuss how to work with intention, and learn how to self-edit from the very beginning.

"From a distance it might look straight, but when you get up close, you can see the line waiver. And I think that's where the beauty is."

—MARGARET KILGALLEN

EXERCISE EIGHT

blind contour

drawing what you see, not what you know

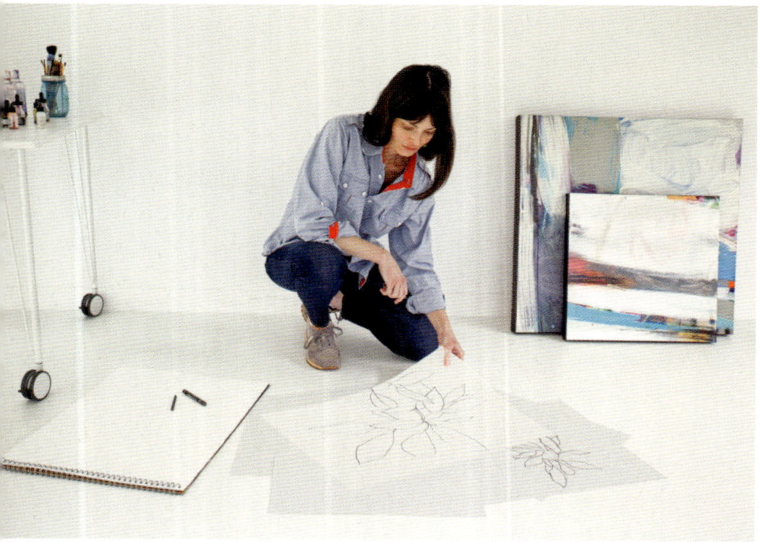

MATERIALS

- sketchbook
- pencil
- drawing subject

The contour line is simply the line that defines a form or edge. It is one of the fundamental elements of art and drawing and provides the foundation on which to build your more involved work. I love focusing on contour lines when drawing because it removes the challenges that can come with color, shading, texture, etc. Working with intention is learning and understanding what is most important in your art. Once you have this base, the rest of the piece can be constructed.

Blind contour drawing is an exercise commonly taught in college classes and involves drawing an object or figure without looking at the paper. Although it might seem odd, this practice is a great way to connect your eye, mind, and hand. It also forces you to truly observe your subject. Intention in art is created through focus and purpose and blind contour drawing is a great method for achieving both of these things. It teaches you to self-edit, stay aware, and be present. A common phrase used by one of my former professors was "draw what you see, not what you know."

prepare

For this exercise, I suggest using pencil as opposed to pen or ink to keep the same line variation. Set up a still life or choose a live model. Keep your still life simple and focus on choosing clearly defined and shaped objects. Vases, bowls, bottles, and fruit are all good examples. Avoid using cloth or drapery, as fabric can be tricky to draw.

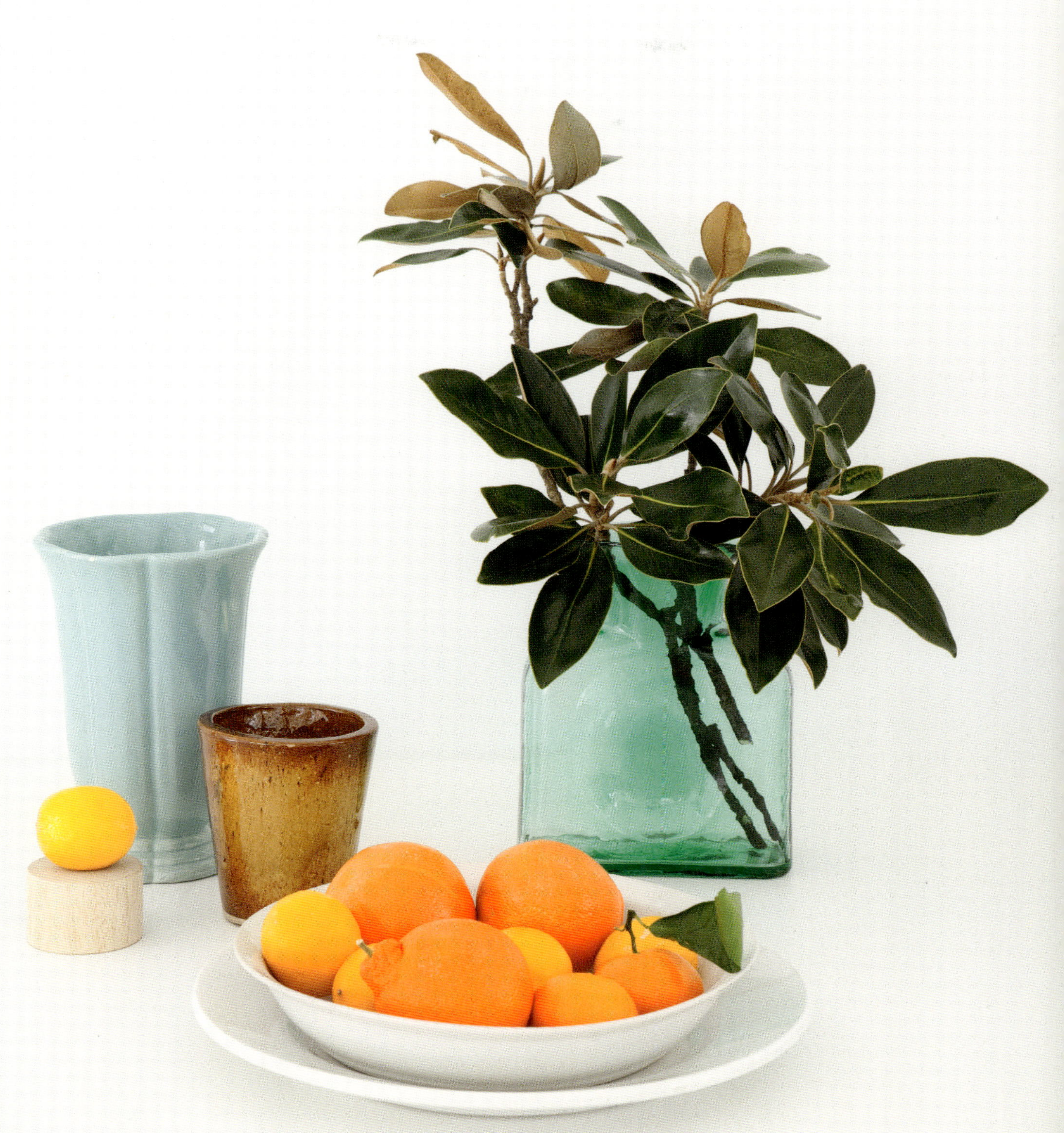

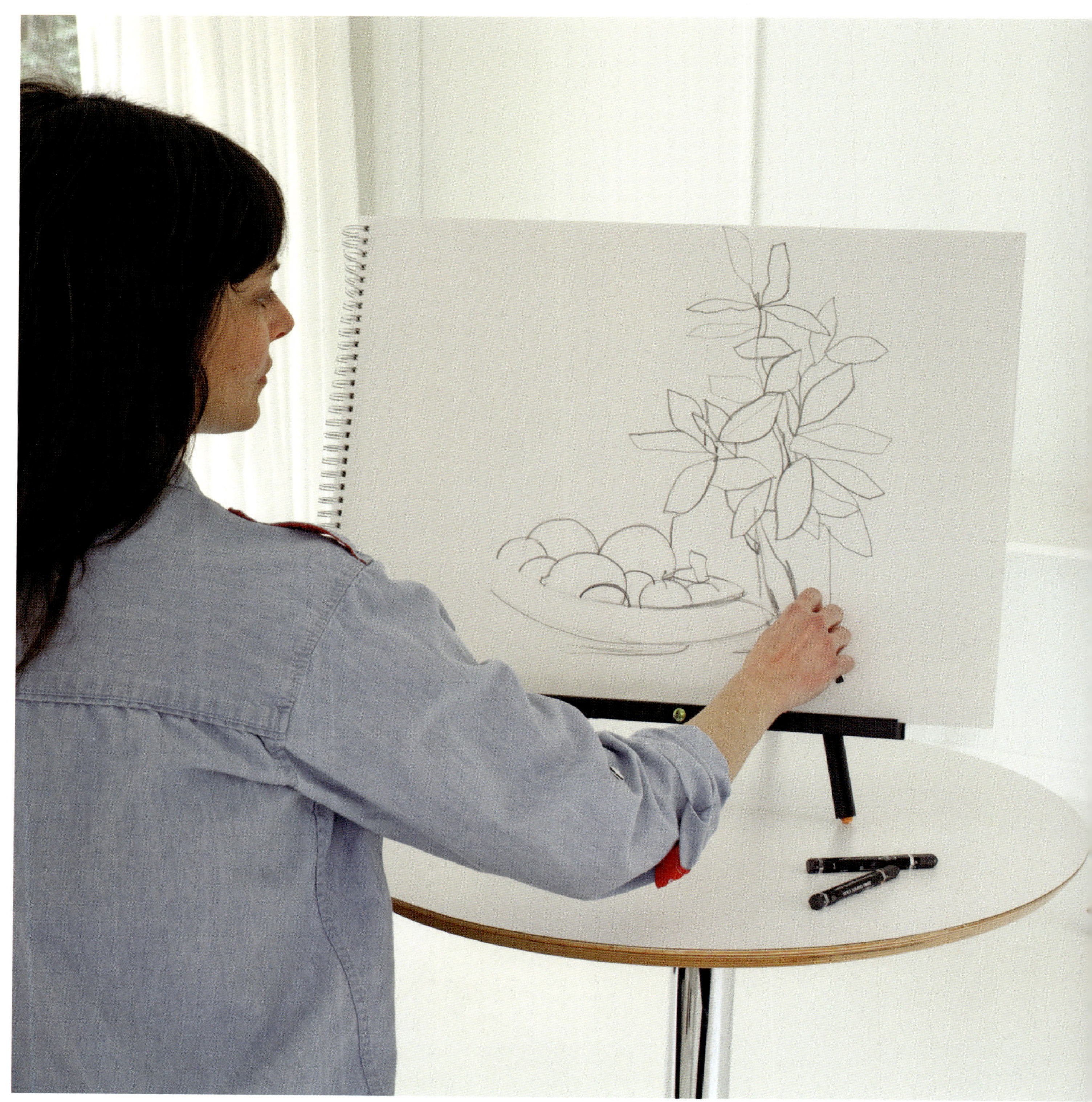

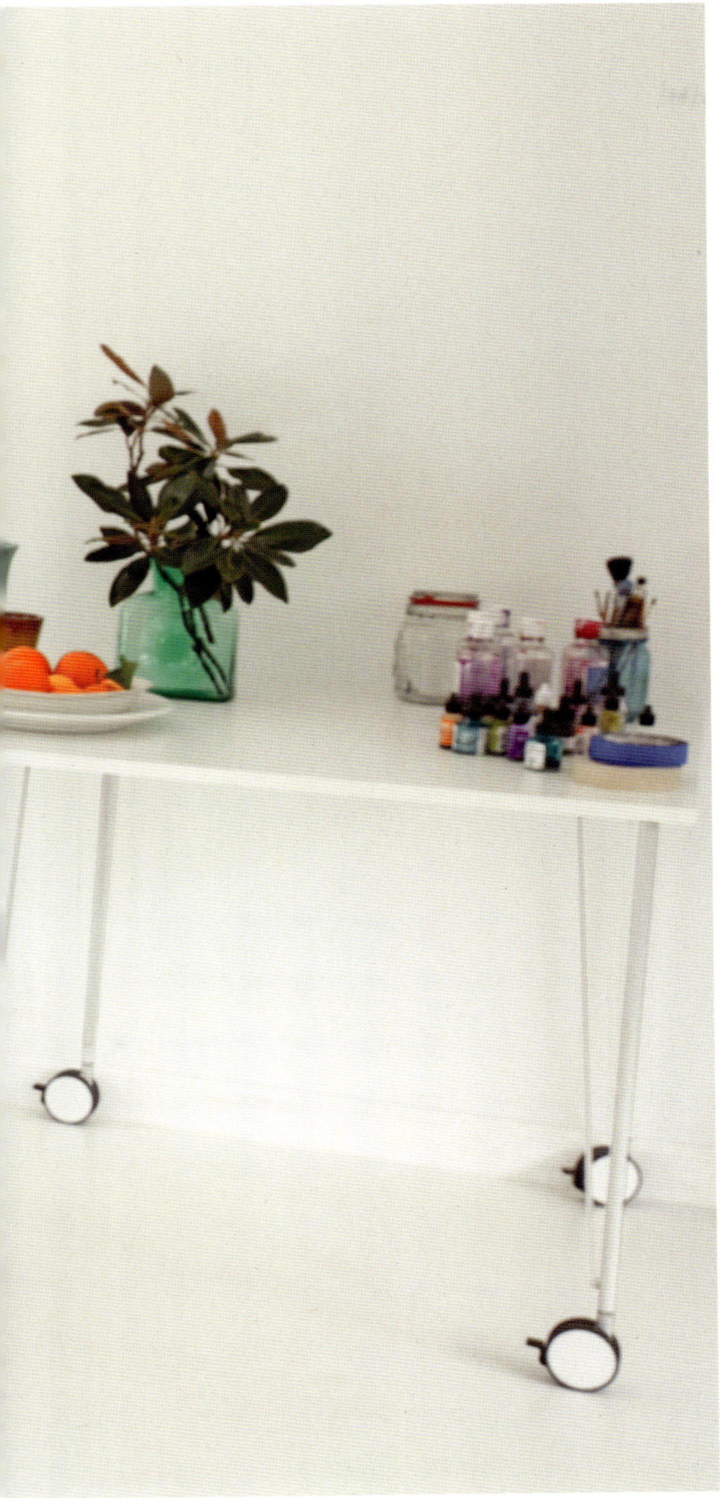

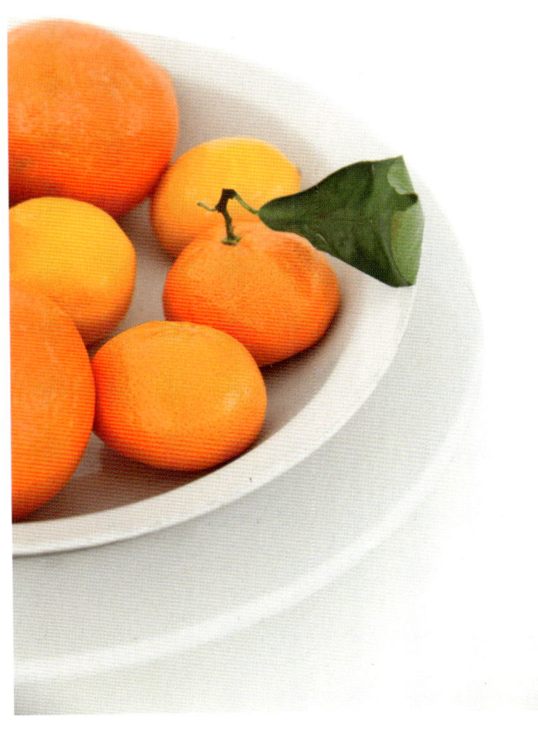

create

- To begin, direct your eye to the outermost edge that defines your subject. Keep your eye moving along that line as you slowly draw it in your sketchbook. This practice can be awkward and challenging. Remember the point is not to render the subject correctly, but rather to see the subject you are drawing with intention.
- Repeat the exercise several times. Try to draw the same subject several times on the same sheet of paper. Then compare your different versions.

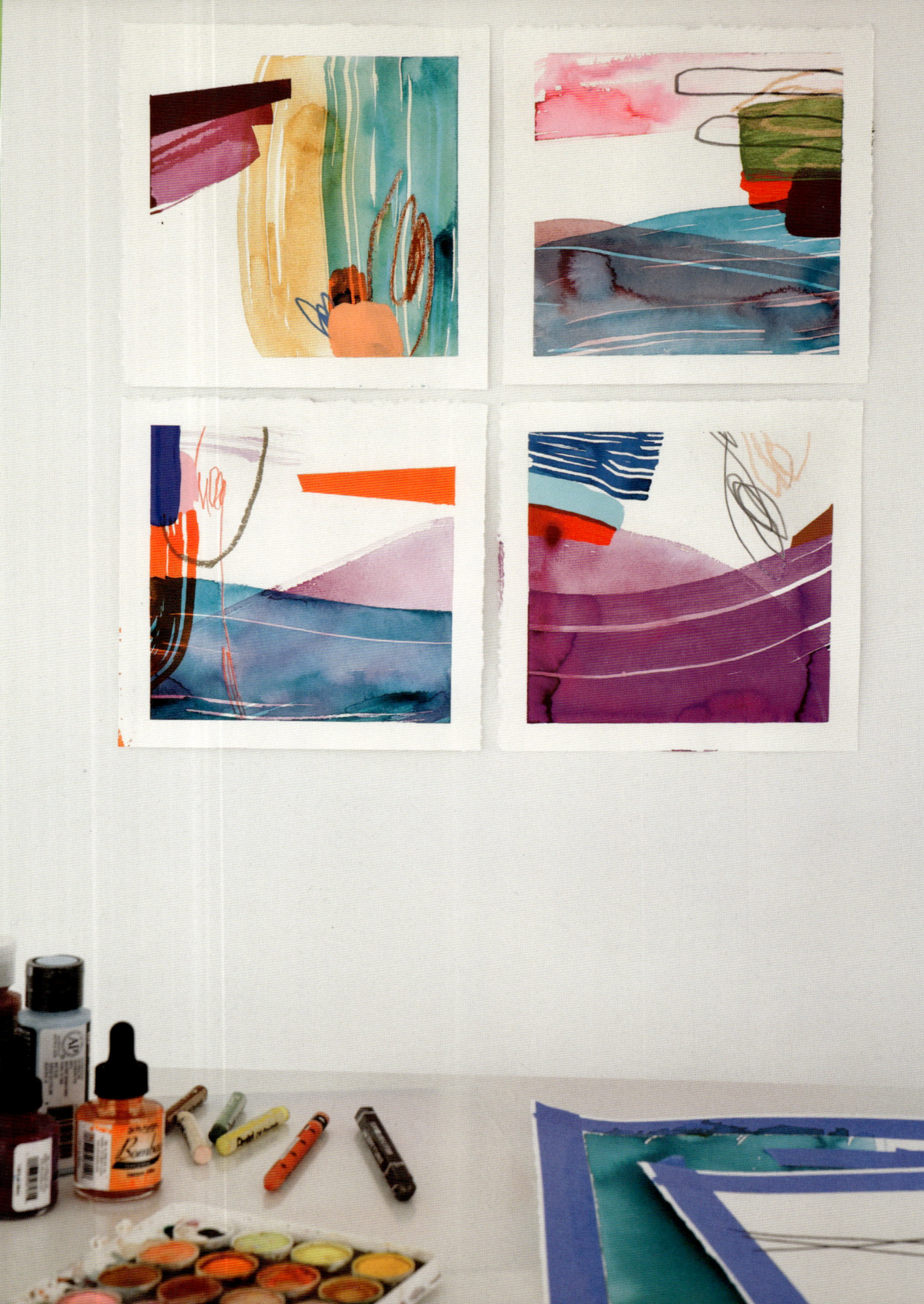

EXERCISE NINE

discover the essential elements

planning your mark making

This exercise is based on the internal thought processes in creating art, so that you begin to ask yourself questions and plan your mark making and brush strokes first before making a move. It means subtracting all that is unnecessary so that you can discover the elements that are most important.

MATERIALS

four cut or torn pieces of 12" × 12" (30.5 × 30.5 cm) 140 lb (300 gsm) cold-press watercolor or heavyweight mixed-media paper

several acrylics, inks, or watercolors of your choice

round and flat brushes in various sizes, including at least one large 2" or 3" (5 or 7.5 cm) flat brush

1" (2.5 cm) painter's tape

drawing pencils, colored pencils, pastels, or oil crayons for line making

prepare

- Prepare a well-protected flat working surface either on the floor or on your table.
- Gather several clean water containers for brushes.
- Draw and then tape a 10" × 10" (25.5 × 25.5 cm) square inside your 12" × 12" (30.5 × 30.5 cm) sheets of paper.

create

- Start each of the four pieces using a different method.
- For the first, make some fluid marks and lines using your pencils, crayons, or pastels.
- For the second, create a wash with either your inks or watercolors using your 2" or 3" (5 or 7.5 cm) flat brush.

- For the third, pick a bright statement color, one that is vivid and eye catching. Create a shape or solid form with it using one of your smallest brushes.
- For the fourth, become creative in your mark making. For example, tape off a certain area and form a solid, bold shape or use an unconventional tool such as a toothbrush, sponge, or even a stick to create lines or colored areas. Enjoy experimenting with how many beautiful and surprising effects that you can achieve.
- Alternate between each of these four approaches for at least three cycles.

Changing your method of mark-making and brush work each time slows down the overall art process to allow you to mentally pause between each decision and envision the outcome first. Also, because each of your marks cannot be erased or painted over, you must consider clearly what your composition blueprint will be and how you will achieve it. This is one way to work with intention.

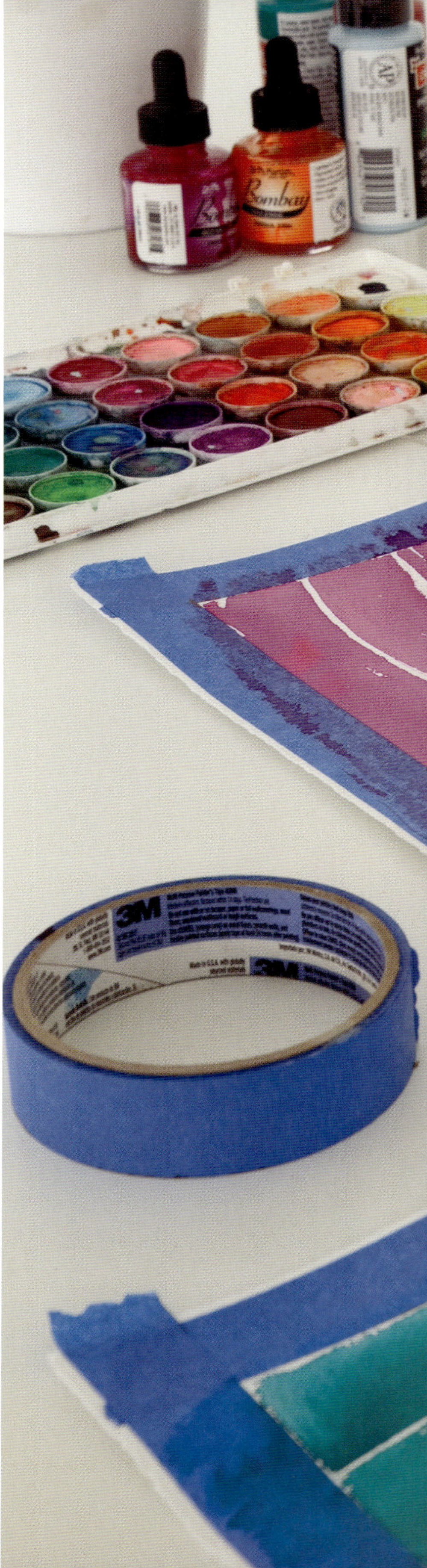

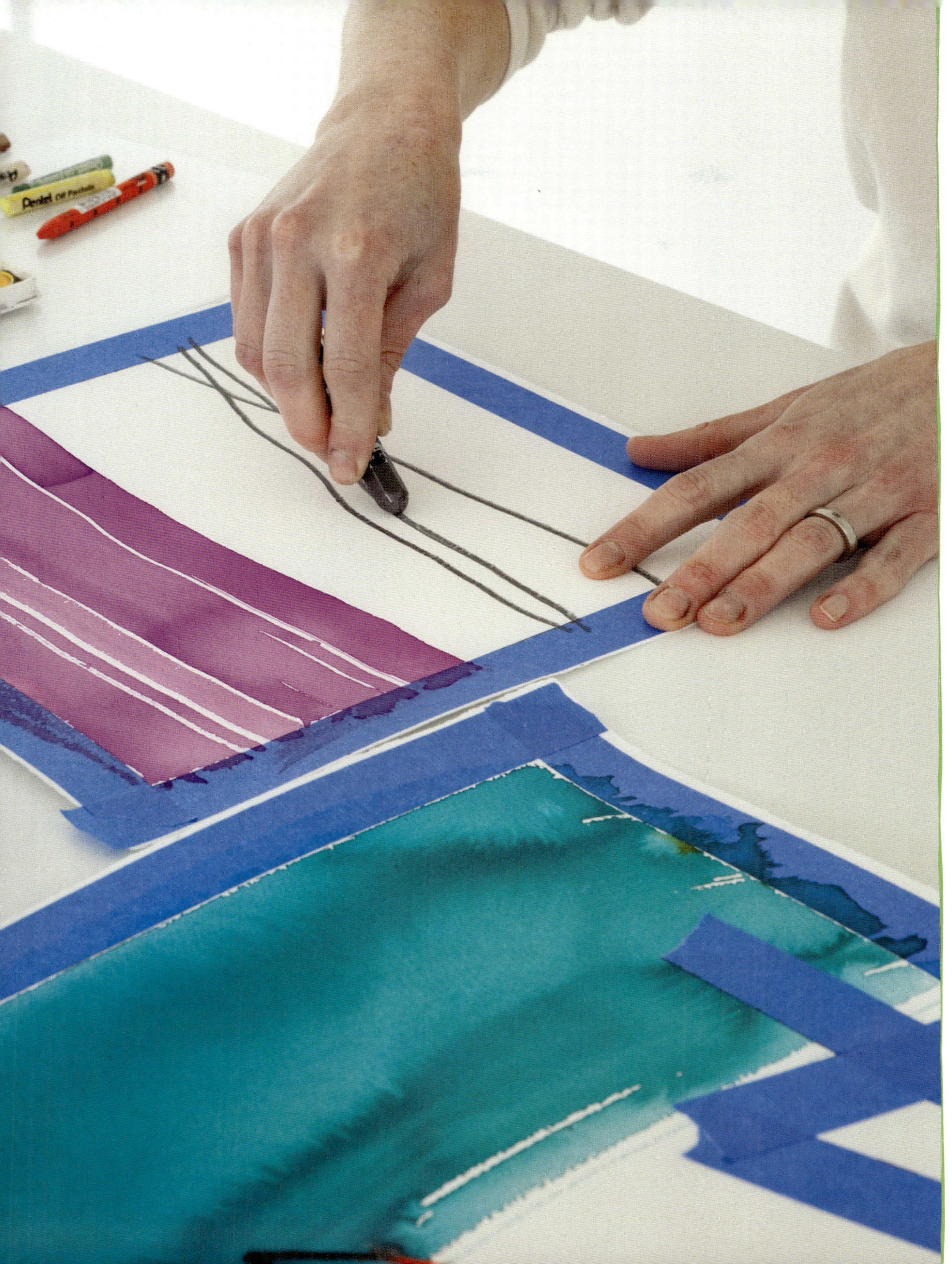

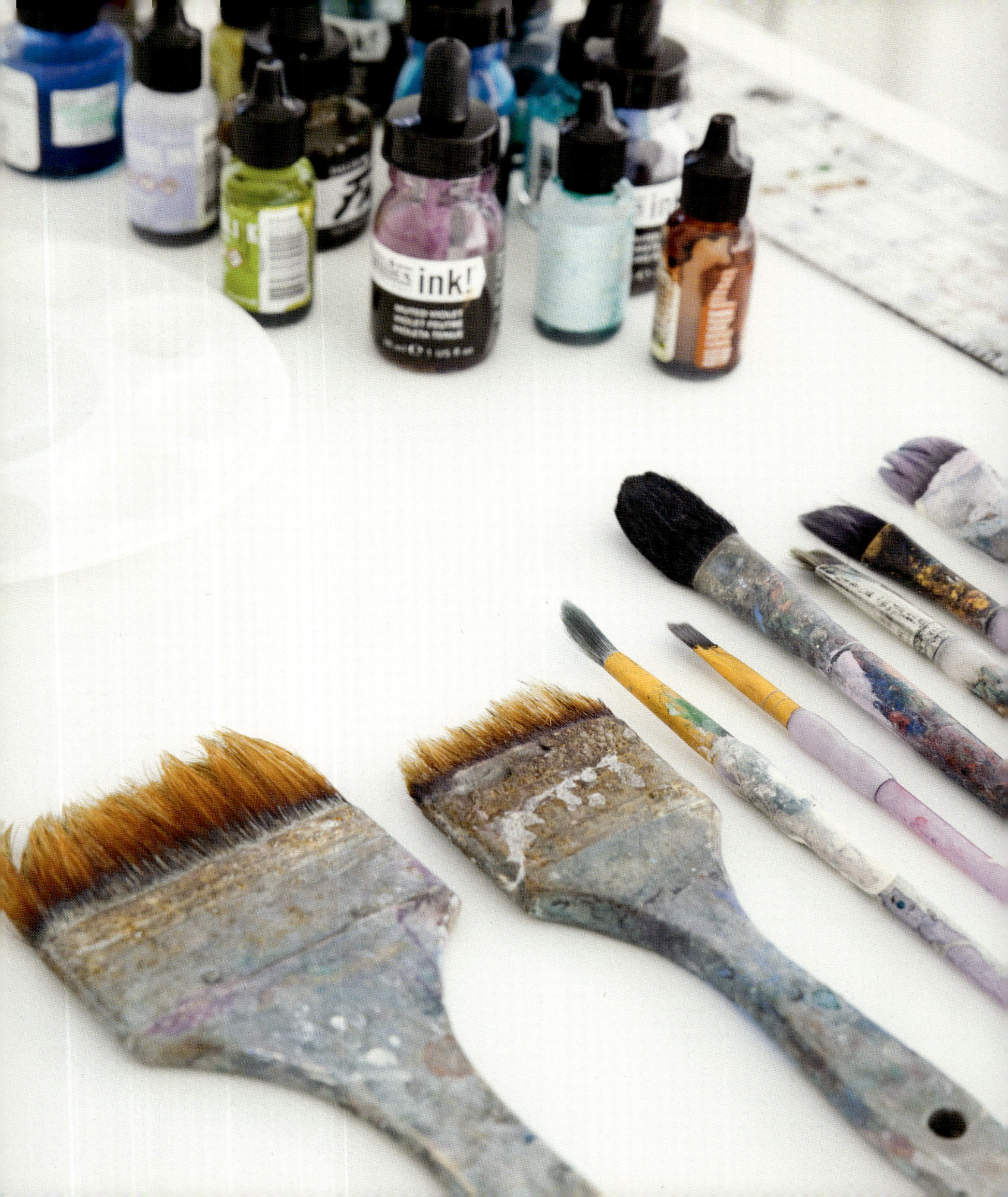
ink!

CHAPTER FIVE

EXPLORING MIXED-MEDIA TOOLS

"You have to know how to use the accident, how to recognize it, how to control it, and ways to eliminate it so that the whole surface looks felt and born all at once."

—HELEN FRANKENTHALER

When it comes to creating, especially if you are working in abstraction, the sky is the limit in terms of supplies. Formal art education tends to focus on traditional painting and drawing materials and techniques. This approach provides a strong base of knowledge, but it can also be limiting.

Changing up your materials and supplies can motivate and inspire. I am always researching and seeking out new paints, mediums, inks, pencils, markers, and so on. In parallel, I am constantly experimenting, attempting to create new art and designs using materials that are not always found in the art supply store. Sometimes these attempts fail, and sometimes, they can become a real breakthrough and help to push a body of work toward a completely new and fresh direction.

Get an understanding, through your own experimentation, how these new and different materials react. Once you have a clear idea of their effect on the work, you can then begin to use them more skillfully and with more purpose. For these exercises, we will focus on a few of my favorite, nonconventional art supplies. Of course, I have a more expansive list of materials, on the following pages. I encourage you to experiment with all of them in an attempt to open up new frontiers in your own work.

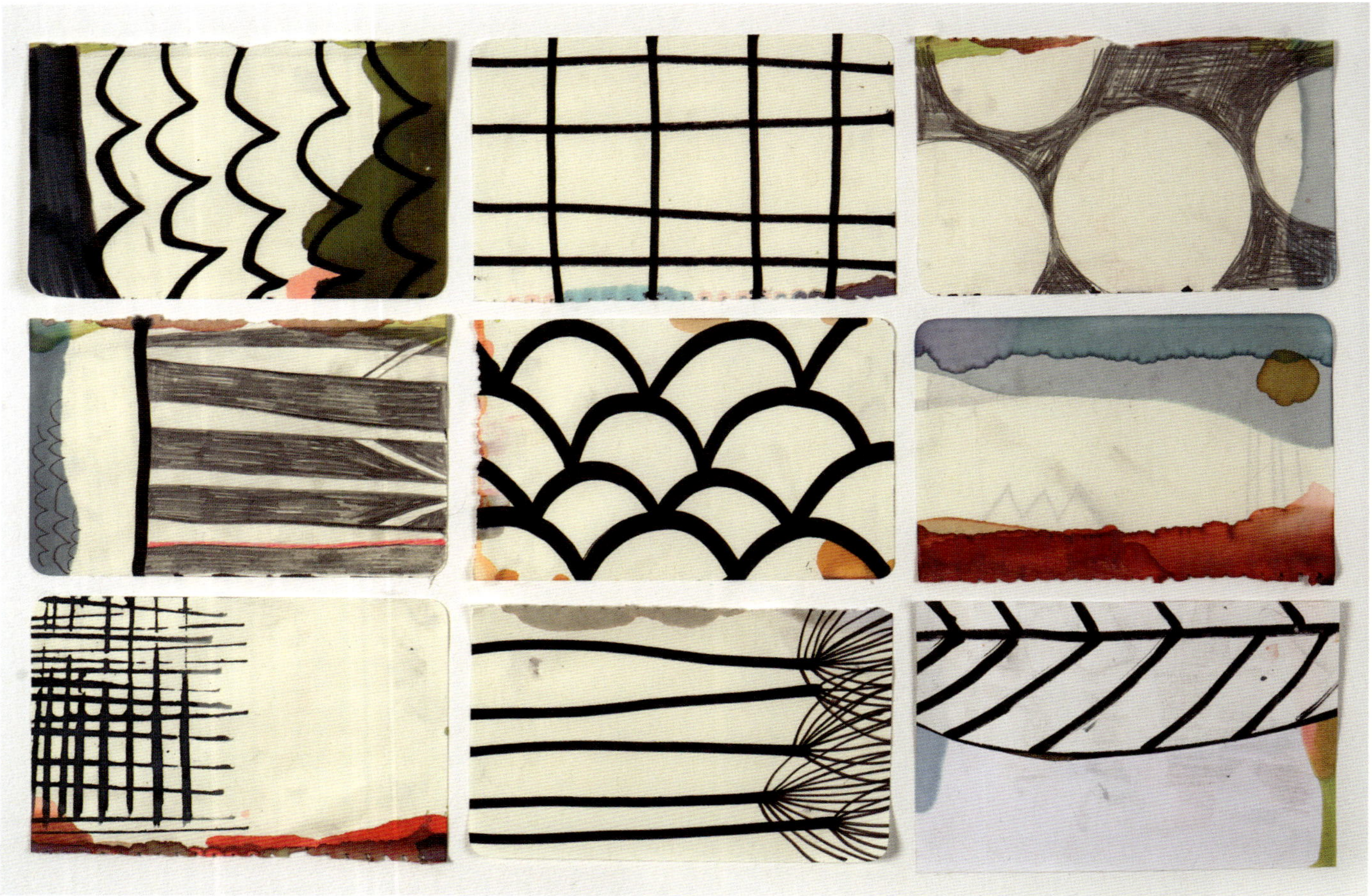

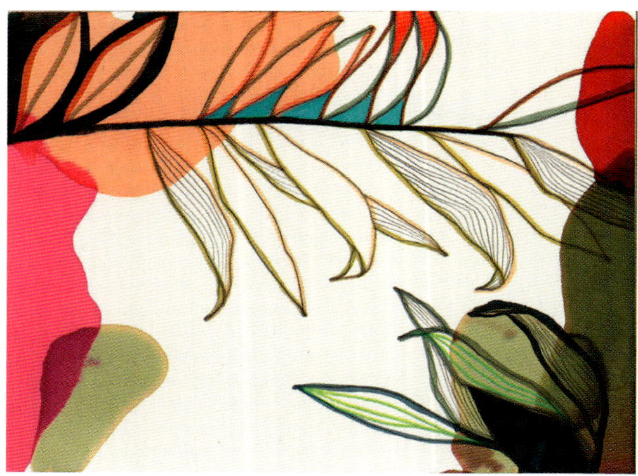

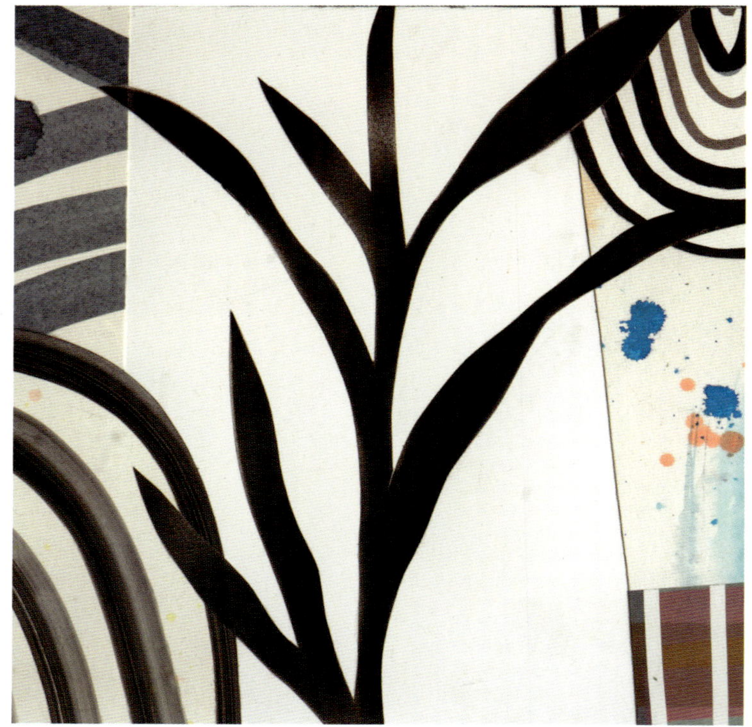

Artwork created with unconventional materials, including sponges, straws, spray paint, correction fluid, permanent marker, and wood stain

unconventional materials list

- spray paint
- white glue
- salt
- wood stain
- plastic straws
- yarn
- food coloring
- permanent markers
- coffee/tea
- correction fluid, such as Wite-Out
- sponges
- polyurethane
- masking tape/painter's tape
- rubbing alcohol/witch hazel

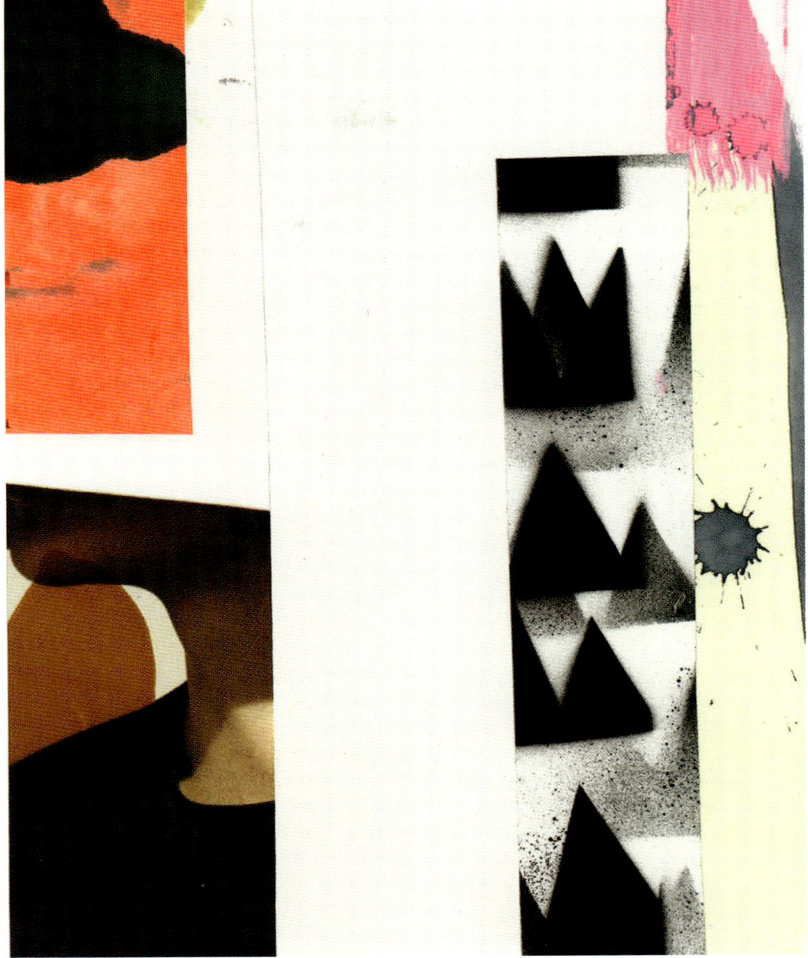

SPRAY PAINT

Spray paint is a great material to use when creating abstract work. Although it is important to add, spray paint should be used outdoors or in a well-ventilated area. You can also use a facemask. Spray paint can make both thin and thick lines, shapes, and it can even be used to fill in and create solid forms. It is quick drying, which helps immensely in keeping your process moving. To create thin lines, position the tip only an inch or two (2.5 to 5 cm) away from the surface. To enlarge the line, move the tip farther back to achieve the desired thickness.

WHITE GLUE

This inexpensive material is perfect when you want to create a "resist" in your work. It functions in the same way that wax is used in batik fabric. The paint or ink will not adhere to areas where the glue is applied anc allowed to dry. The glued area will be left paint-free and white, which can be beautiful when trying to create patterns, line, movements, and so on.

SALT

Salt is best used with inks and watercolors. If you apply it sparingly while the inks and watercolors are still wet, the salt will act like a sponge and absorb the surrounding paint. Once everything is dry, you can simply brush the salt away. This method creates natural effects that emulate water or night skies. Sometimes it can even produce a luminescent and ethereal effect.

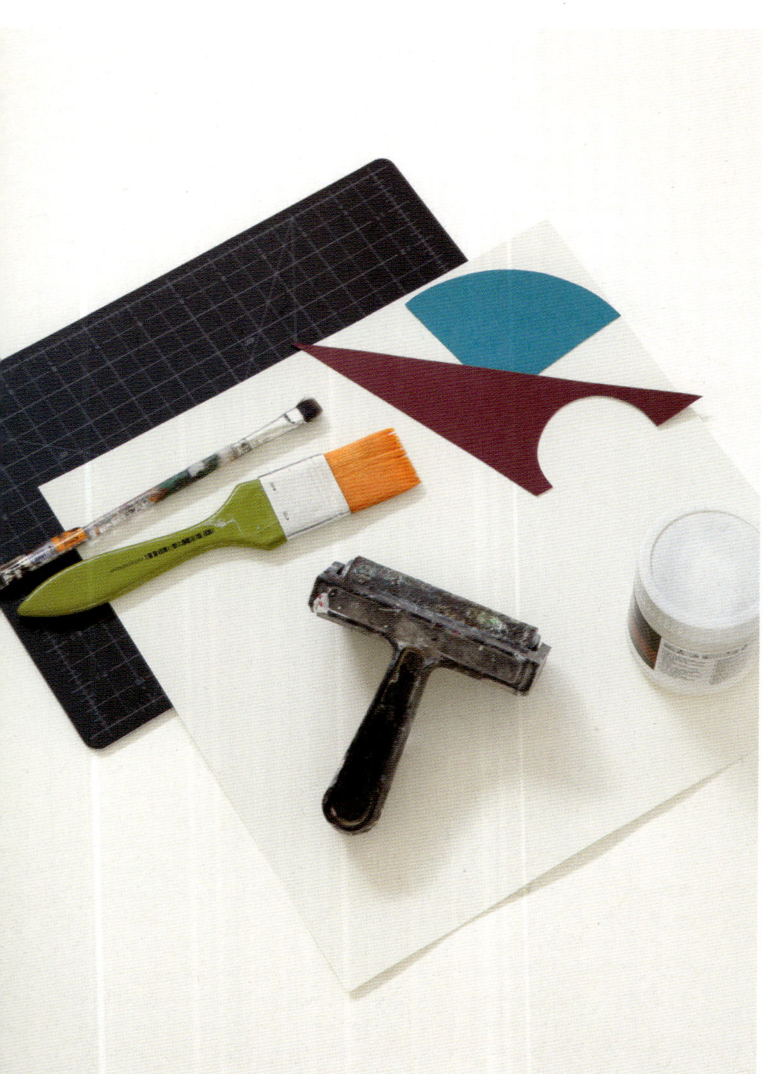

WOOD STAIN

Wood stain, available in both oil and water based, is a great substitute for paint. It comes in a variety of rich, warm tones. Because of its translucent nature, you can create brush marks that vary in contrast and depth. You can also use stain as a finishing glaze or varnish. Once a painting is completely dry, you can apply it and then wipe away the excess. The stain will stay in the areas that have texture and create a wonderful richness to a painting that might otherwise appear flat.

PLASTIC STRAWS

I did not discover the use of straws until I had my son. I was participating with him in an art class when he was around four years old. The class was amazing on two counts. First, I discovered that you can blow through a straw in an effort to move wet paint around your paper or canvas to create beautiful, organic shapes and movement. Second, I learned about concentrated watercolors, which we used for the project. They are sold at any online discount school supply store.

YARN

Many objects other than brushes can be used to print onto your paper or canvas. Yarn is useful because it can absorb a lot of paint or ink and create distinct structured or organic lines. I have even dipped yarn into bleach and used it to make shapes and lines that take away the color of the paper.

FOOD COLORING

Food coloring can be used in its pure form to make a vibrant, rich color. Or it can be watered down to soften the intensity. I have mixed it with inks to create new colors because food coloring only comes in a small selection of color choices. I have also used spray or squeeze bottles to apply food coloring to surfaces. It is always fun to allow your materials to play an active part in your art. Artists and their materials create art in a very natural and collaborative manner.

PERMANENT MARKERS

Permanent markers, such as Sharpies, are a must in my studio. I use them constantly! They can be used quite literally to draw or fill in, but they have myriad other uses. I use them to sign the backs of my paintings and to create stencils (see chapter 6). I also use them to cover up small dings or scratches on the surface or sides of a canvas.

COFFEE AND TEA

I have used both of these in varying strengths to create warm, sepia-colored stains and washes. Another technique is to submerge the entire sheet of paper in the coffee or tea, remove it, and then allow it to dry. This makes the paper seem old and weathered.

LIQUID CORRECTION FLUID

Correction fluid, such as Wite-Out, is great to experiment with when brainstorming new designs or ideas. Note, however, that it is not archival, which means it can easily be scratched or scraped off the surface of paper or canvas. That being said, correction tape has been one of my go-to tools when creating designs in my sketchbooks. It makes clean white lines or shapes that would be almost impossible with traditional paint. These drawings and designs are not permanent, and in a way, that it the beauty of it. You are creating in the moment for yourself and for your art—art for art's sake!

SPONGES

Sponges are useful when painting because they come in a large variety of shapes and sizes. Plus they are relatively inexpensive. Natural sponges, which are found in most art supply stores, are often used in watercolors to create the effect of foliage or water or to add texture and depth. I also use every-day synthetic sponges to make textures with acrylic paint and create broad strokes that can be hard to produce with paintbrushes alone. The inexpensive foam brushes found at most home improvement stores can soak up a lot of paint at once, so in one application, you can create bold, clean lines and shapes effortlessly.

POLYURETHANE

Polyurethane creates glazes or can be used as a finishing varnish. Water-based polyurethane has fewer fumes than the oil-based version, which also requires mineral spirits or paint thinner to clean your brushes. Oil-based polyurethane can be mixed with oil paints to create transparent, rich glazes. When mixed with a warm sepia or burnt umber oil color, it can be used as a final finish either over acrylic or oil paintings. Once applied to the entire surface, wipe away the excess. The remaining residue settles in the texture of your painting, which adds a beautiful depth and lush quality to the work. It also works as an aid to make your colors pop.

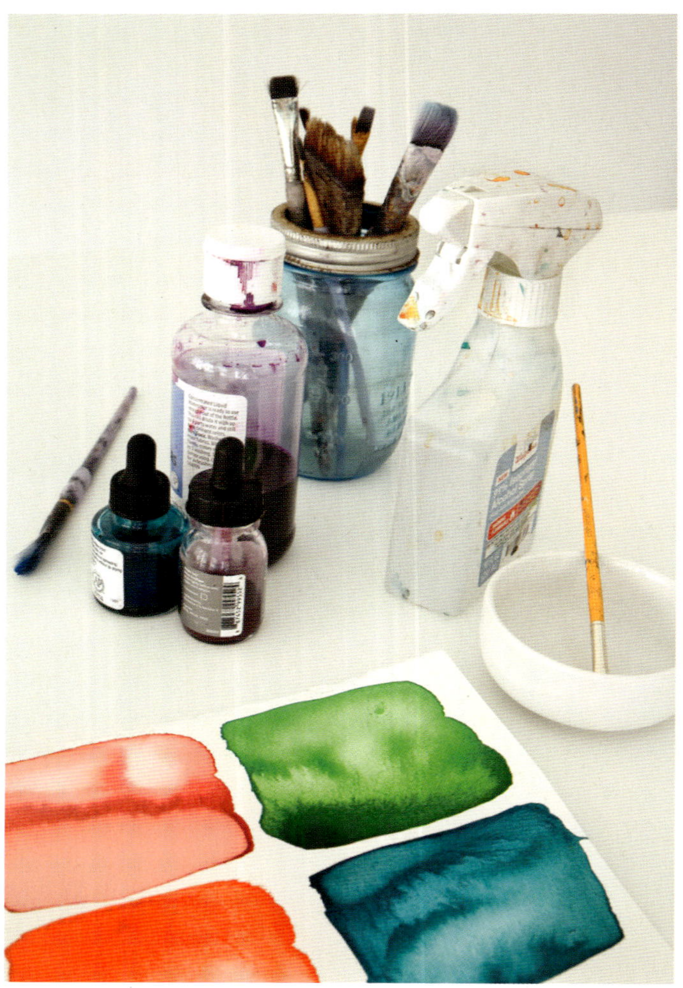

MASKING TAPE/PAINTER'S TAPE

Masking tape and painter's tape are another studio staple for me, and I use them interchangeably. In most cases, I use them to tape off the edges of a finished painting in order to paint and clean up the sides. This is a final step I often do to cover up the drips that occur on the edges of the canvas. They can also be used to create sharp edges and shapes, frame the paper as you paint, or cover or protect certain areas you wish to remain untouched.

Tape can also be used to create stencils. Place strips of tape flat on a table and slightly overlap each one to make an adhesive square. Then cut out the shapes you wish from the square to make the stencil. One benefit of these stencils is that they are adhesive and stay in place as you work. Therefore, you can keep your stencil outline exact.

There is a print-making technique using tape called *collagraph*. You place strips of tape onto a flat surface overlapping one another each time. Then you use this textured tape surface to print onto the paper or canvas. Simply apply paint to the tape and use it as you would a stamp to create interesting lines and texture in your work.

RUBBING ALCOHOL/WITCH HAZEL

Both of these common antiseptics work in a similar way, but the witch hazel is much less potent. Rubbing alcohol can be sprayed or brushed onto wet ink or watercolor paints, causing a chemical reaction that pushes the paint away from where the alcohol was applied. This effect creates the illusion of water and has an almost ethereal look. Witch hazel also does this, but in a much softer and more subtle manner. I have used witch hazel often when painting leaves. When applied, it lightens the area on a leaf that the sun might highlight and the paint puddles on the edges where the shadow would naturally occur.

EXERCISE TEN

incorporating unconventional materials

adding rubbing alcohol to watercolor and ink

I usually paint and create artwork that is inspired by nature. That is why this simple technique used with rubbing alcohol and witch hazel is a favorite of mine. Once the chemical reaction has occurred and settled, it mimics the variations and reflections in water and atmospheric clouds in such a clear and beautiful way. I utilize it both on paper and canvas, and it can be applied on top or underneath acrylics, pencil, marker, or other inks and watercolors. I often use it as an underpainting on my larger canvas works to create the illusion of movement and help build interest in the piece. This technique is also appealing because of the unpredictable nature of the materials, which plays a role in the creation of the art.

MATERIALS

- several sheets of 140 lb (300 gsm) cold-press watercolor or mixed-media use paper, 8" × 10" (20 × 25.5 cm), 11" × 14" (28 × 35.5 cm), or another standard size
- three colors of ink
- three colors of watercolor
- rubbing alcohol

prepare

→ Choose three different colors each of inks and watercolors. Each one has different properties and reacts differently to the rubbing alcohol because of the varying ratio of pigment to water.

→ Choose three from the cool range of colors (e.g., blues, teals, and greens) and three from the warm range (e.g., reds, pinks, and oranges). This will give you a better understanding of the reaction of the materials as well as the effect on different color palettes.

create

- Create a simple, gridlike formation, organizing the warm colors on one side and cool colors on the other.
- Experiment with two application techniques. The first is wet on wet, in which you start by wetting the paper with water before applying the paint. The second is dry brush, or painting directly onto dry paper.
- After applying the color, but before it dries, use rubbing alcohol sparingly and apply it to each color. You can experiment with application techniques by spraying, dotting, brushing, or tapping the alcohol onto the page. You can also experiment with the amount of alcohol to see different results.

I love this practice because you are letting go of control and allowing the properties of the materials to create the final outcome.

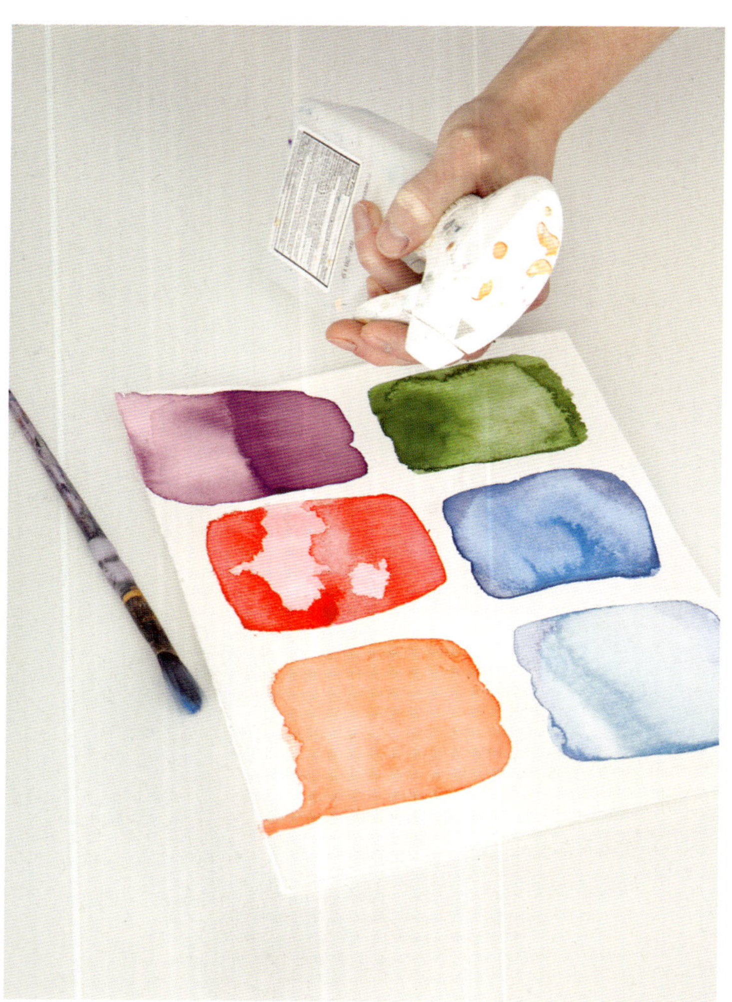

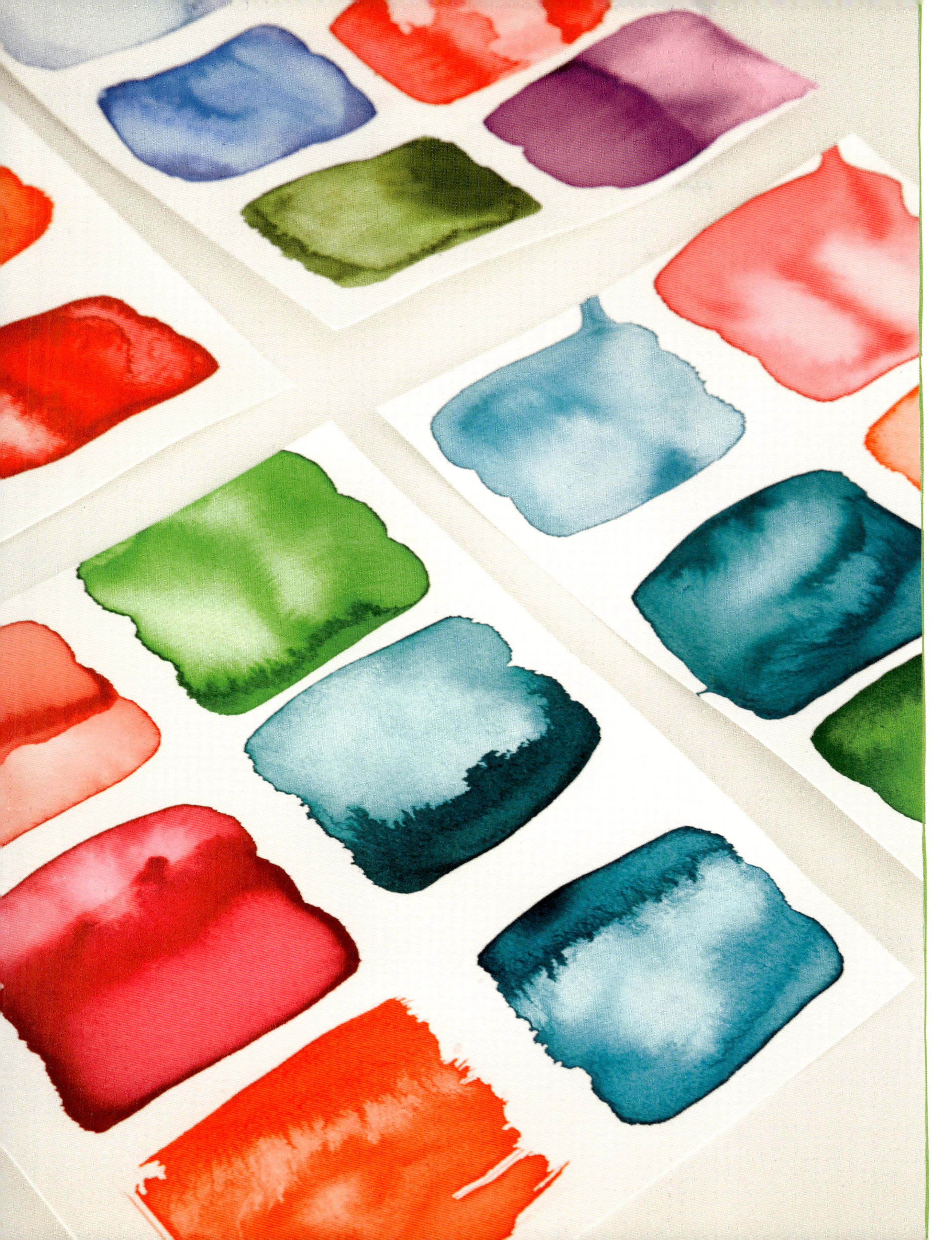

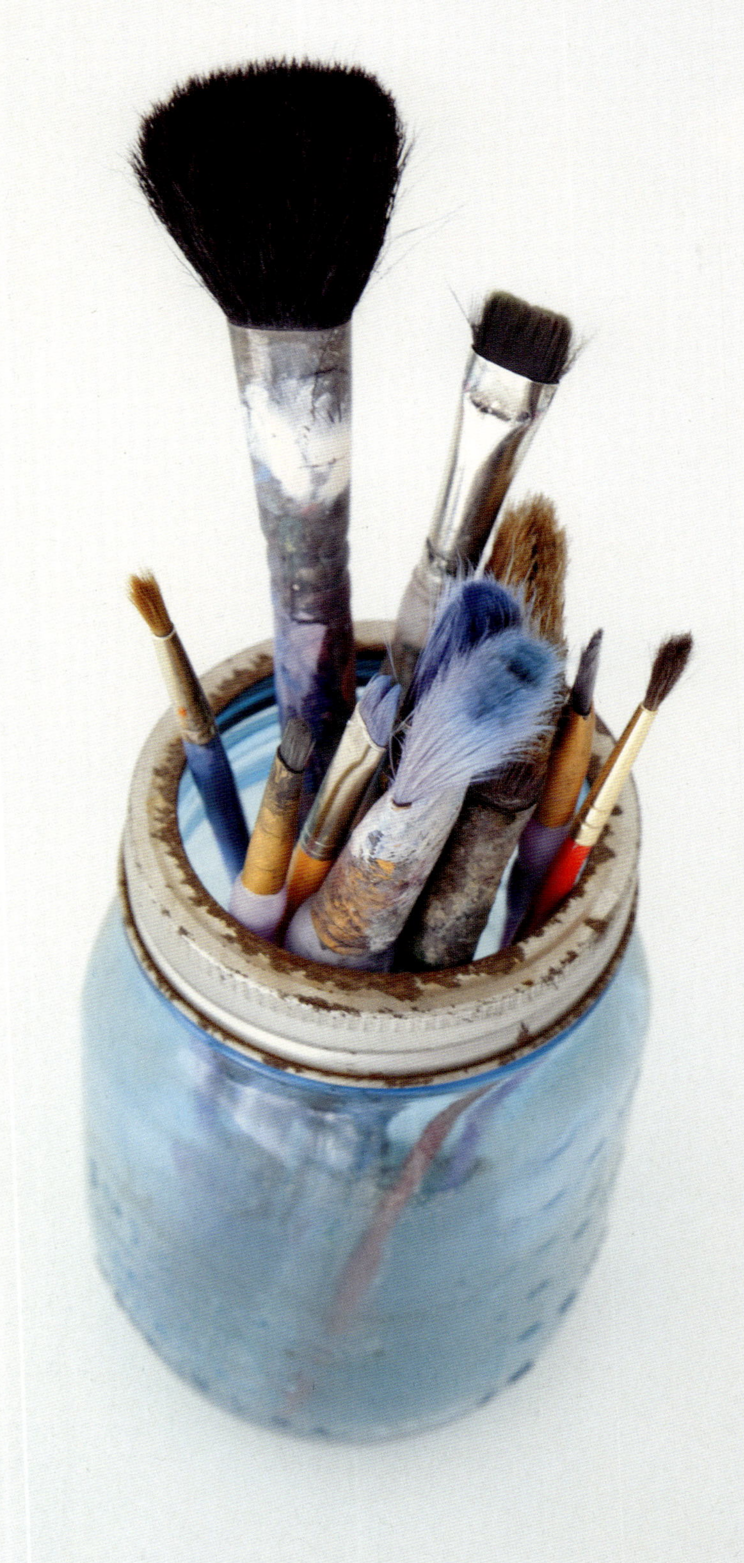

EXERCISE ELEVEN

playing with color, texture, and uncertainty

experimenting with three unusual materials

MATERIALS

- three items from the unconventional materials list (see page 67)
- small primed canvas or heavyweight mixed-media paper
- round and flat paintbrushes, in a variety of sizes
- containers for water

Even though you are the main, proactive force in your art, your materials also play a major role. Your ideas and intentions when planning a new piece can be very well thought out and constructed. Yet even the most seasoned artist has to factor in the materials. We can only go as far as our materials allow us. It is the responsibility of the artist to always be innovating and learning new ways to be creative and to express themselves. As you develop and your tastes and ideas change, so do your choices and decisions concerning your materials and how you apply them.

This interaction with your materials is especially evident for mixed-media artists. There is always an element of uncertainty when working in several different mediums at once. A mixed-media piece of art invites the viewer in both figuratively and literally. I love when a viewer steps toward an artwork to study how it was made. When I was studying art, I was equally amazed by how Monet portrayed atmospheric light, as I was by how Cy Twombly depicted Homer's *Iliad*. Twombly's work is a perfect example of why I love mixed media. His aggressive pencil scribbles and energetic paint strokes are visual poetry and emotion at work.

Another reason I love mixed media is because, with all its levels and variations, it is a reflection of life. Life is never flat, but made up of an endless array of colors, textures, patterns, transitions, and uncertainty.

For this exercise, choose three products from the unconventional materials list in the introduction to this chapter and experiment with them as you paint to discover how new, unfamiliar materials interact.

The materials for this exercise will depend on your choices:

- **If you decide on rubbing alcohol, witch hazel, or salt, then you should work only with watercolors or inks.**
- **The rest of the items can be used with acrylics, watercolors, or inks.**

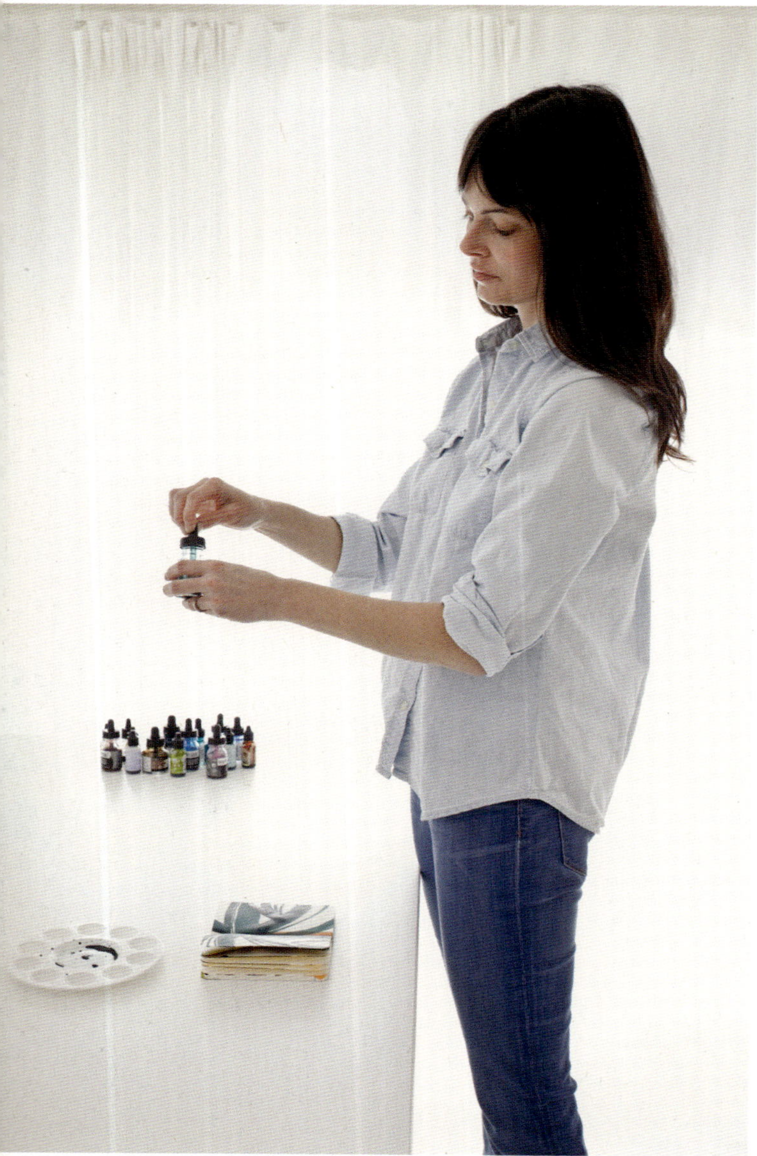

prepare

Make sure you have a well-protected work area. If working with spray paint or polyurethane, set up your work area outside or in a well-ventilated area to reduce fumes.

create

The main goal of the creation process for this exercise is experimentation. I've listed a few suggestions on how to use these materials, but push yourself to try out methods not listed below.

POSSIBLE MATERIAL PAIRINGS

- **Spray paint works best with acrylics. Use masking tape to tape off certain areas on your surface to create lines or shapes. Spray the defined areas, allow for drying time, and then remove the tape slowly in a 45-degree angle toward you.**
- **Salt works well with rubbing alcohol or witch hazel. The salt absorbs the surrounding ink or watercolor and the antiseptics expel it. The combination of these two adds depth and interest to a piece.**
- **Apply coffee and tea with sponges or straws. Blow into a straw to move the stains around your paper. Use various sponges to absorb coffee or tea and then experiment by squeezing out the liquid onto the surface. Or use these materials to make broad, saturated marks and strokes across your paper. The stains will most likely pool in certain areas, creating beautiful variations in the warm colors.**

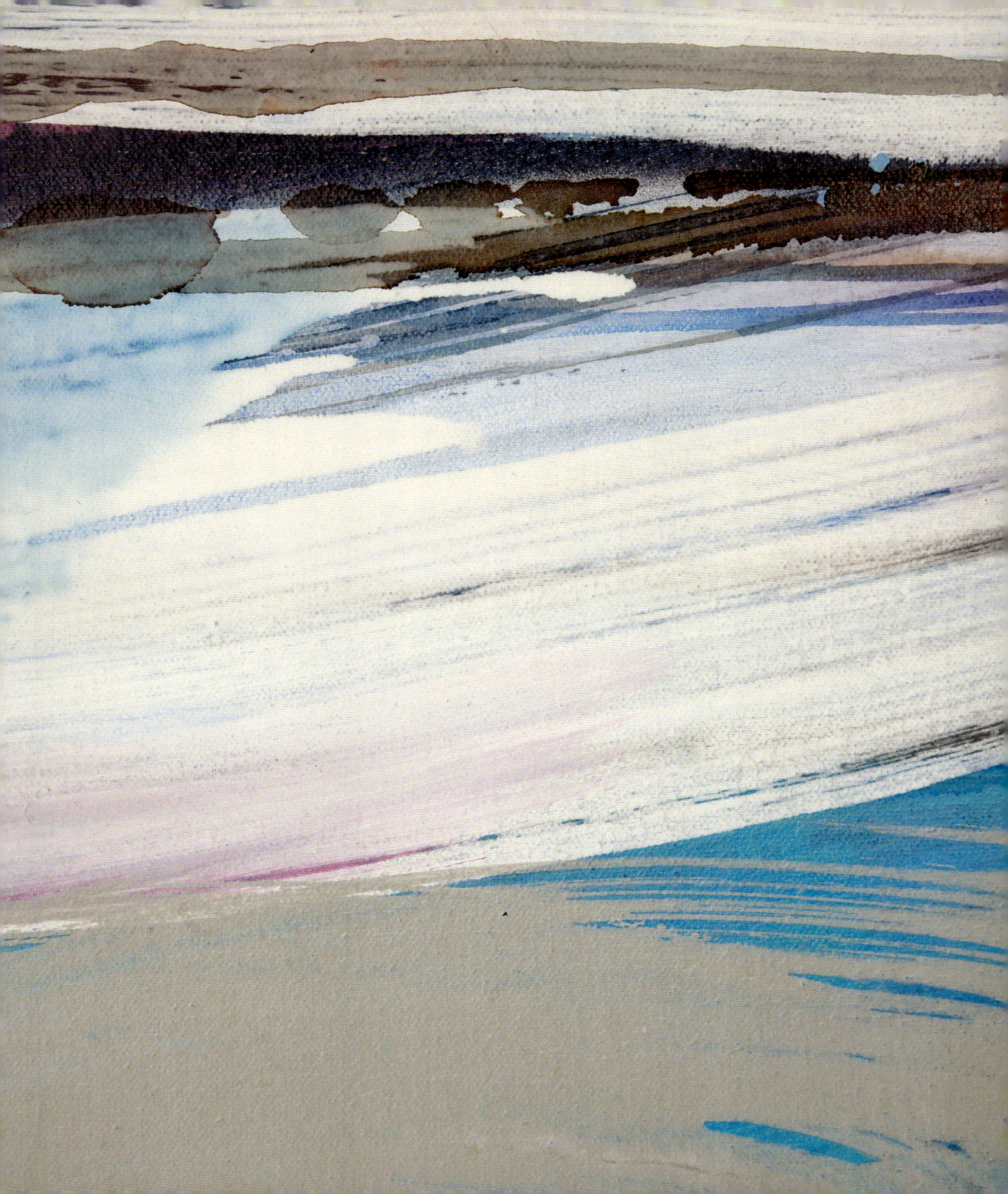

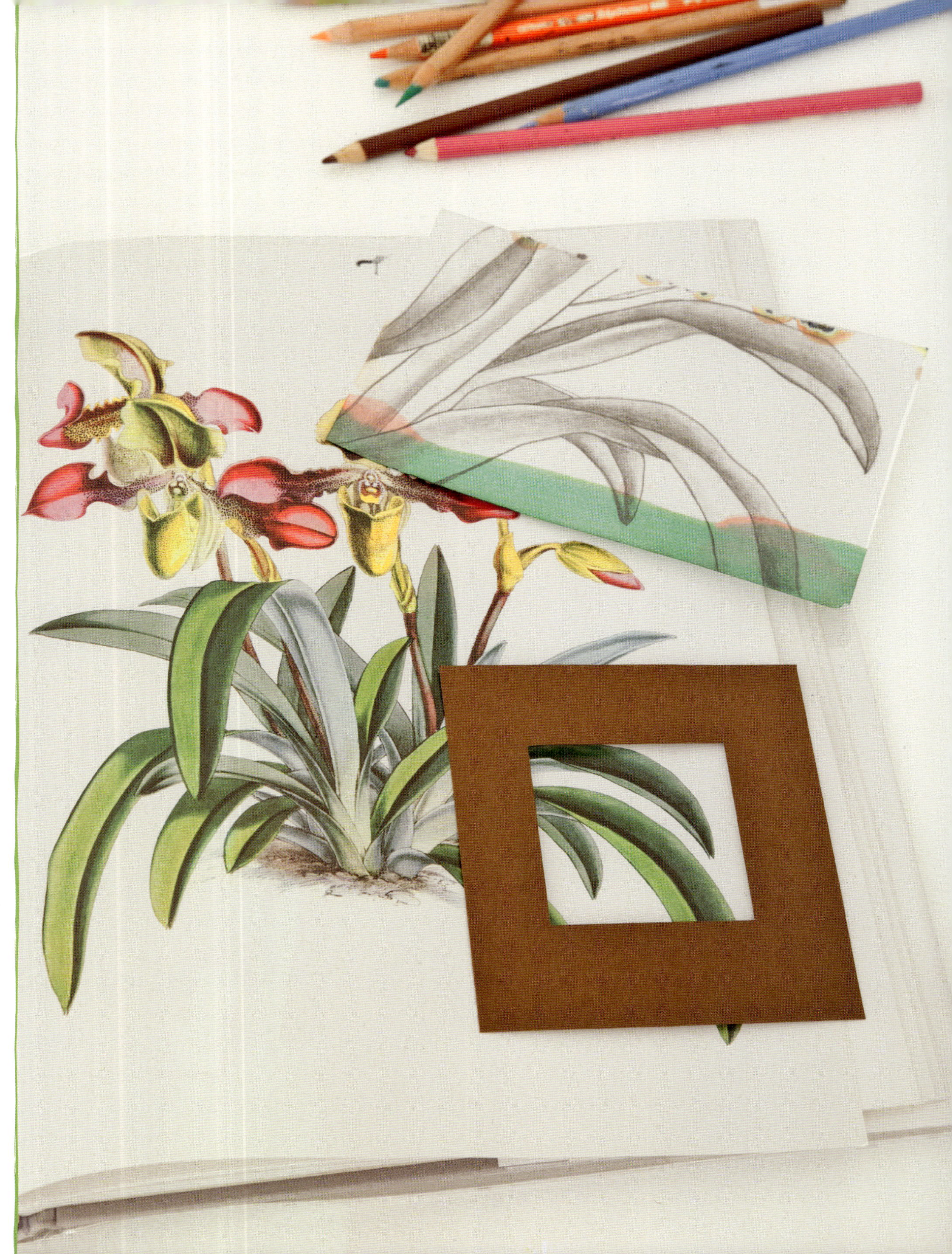

EXERCISE TWELVE

pattern play

discovering and using patterns in mixed media

A pattern, by definition, is the combination of elements or shapes, repeated in a recurring or regular arrangement. They can be found everywhere, in both ancient and modern architecture and in natural patterns of flora and fauna. You can discover them in our everyday lives, such as a crosswalk, the spokes in a bike, or even the tiles on your bathroom floor.

You can use repetition in two different ways in art, including mixed media. One is to bring weight and importance to what you are repeating. Through repetition, you direct the viewer's eye toward the pattern. The opposing method is to repeat something to lessen its importance. Instead of an optical pathway, repetition can lead one's line of vision to the more important imagery. In either approach, pattern can be an effective element when put into practice correctly.

TIP ▸ This small viewfinder can help narrow down and create compositions. The small square format helps to define and enhance your visual focus.

MATERIALS

a book on botanicals (You can find botanical books in either the art or garden section of your library.)

a 4" × 4" (10 × 10 cm) piece of card stock

craft knife

an 18" × 24" (46 × 61 cm) drawing pad

drawing pencils in a variety of types (2B, 5B, 8B, etc.) and colored pencils

The following exercise shows you how to discover patterns found in nature and how to use patterns in your artwork.

prepare

→ Cut out a 2" × 2" (5 × 5 cm) square from the center of your piece of card stock using your craft knife. This will now become your viewfinder.

→ Choose one or two botanical images from your book for this project.

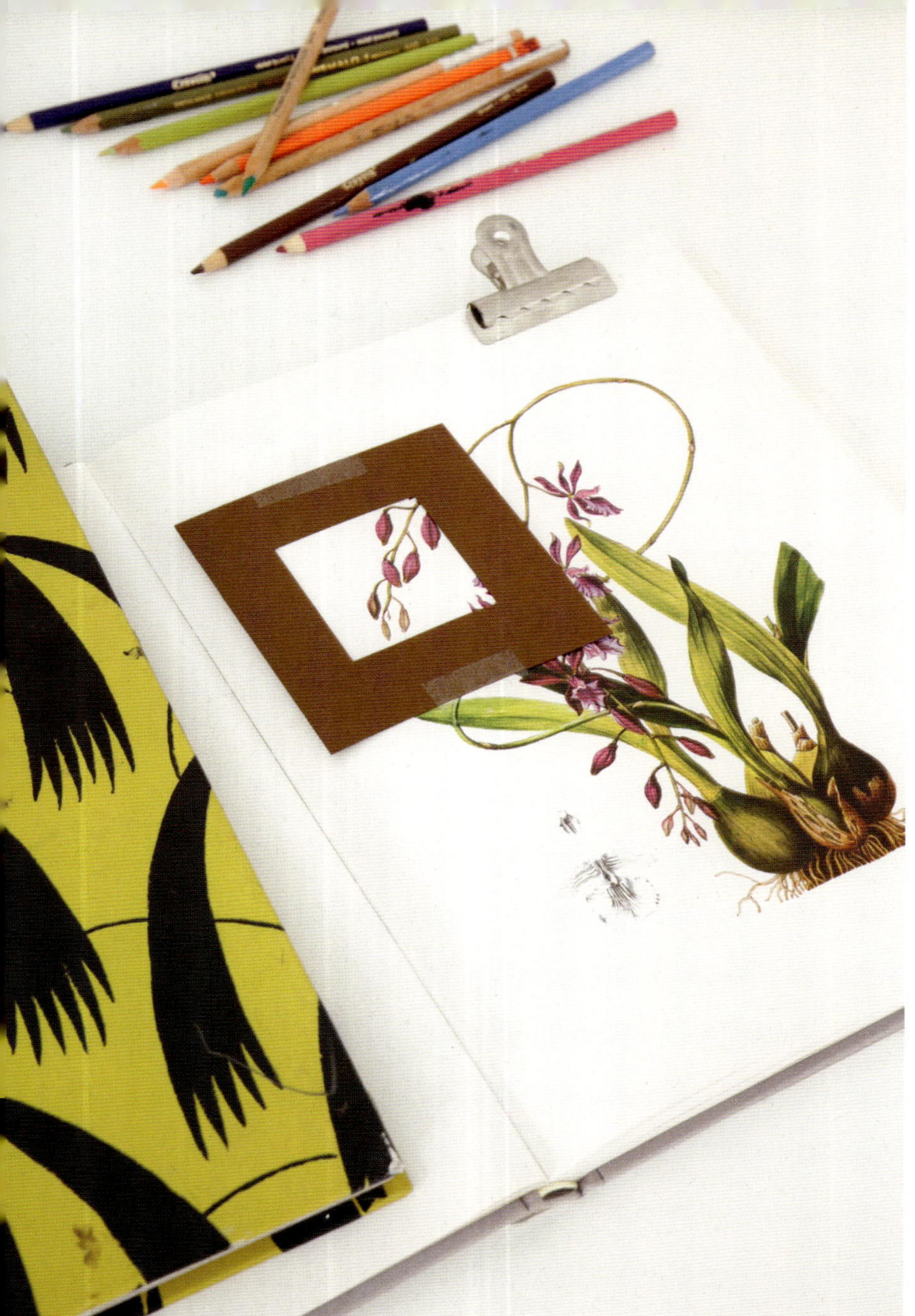

create

- Place your viewfinder in several different areas around your botanical image. I chose to focus on botanicals because their organic nature lends itself well to creating interesting abstract patterns.
- Through the window in the viewfinder, notice that the image has been transformed and abstracted, reduced into a grouping of forms, shapes, and lines.
- Choose an area on your botanical image that interests you the most. Lightly tape the viewfinder on the area and take a moment to observe and discover the organic, abstract composition it created.
- From this small image, use your drawing pad to draw what you see in the window.
- Repeat this one composition, covering the entirety of your drawing pad. The repeated forms and lines will turn into a pattern that is discovered and created by you. Feel free to add color with your colored pencils, but do so in a consistent and repeating manner.

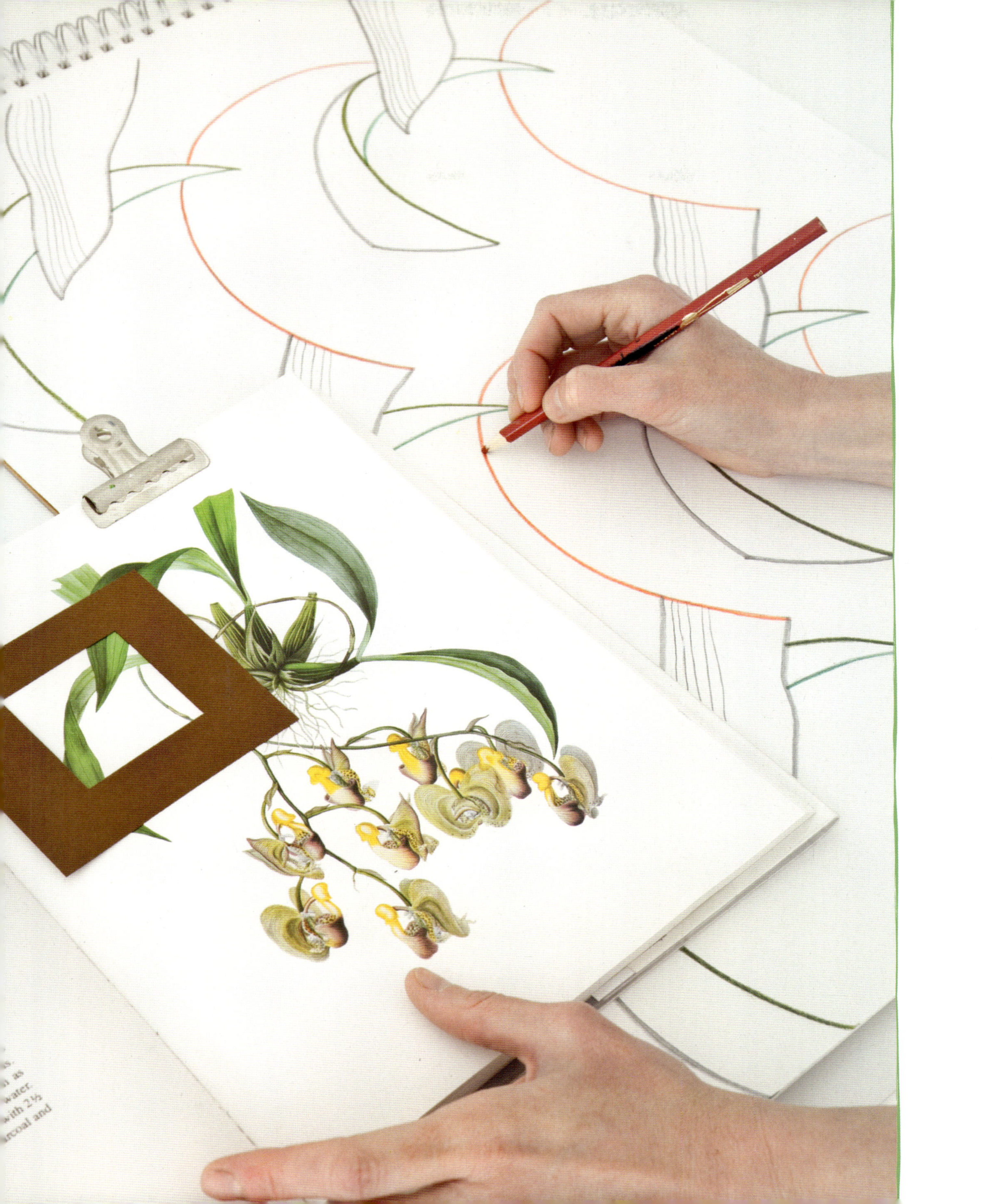

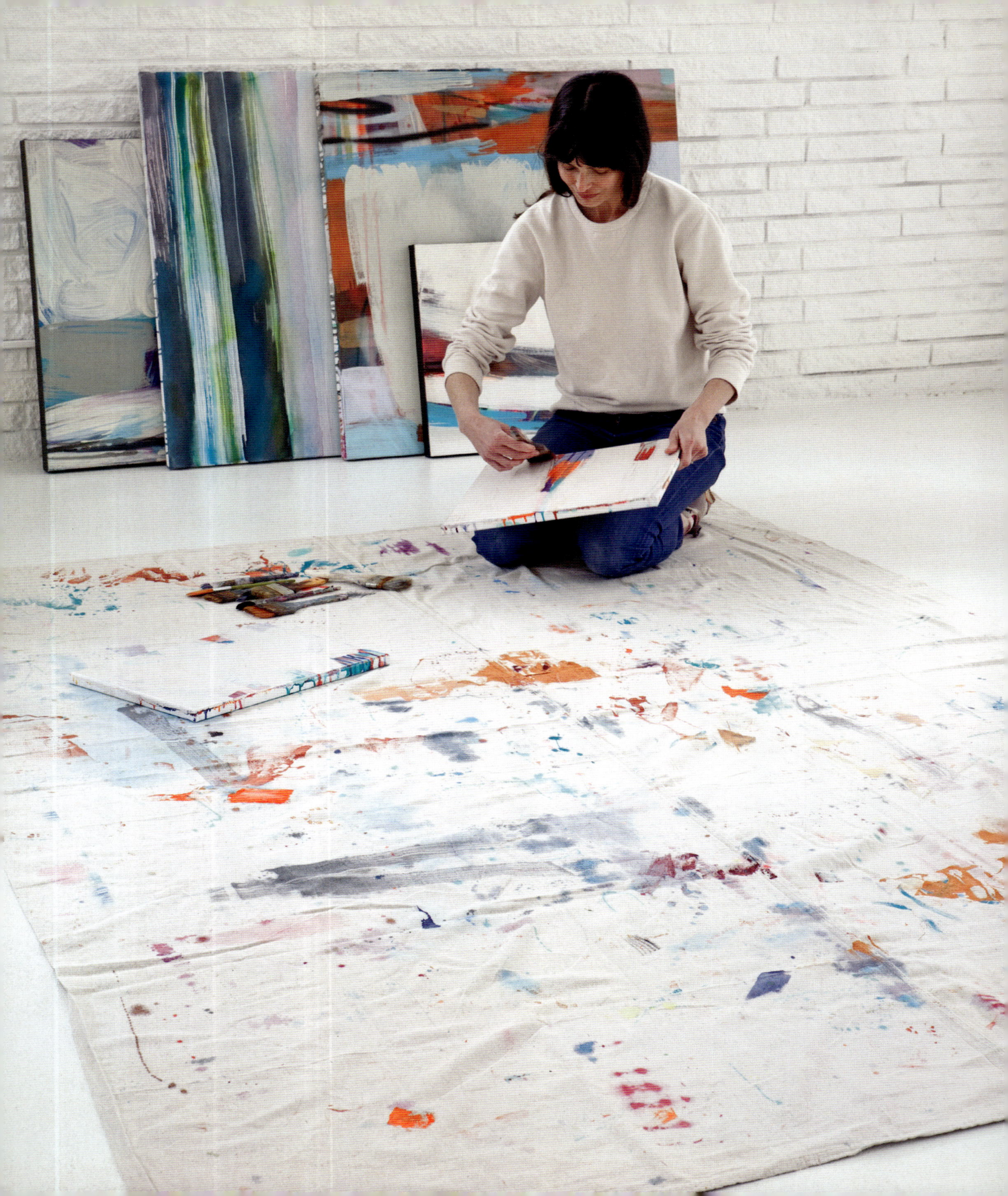

CHAPTER SIX

SPACE, COMPOSITION, AND FORM

"I consider space to be a material. The articulation of space has to come to take precedence over other concerns."

—RICHARD SERRA

People often discuss abstract art in terms of shapes, forms, lines, and color. All of these elements are important; however, learning, understanding, and controlling the positive and negative space is vital as well. Negative space is the area around and between the subject(s) of an image. Negative space can create areas of visual rest, which can boost the overall success of the composition. In my own work, I allow some breathing room in a composition. A busy painting saturated with colors, lines, shapes, and marks makes me want to turn away instead of pulling me in.

This chapter focuses on two exercises that will allow you to begin to understand how to pinpoint and value what is most essential to your composition and how to make the viewer's eye and mind focus and stay connected. Having larger areas of negative space does not mean that a certain area is void or uninteresting. On the contrary, it gives the painting and the viewer space to breathe. The wonderful thing about painting is that through layering, texture, and subtle marks, negative space can hold just as much weight as the positive. This creates balance, which is your ultimate goal.

EXERCISE THIRTEEN

negative space

create breathing room in a painting

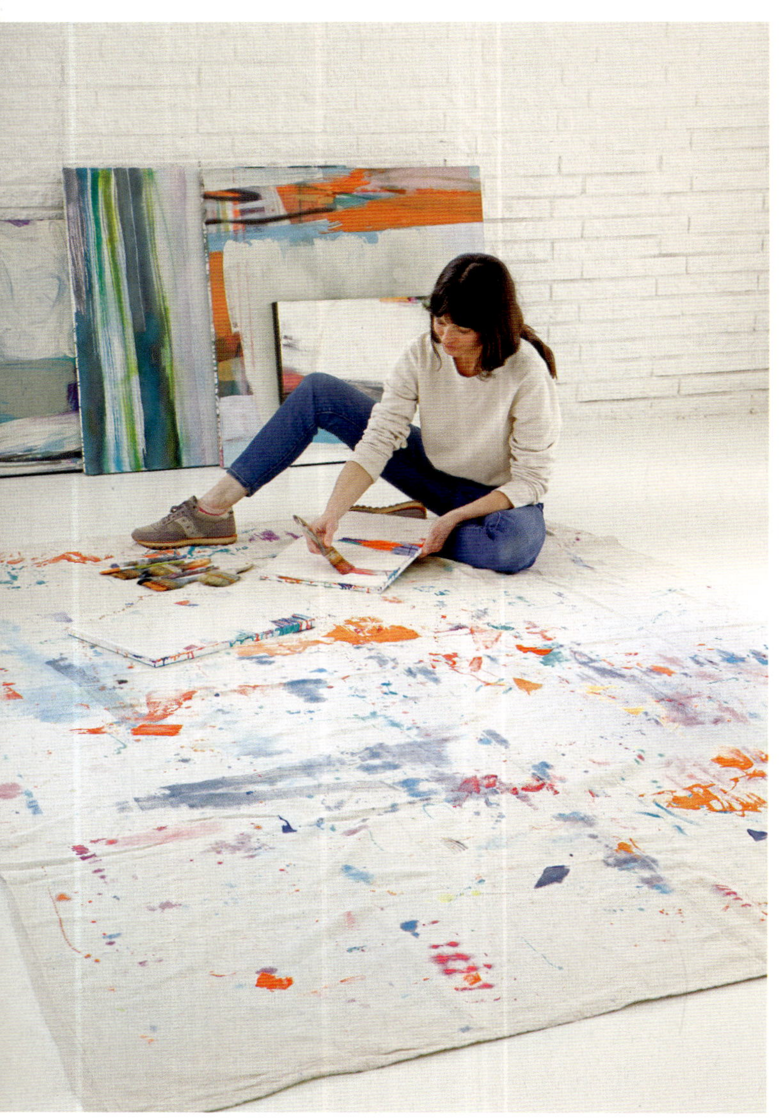

MATERIALS

small, primed canvas
(e.g., 11" × 14" [28 × 35.5 cm] or smaller)

acrylic paint, in a variety of colors

large tube of white or off-white acrylic paint

flat and round paintbrushes, in a variety of sizes

several containers of water
to clean paintbrushes quickly

several household items used to create
texture and interest, such as

- sponges
- scrub brushes (Old toothbrushes work well.)
- scrapers/palette knife
- spray bottle
- old rags
- drop cloth or old sheet for floor protection

Allowing for breathing room in a painting is the same as having moments of silence in a musical piece or when a speaker pauses for emphasis. It is an essential technique for bringing a clear voice to your work and functions as a complement to the more energetic and poignant areas of your art.

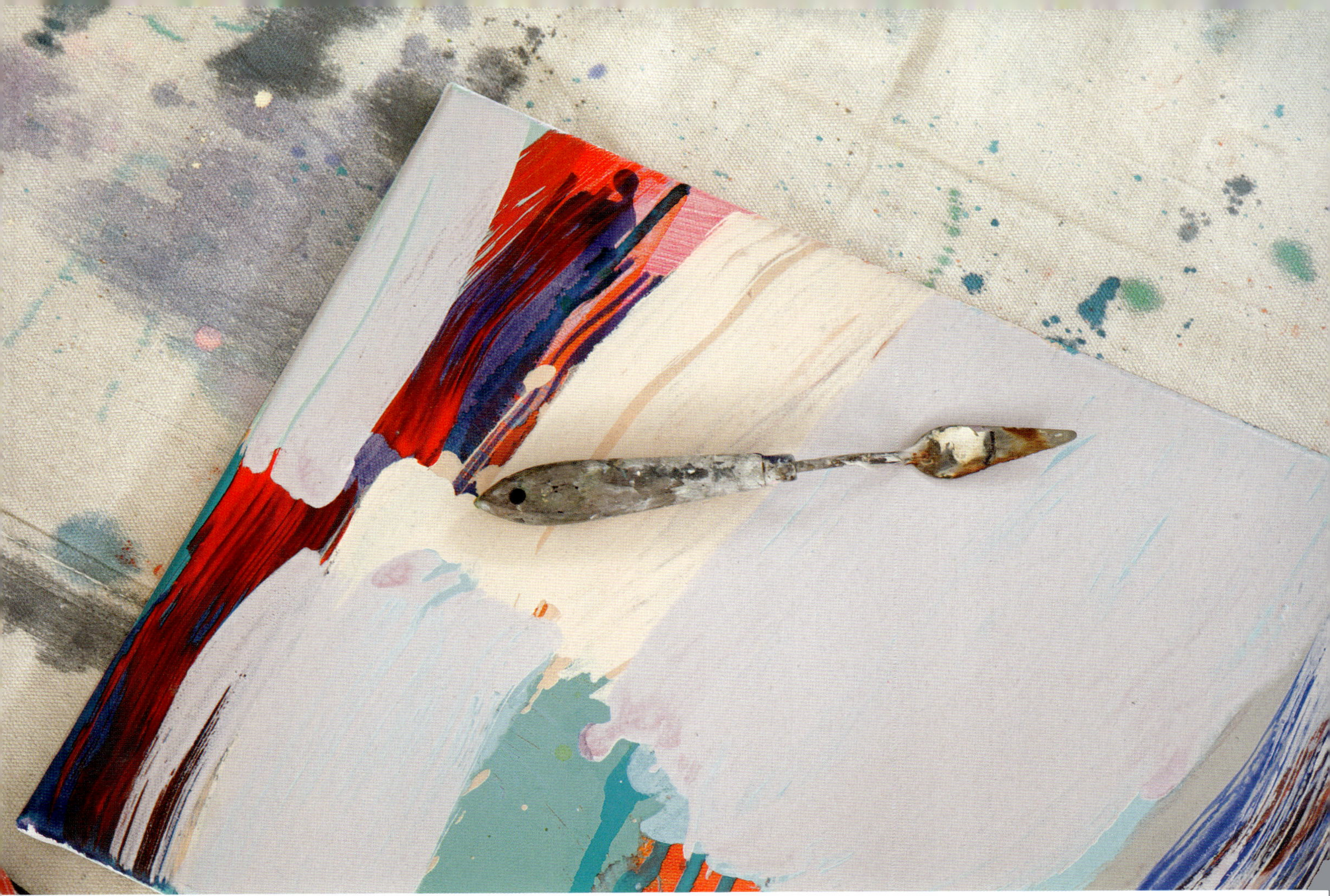

TIP ▸ Hardware and home improvement stores are great places to find inexpensive plastic containers to use for cleaning your brushes. I also recycle old jars and gallon (3.8 L)-size paint containers.

prepare

First, protect your work area with the drop cloth or sheets. Have several containers of water nearby to clean paintbrushes right away to keep the process moving quickly.

create

→ Often when I begin to paint, I just start and don't try to overthink it. This is what I want you to do here.

→ I almost always paint on the ground or on a flat surface, so the paint doesn't run or drip.

- Vary your color selection and brush size periodically, but other than that, have fun experimenting.
- This is a great time to practice different techniques, such as the following:

  Pick up the canvas on one side and allow the paint to run down.

  Use your wrist to fling paint and make energetic marks.

  Hold the brush high above the canvas and allow the paint to drip onto the surface.
- This exercise is about creating interesting negative space. So allow your paint to dry completely and then use your solid white or off-white paint to apply a new, thin layer. Be sure not to cover all areas of interest, leaving two to three sections uncovered. These will "peek-a-boo" through the white, creating interest, texture, and depth.
- I chose white for this exercise because white effectively highlights and accentuates the brighter colored areas, making it more vibrant and contemporary. But you can create more open areas using any color.
- Apply more coats of white (or other colors) using your household items to scrape into the wet paint. For example, you can employ scrub brushes to create texture. Use spray bottles of water and rags to rinse, smudge, or wipe away certain areas. All of these techniques create visual effects that allow for breathing room while also engaging the attention of the viewer. In other words, these sections are not dull or flat, but complement and enhance the focal points of your work.

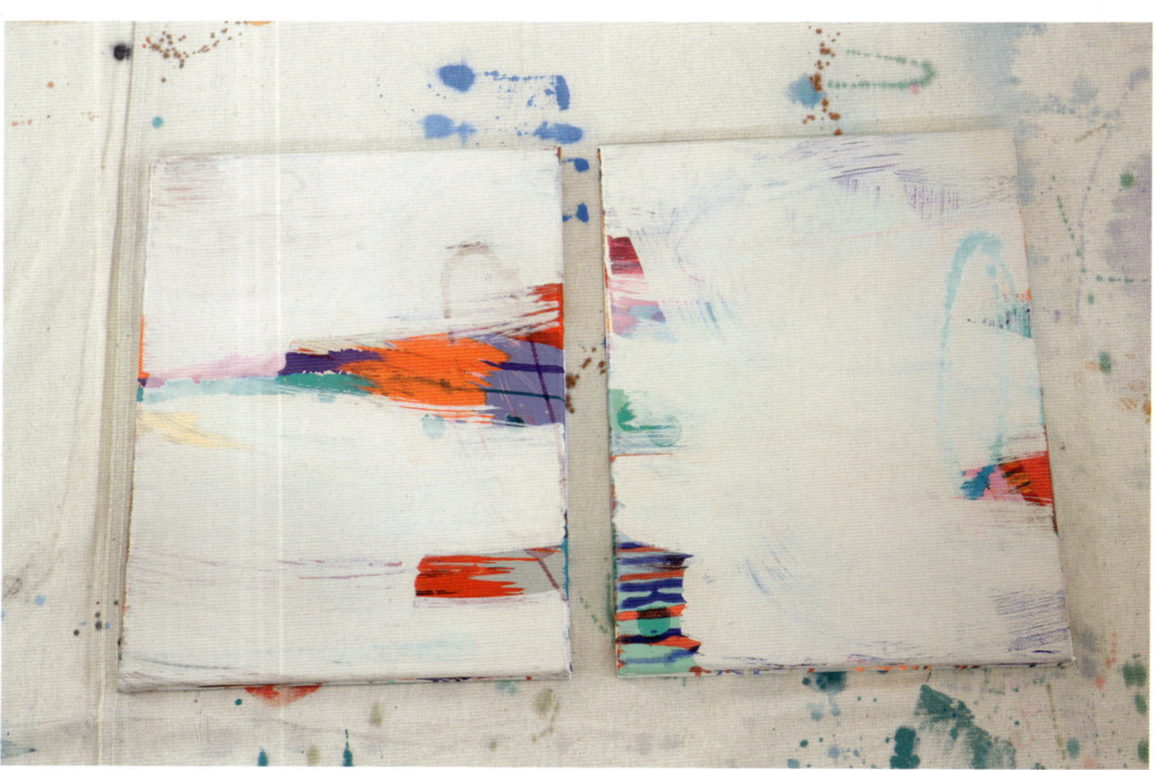

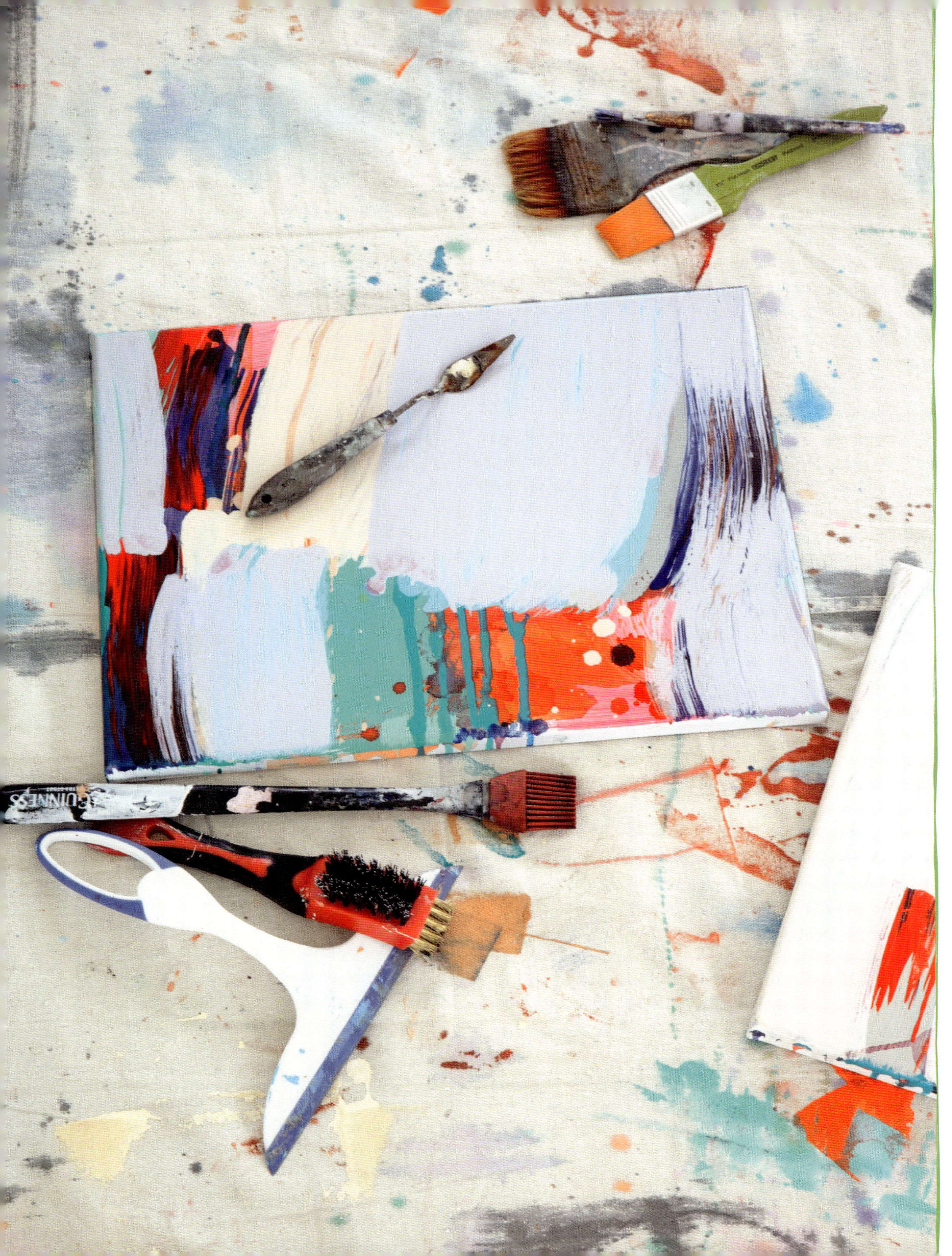

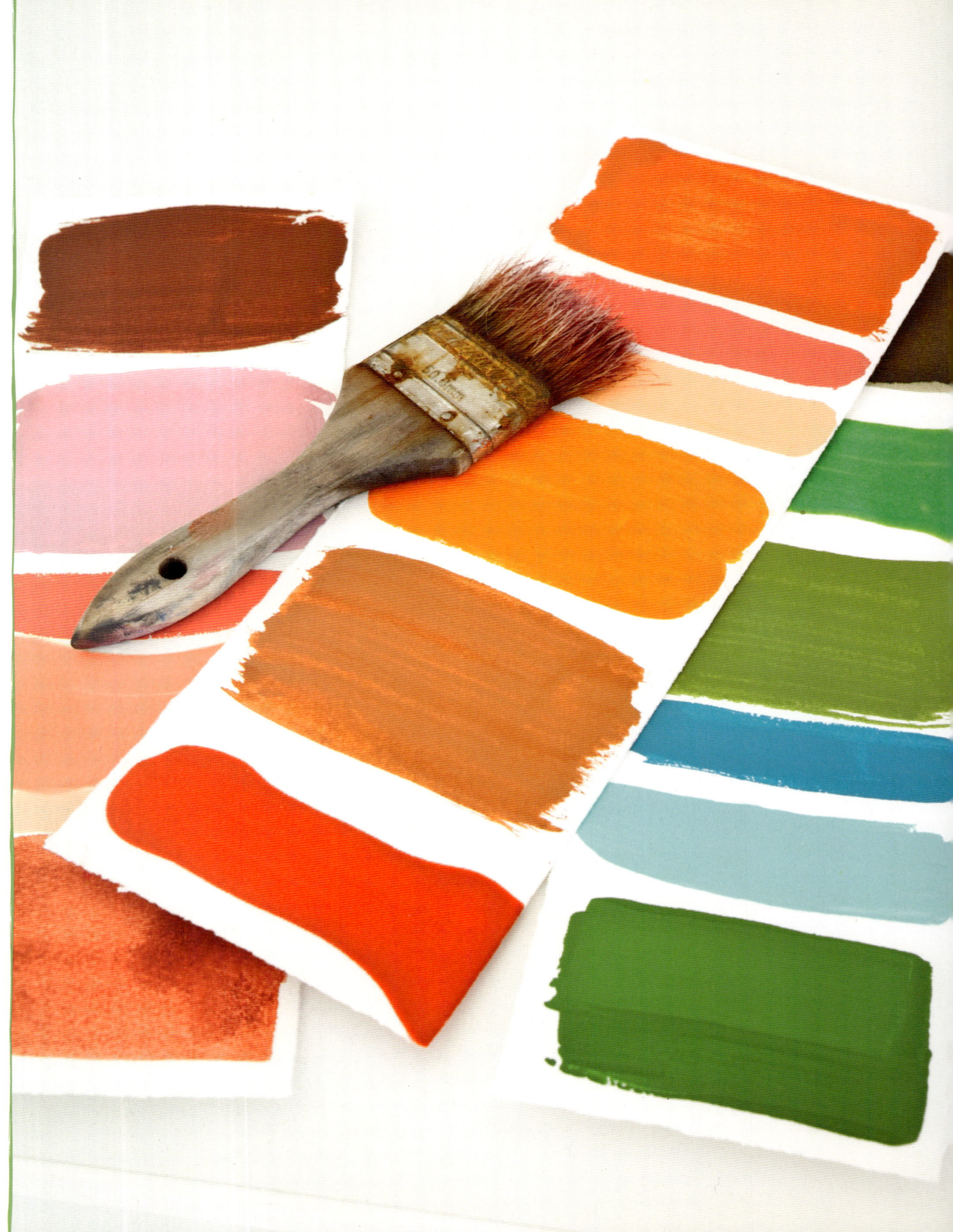

EXERCISE FOURTEEN

finding your focal point

emphasize an area with complementary colors

MATERIALS

- a well-protected work surface
- a 10" × 10" (25.5 × 25.5 cm) primed canvas
- flat and round paintbrushes, in a variety of sizes
- acrylic or watercolor paints, ink, cr other pigment, in a variety of colors
- several containers of water for cleaning brushes
- one piece of 8" × 10" (20 × 25.5 cm) 140 lb (300 gsm) cold-press watercolor paper

It is important to have a central focal point, whether your art is abstract or representational. Even though the painting may have several areas of interest, it still needs to have one area of emphasis and visual impact where the viewer's eye can rest. In realistic art, this practice is relatively straightforward, but for abstract paintings, creating a focal point is not as obvious and calculated. By focusing on color, contrast, placement, shapes, and lines, you will begin to build a visually concentrated area of interest. This area will develop into your work's prime focus.

There are no concrete rules when it comes to focal points in abstract art. Various artists, such as Jackson Pollock and Andy Warhol, chose to have the entire piece of artwork be the center of attention. Pollock's action paintings were made up of drips and splatters that carried your eye over the entirety of the painting at once. Warhol's iconic screen-printed portraits created a pattern that made no one section more relevant than the next. It is possible to create successful works without any real focal point; however, as the saying goes, you have to learn the rules before successfully breaking them.

Because there are so many variables to consider when creating a focal point, I want to focus on only color in this exercise. Color, discussed in chapter 8, can have a language and life all its own. This exercise will help you celebrate it, study it, and learn how to elevate it to the center of attention in your artwork.

prepare

- Select three main colors that you would like to highlight as your focal point. Then choose a variety of shades of these colors. You can include inks, pigments, watercolors, etc., just be sure they are in the same color family.
- Cut or tear the watercolor paper into three strips to use for your color testing.

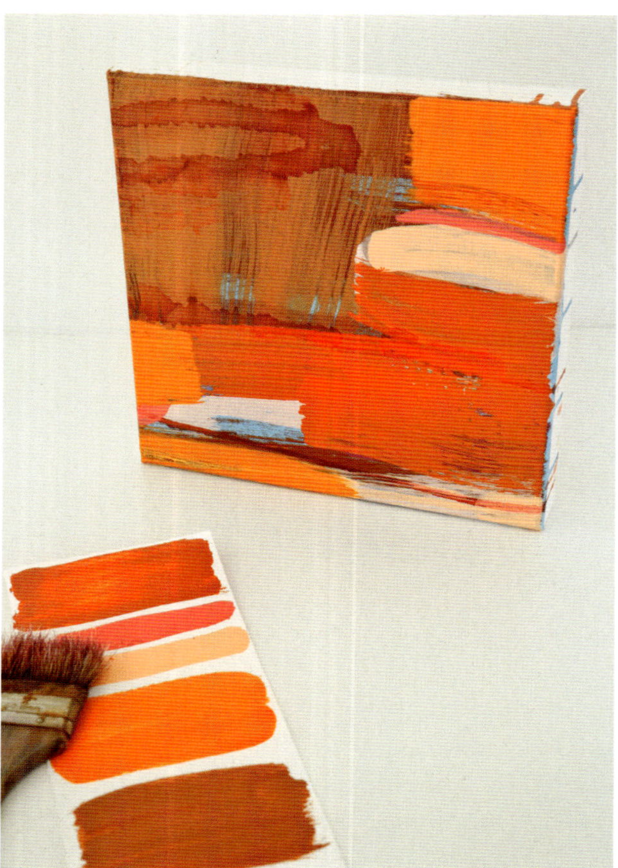

create

- Gather your three main colors and use the paper strips to test each of them (dedicate one strip to each color).
- Look at the strips, choose one color that speaks to you the most, and have it become the focal point for your painting.
- To highlight your chosen color, use its complementary color as you paint.

Complementary colors are colors that are found directly opposite one another on the color wheel, such as red and green; yellow and purple; and orange and blue. When used in correct proportions, each can highlight and accentuate the other.

For this exercise, I decided to focus on orange and its complementary color, blue. When used in small amounts and alongside each other, they do their jobs perfectly and complement each other.

- Start by painting a small amount of your complementary color on the canvas.
- Then begin to layer on the different varieties of your focal point color.
- Be sure to allow a small pop of your complementary color to peek through.
- As the layers build, you can begin to see a visual dialogue happening among the color variations and overall harmony and focus beginning to develop. Pause between each layer and step away from the work in order to see if more needs to be added and where. How many layers to add and knowing when the piece is finished can be personal and intuitive decisions. Sometimes your layers will be quite small and more of an accent, and other times, they might cover an entire section.

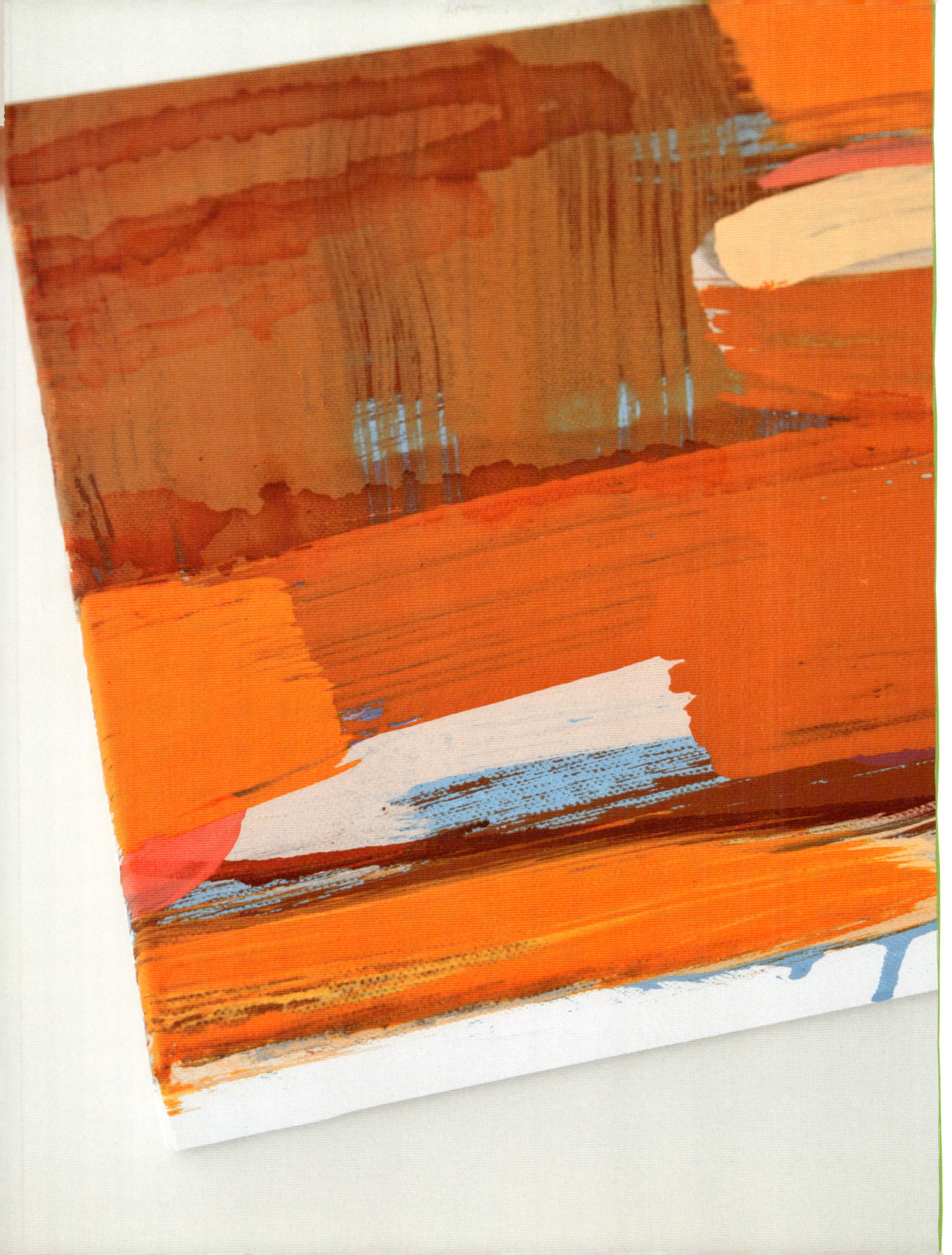

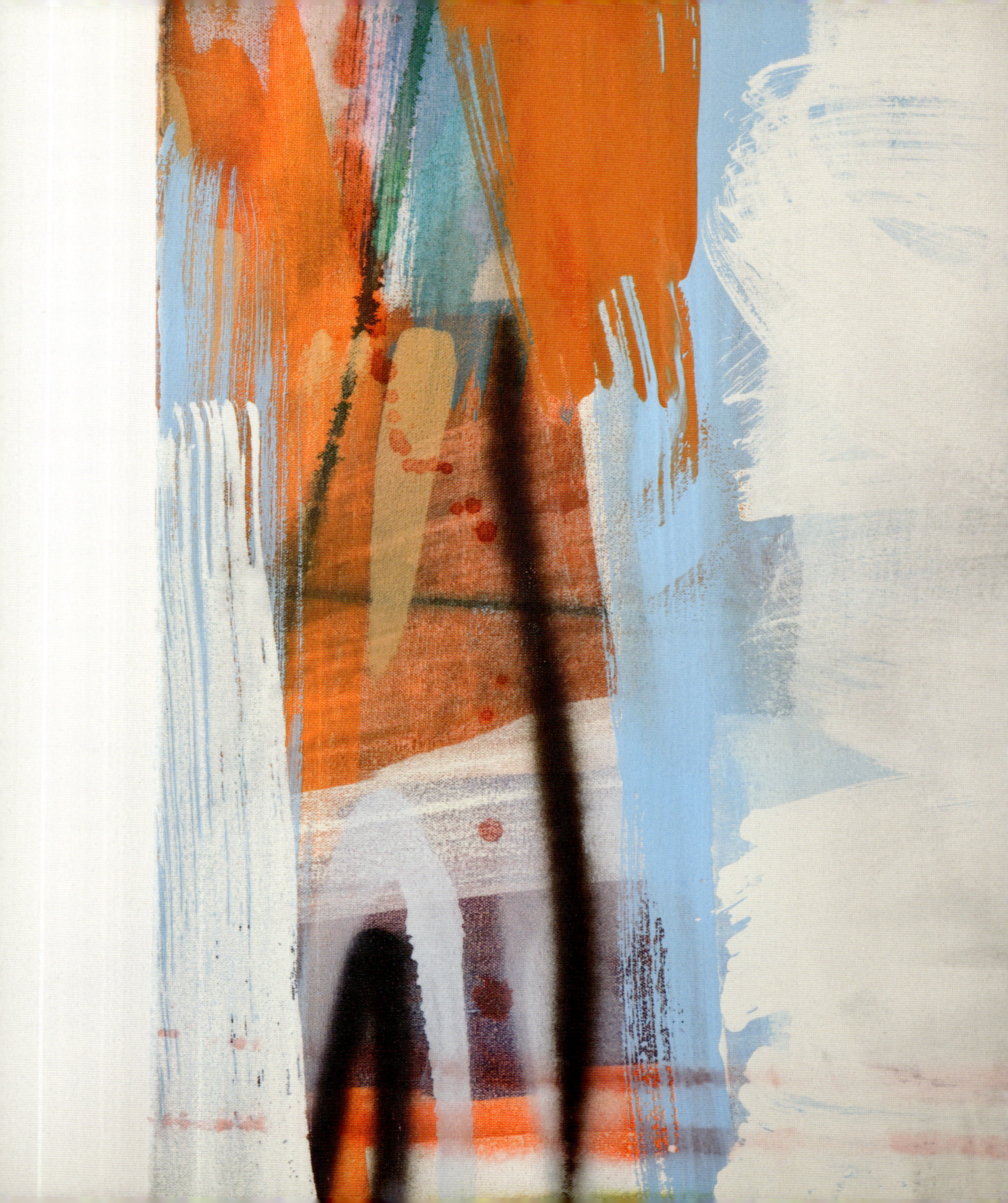

CHAPTER SEVEN

IMPROVISING WITH ACRYLICS

"All intervening steps, scribbles, sketches, drawing, failed work models, studio thoughts, conversations, are of interest. Those that show the thought process of an artist are sometimes more interesting than the final product."

—SOL LEWITT

Being capable of improvising while you paint is a learned practice, but can save you time and frustration. Acrylics, unlike oils or watercolors, are a very forgiving medium. You can easily and quickly paint over areas you dislike when you can't find a solution. Or you can lightly sand the surface, gesso over the entire piece, and begin on a completely fresh canvas. There are so many variables that occur as you paint that it is hard to be in complete control the entire time.

Feeling a little more comfortable in handling these unplanned events will help you to take chances. Art is a lot about taking chances and experimentation—with new materials, concepts, techniques, and so on. It is inevitable that during experimentation, unexpected things will happen. It is how you react and improvise that will build your knowledge and confidence.

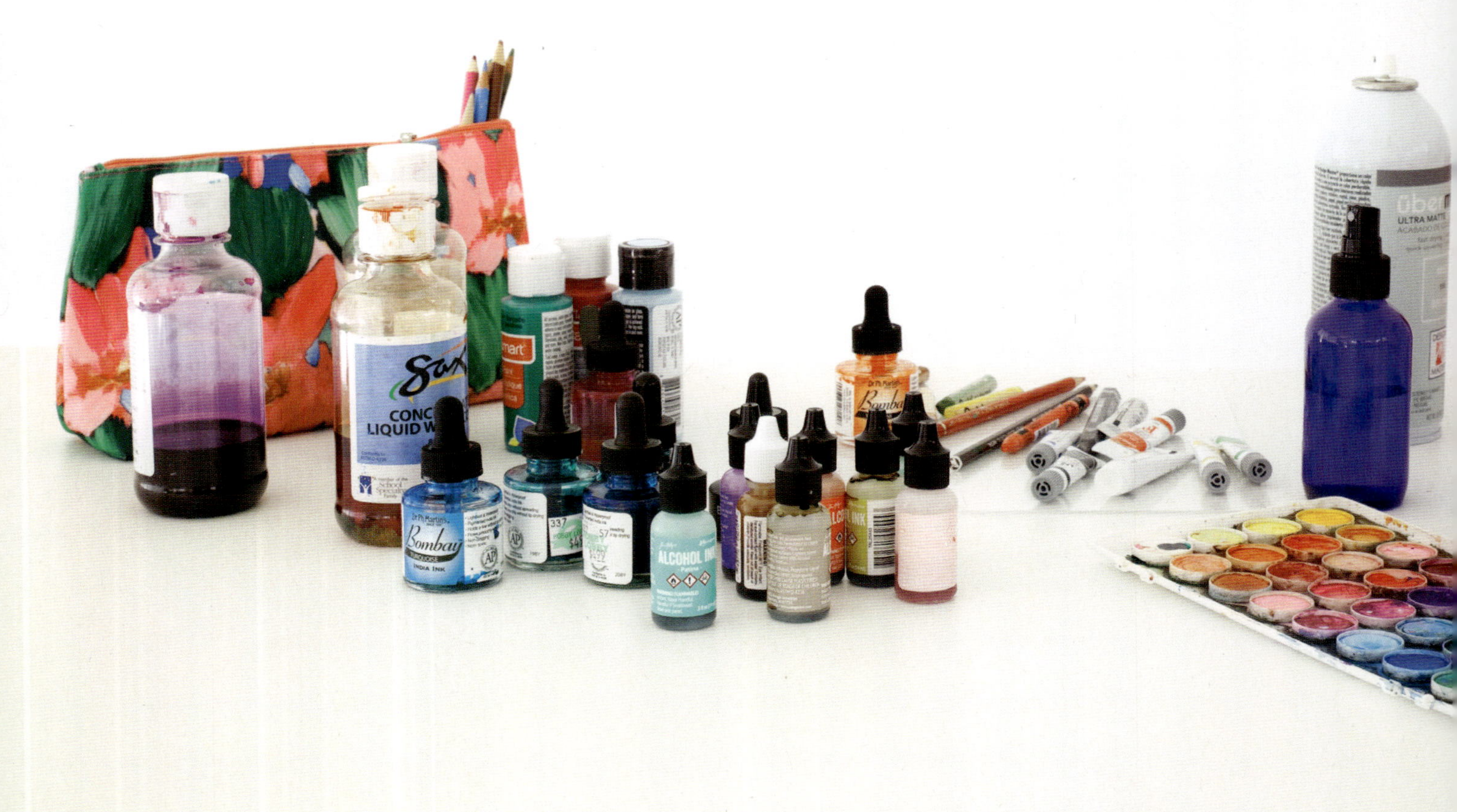
Bombay
INDIA INK
ULTRA MATTE

EXERCISE FIFTEEN

reacting with confidence

overlapping colors to create something new

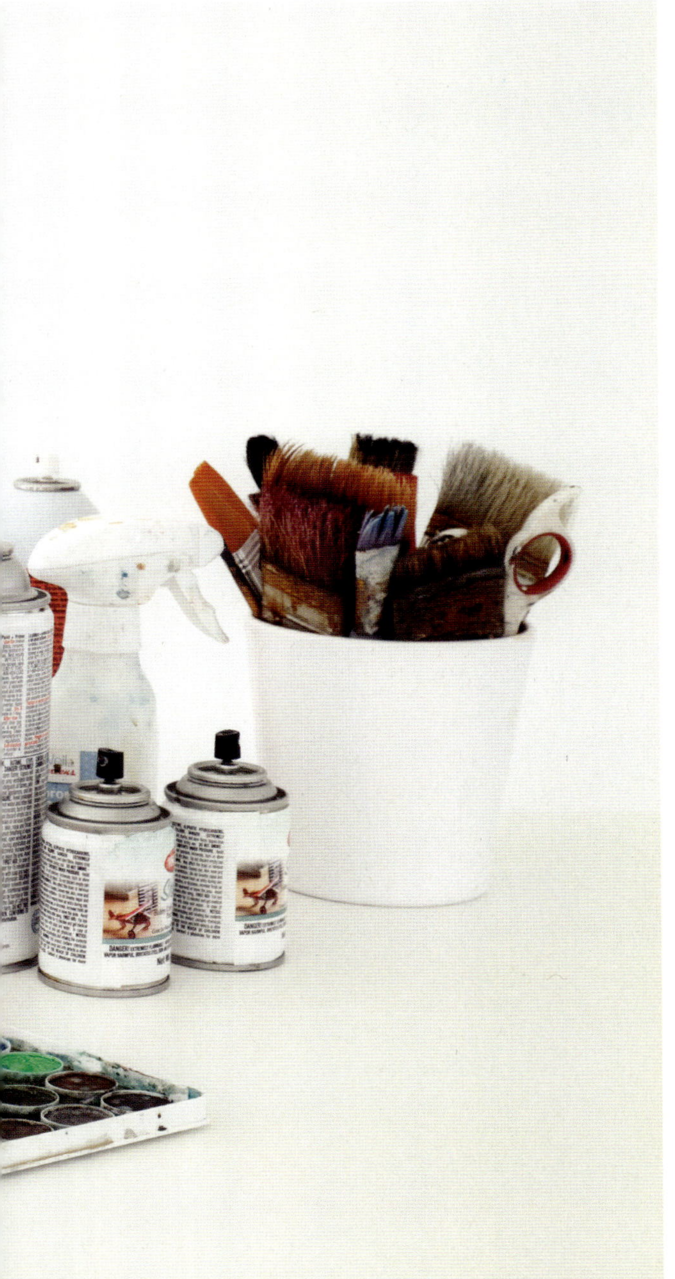

MATERIALS

- one primed canvas, 12" × 14" (30 × 35.5 cm) or smaller
- flat and round paintbrushes, in a variety of sizes
- acrylic paints, in a variety of colors
- watercolors, inks, and other pigments of your choosing
- choose at least two items from the unconventional materials list in chapter 5 (see page 69) to experiment with on this project.

Reacting with confidence in painting, as in life, has a lot to do with being prepared and feeling in control. If you are prepared, you will feel more certain in your decision-making as you create. Experience is the clearest path to confidence, but it cannot be achieved without making many, many mistakes. It is through these mistakes that knowledge is gained.

For this exercise, I would like you to create, make marks, experiment with materials, and, above all, feel uninhibited and unrestrained. You will learn the most about painting here from the process itself rather from the final outcome.

prepare

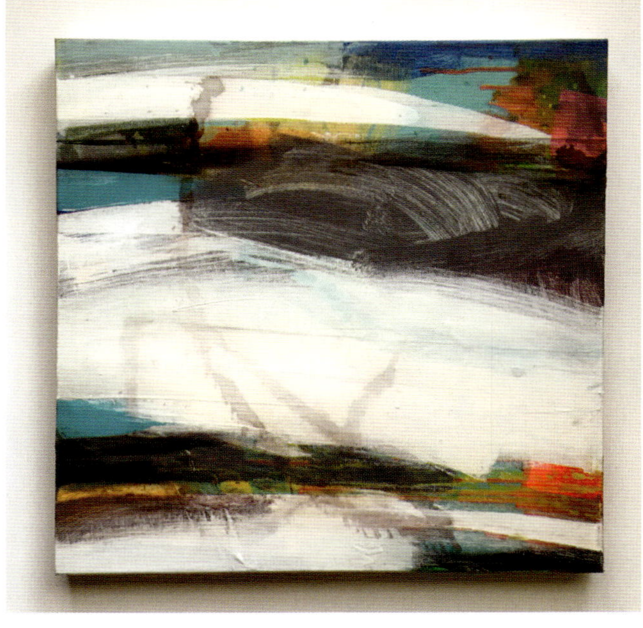

- Work on a well-protected surface.
- Prepare a well-ventilated area to work in if you are planning to use spray paint or other toxic materials from the unconventional list.
- Have several clean water containers for cleaning brushes. You should also have all your supplies ready and nearby to facilitate the process.

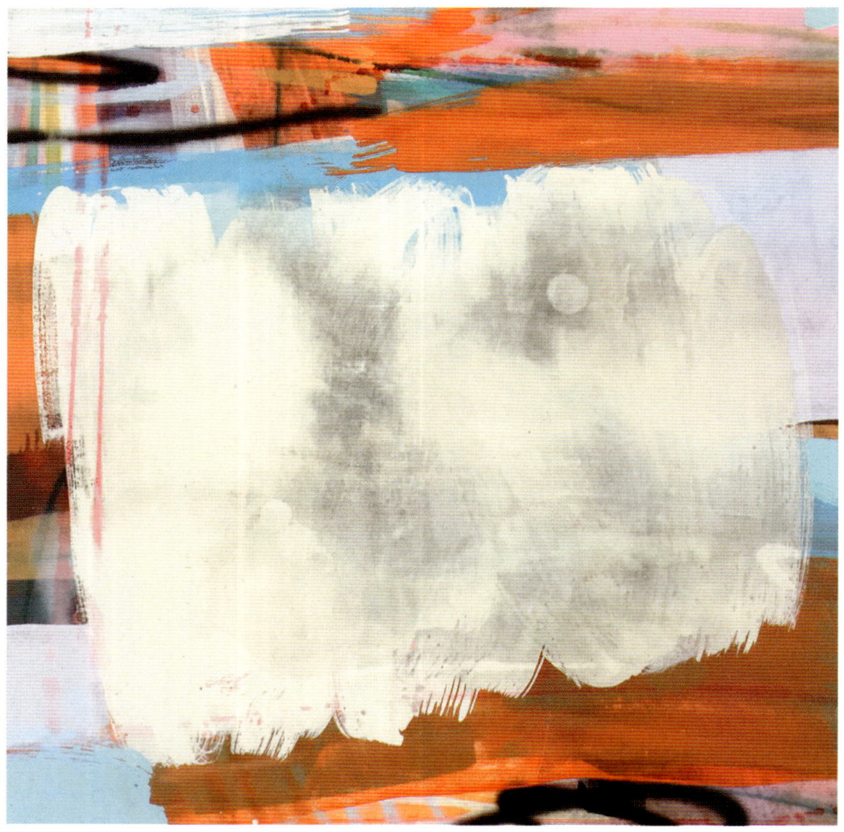

create

- This exercise is all about learning and experimenting. If you don't experiment and try out new ideas, then you will never know which ones are going to produce the best results in your work. There are always different paths to explore.
- Begin by applying large areas of color to cover the canvas. It's a good practice to think of the canvas as a whole while you work and to add more detailed focal points as you progress.
- Allow for each application of paint to dry before applying the next. This helps to keep colors true and avoids unintentional mixing, which can lead to muddied colors.

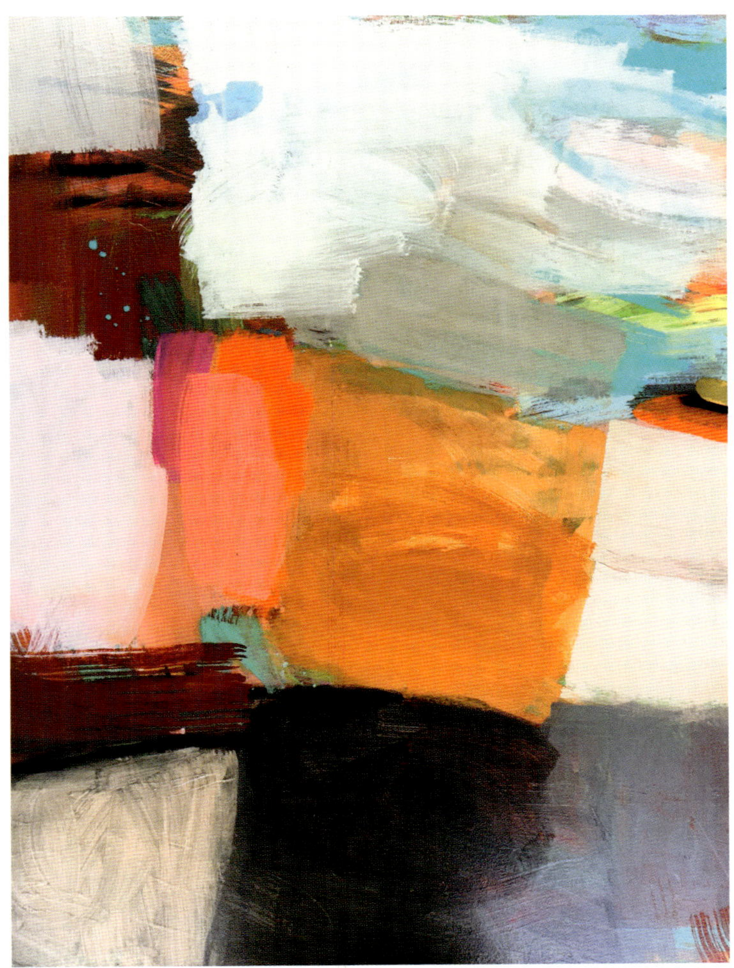

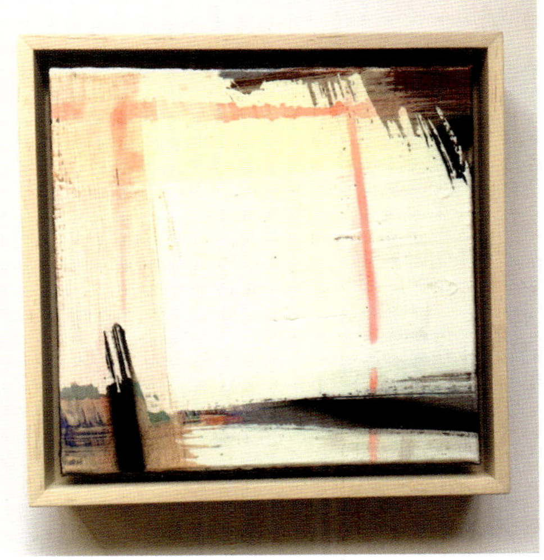

- After adding each layer, take note of your results. Ask yourself:

  Are the relationships between the materials working or fighting against one another?

  Do certain materials complement one another or lead to confusion?

- Notice how certain color combinations are created through layering, color washes, and transparencies. Transparencies and color washes refer to overlapping translucent colors to create new colors and add depth.

  Do the marks and lines make interesting textures and defined areas?

  Were your choices from the unconventional materials list a success?

  Would you use them again in future projects and paintings?

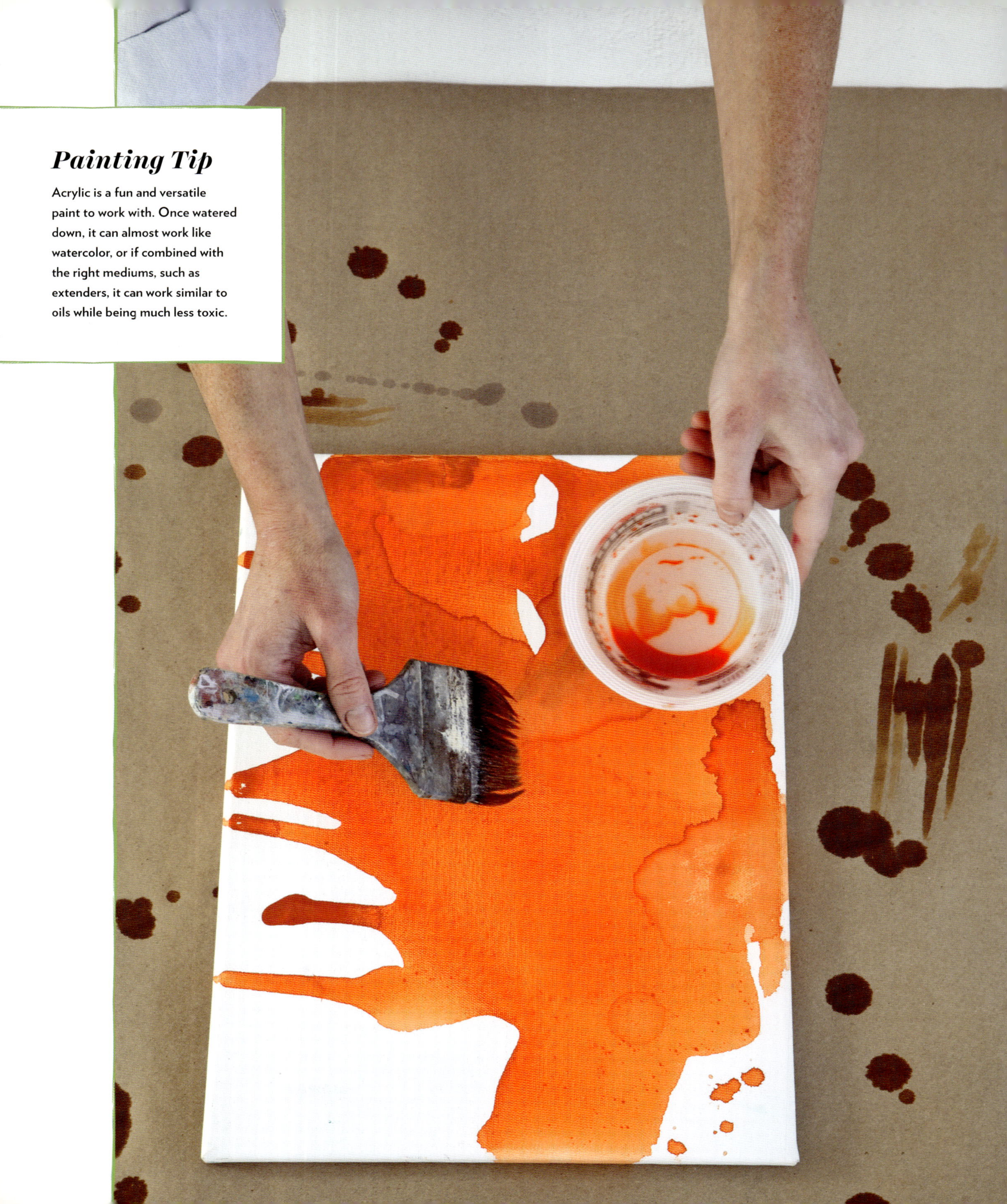

Painting Tip

Acrylic is a fun and versatile paint to work with. Once watered down, it can almost work like watercolor, or if combined with the right mediums, such as extenders, it can work similar to oils while being much less toxic.

EXERCISE SIXTEEN

adlibbing in art

improvising with poured paint

For this exercise, I want you to be an active participant in facilitating a situation in which you must improvise. This will help you learn to be more open and mindful when creating art and learn how interact with your materials. This practice also aids in sharpening your eye and mind to think and see intuitively and allows for your gut reaction to take over.

MATERIALS

12" × 16" (30.5 × 40.5 cm) or smaller primed canvas or heavy mixed-media paper of the same dimensions

acrylic paints, in a variety of colors

paintbrushes, in a variety of sizes and shapes

containers with water for mixing

prepare

→ Before you begin, make sure that you have a well-protected work area.

→ Choose a variety of colors for this exercise. Try to vary them in value because it will help in seeing the layers as you create them and will add interest to the overall composition.

→ Pour a small amount of acrylic paint into a cup and add an equal amount of water. Mix them together until they are well combined. The added water helps to increase the viscosity of the acrylic.

create

→ Slowly pour the paint and water mixture onto the flat surface. This will allow chance to play a significant role in the outcome of your composition.

→ Let the paint dry completely—for several hours or overnight—without manipulating it in any way. Because of the added water, it will take longer to dry. The time will also vary depending on whether it is on prime canvas or paper. If using paper, the time will be shorter as some of the water will be absorbed into the paper itself. Also, humid or wet conditions can significantly extend drying time.

→ Observe what forms and shapes the paint created. Study how it pooled, spilled, and dripped on the surface. Turn and observe it from different perspectives and decide which angle interests you the most.

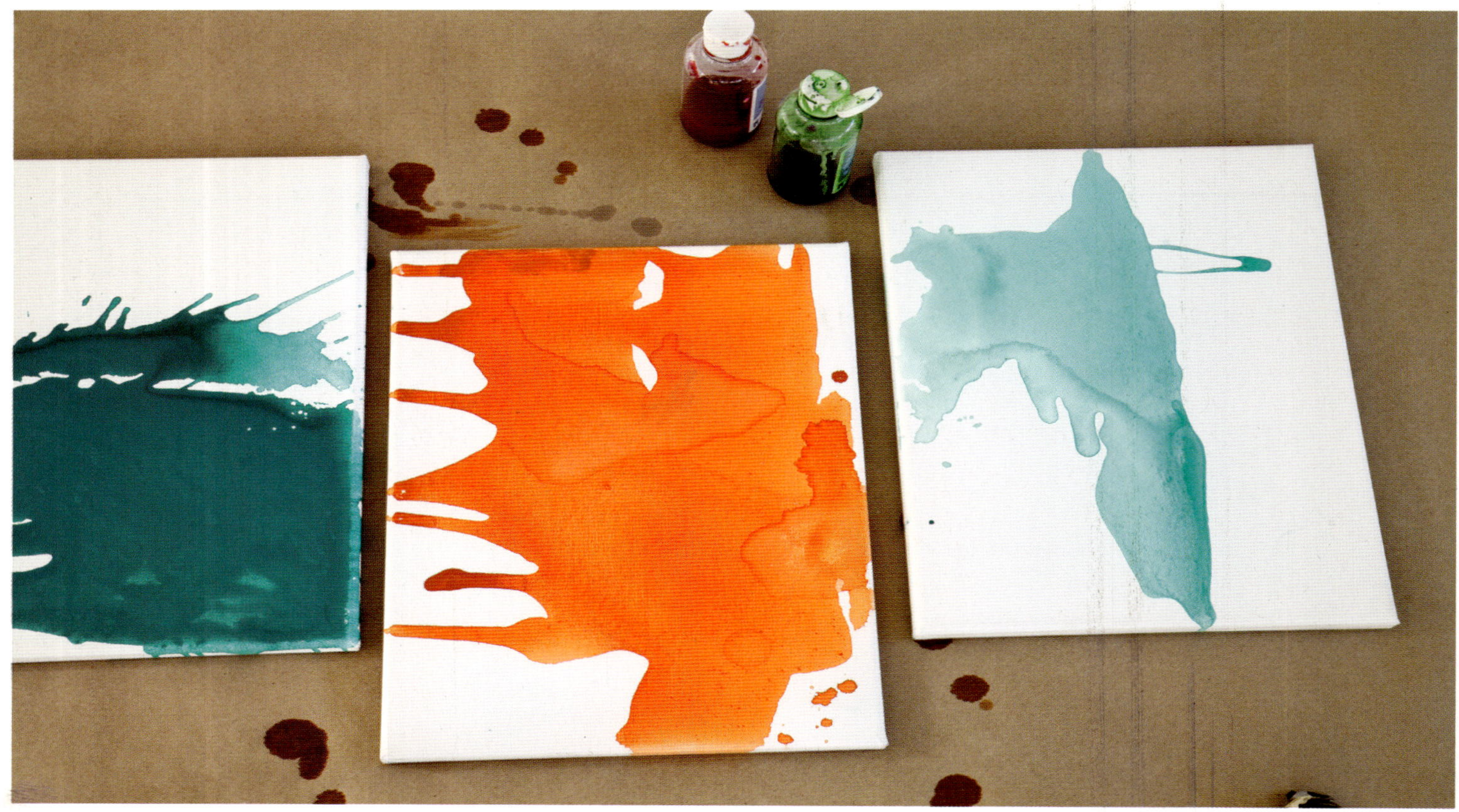

- This is where the improvisational part of the exercise comes in. Often when making art, your materials act in unexpected ways. It is up to you to accept and embrace these events and incorporate them into your work.
- Add more colors, one layer at a time. Allow each one to dry completely before adding the next one. Sometimes mixing colors can cause them to become muddy and lose their original vibrancy.
- Leave some of the unexpected and visually interesting drips and pooling you initially started with.
- As you add each new color, use the drying time as an opportunity to step back a few feet (or a meter) and simply observe and reflect on the work as a whole.
- Let your instinct guide your decision-making. Add more layers, cover certain parts, or simply leave it alone.

This short practice will help you to become comfortable committing to decisions. You will begin to see which parts are and are not important to the composition. Most importantly, this exercise helps you learn restraint. Practicing restraint is an important aspect in creating art, particularly abstract art.

In realism, the viewer can easily understand a painting. There's no guesswork in what they are seeing. Our minds automatically recognize certain objects, colors, and shapes. Abstraction has to be contemplated and dissected by both artist and viewer. Restraint plays a part in this for the artist in regards to the successful comprehension of a work. A piece that is overworked, saturated, overcomplicated, and/or muddy will leave the viewer confused and unfulfilled.

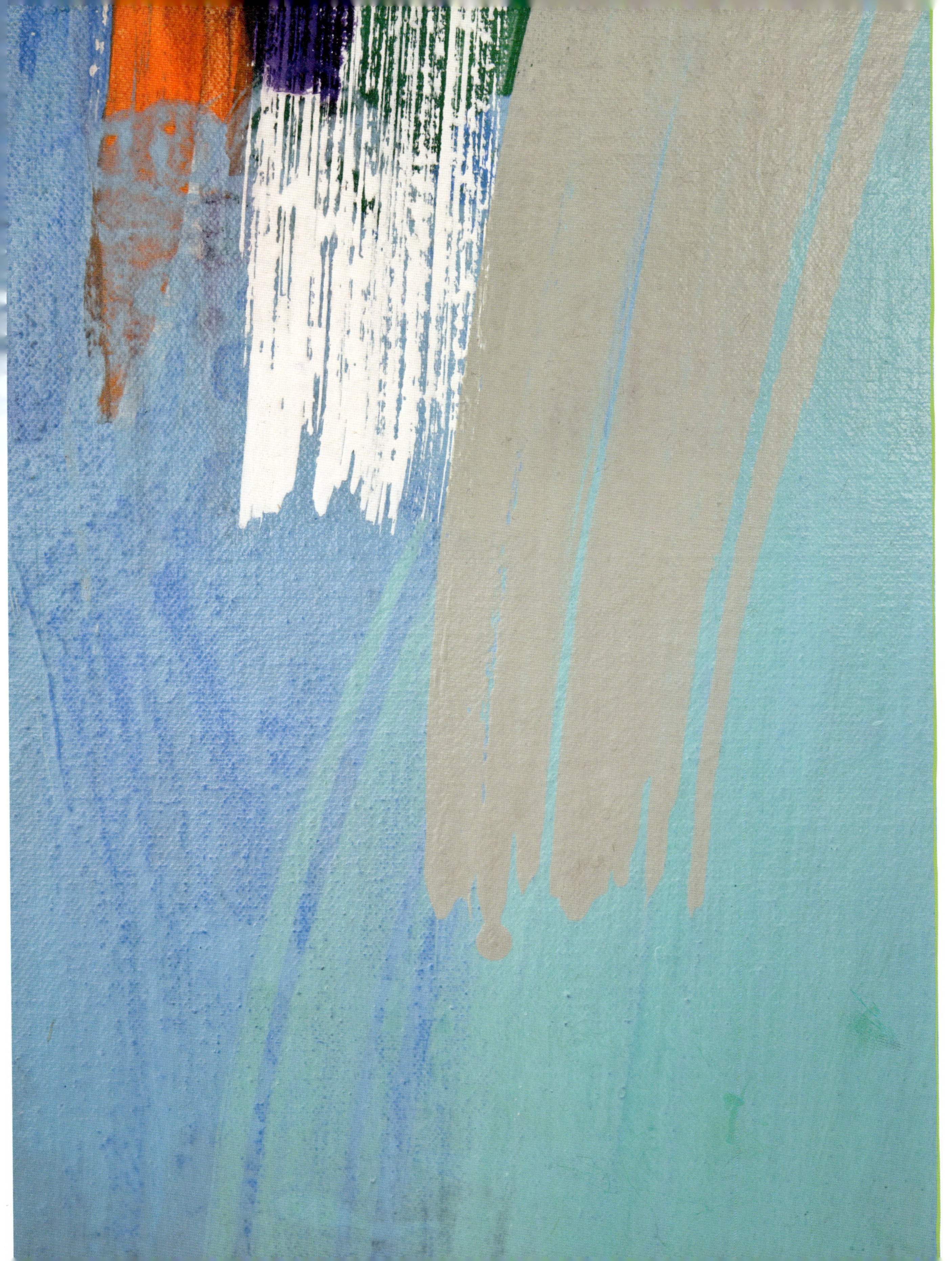

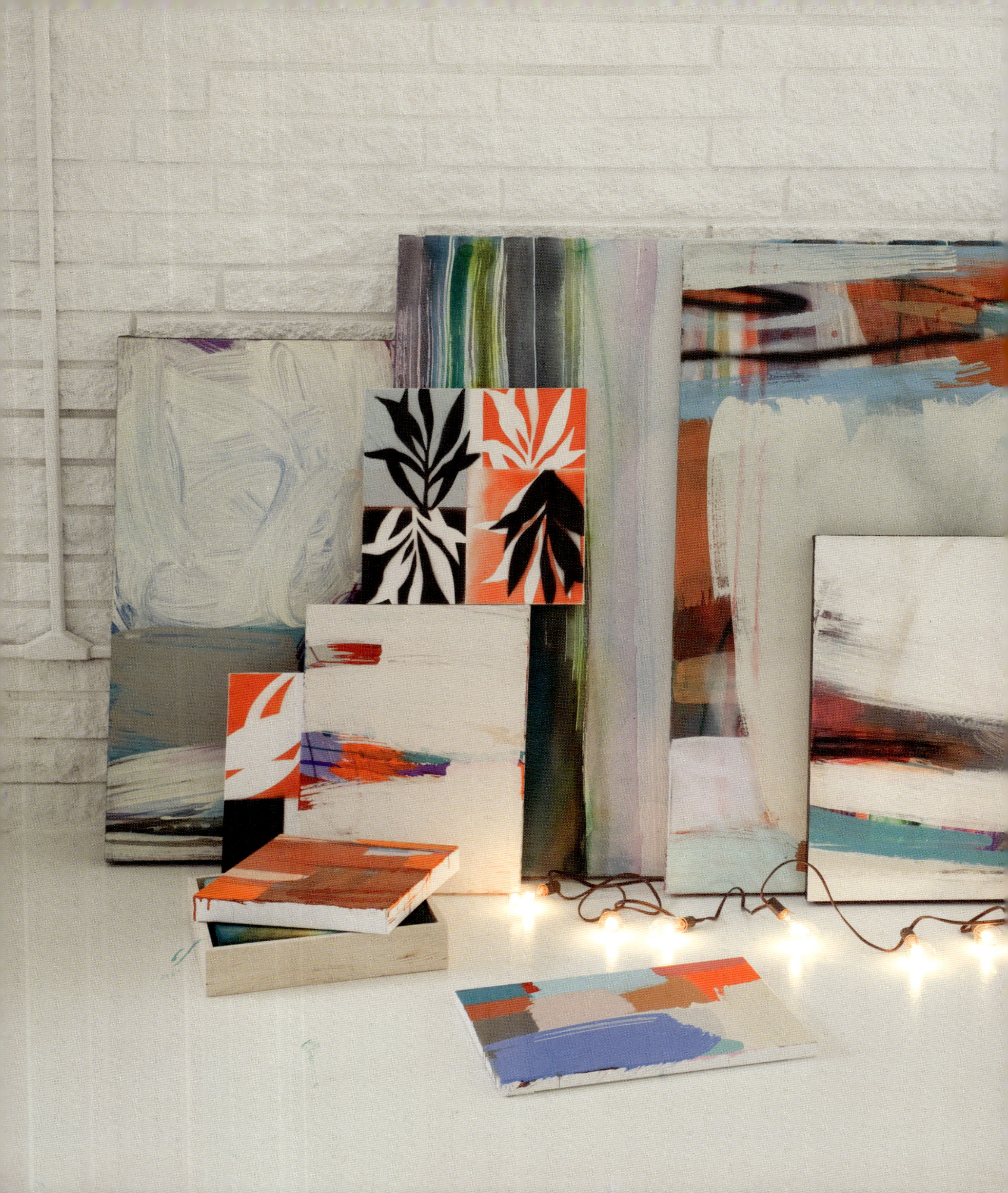

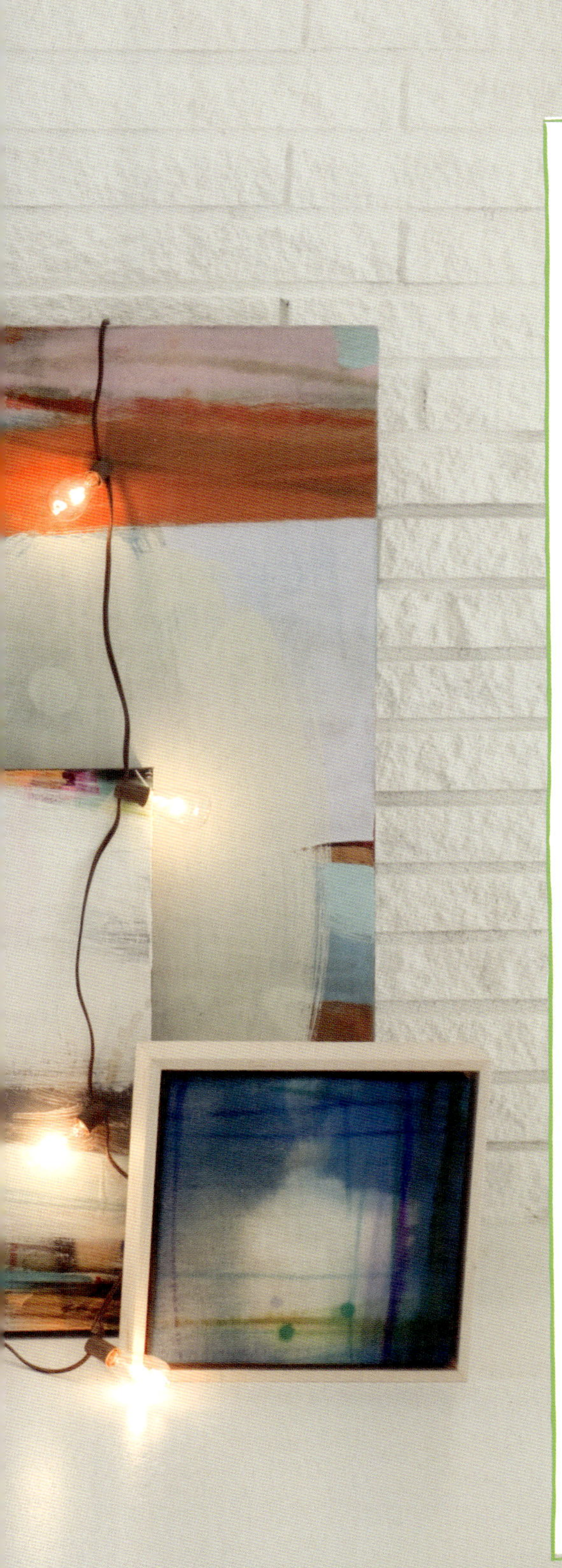

Learn to Push, Pause, or Start Over

Many artists find it difficult to make the choice to let go and start over. They feel as if they have already invested so much time and effort in this work that they don't feel like it is a choice to give it up. When I was first starting to paint, I would often leave work unresolved and unfinished. I would be unsure, confused, and frustrated with how to complete it—or even know when it was completed! In hindsight, I should not have wasted so much time and energy in this state of insecurity. Learn from my mistakes!

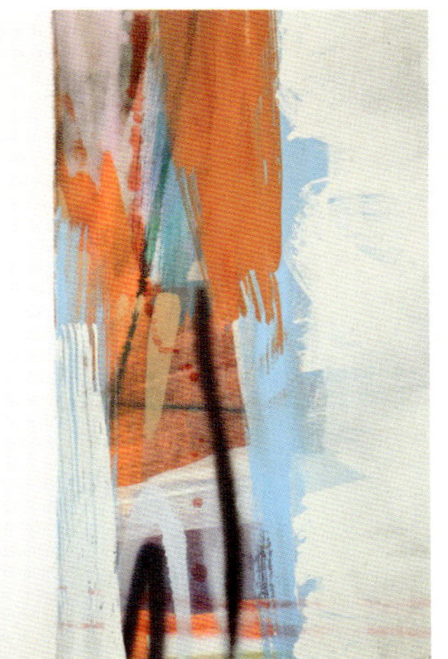

This is a challenging concept, but in the end, by learning, accepting, and ultimately making decisions, you'll gain confidence. Your time, and even more important, your sanity, will be saved by allowing yourself to be the only one held accountable for your artwork. Your work is your personal vision, and it is you who holds the power to either push through times of indecision and frustration, pause, and come back to your work with fresh eyes or simply start over. Artists evolve and develop in tandem with their work, and sometimes what you painted only yesterday is not who you are today.

An artist friend once told me, "In art, nothing is precious." You might think, like I have, that you will never be able to make those same marks again or mix that exact color another time. Although both these thoughts might be true, the knowledge you gain while creating these works will not be lost. Your newfound knowledge will most certainly carry through to your next painting.

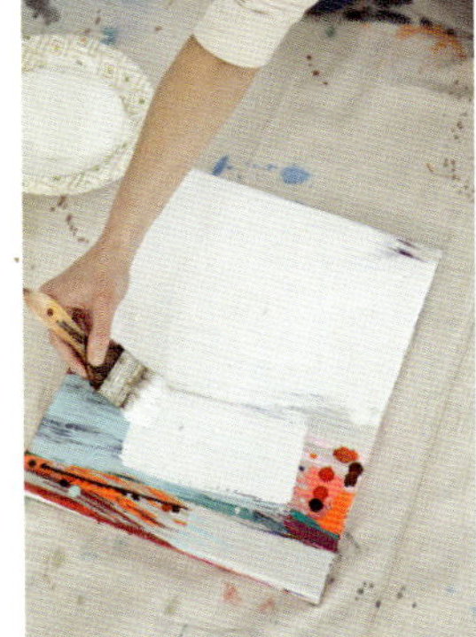

If you are going to create art, then you must take risks. A risk by definition is to expose something valued to harm or loss. Mistakes will happen. What molds and shapes you as an artist, and therefore your art, is the process that led you there. The finished product is the outcome of the desire to create and experience the process. Mistakes are inevitable, so allow yourself to accept them, learn from them, and continue on.

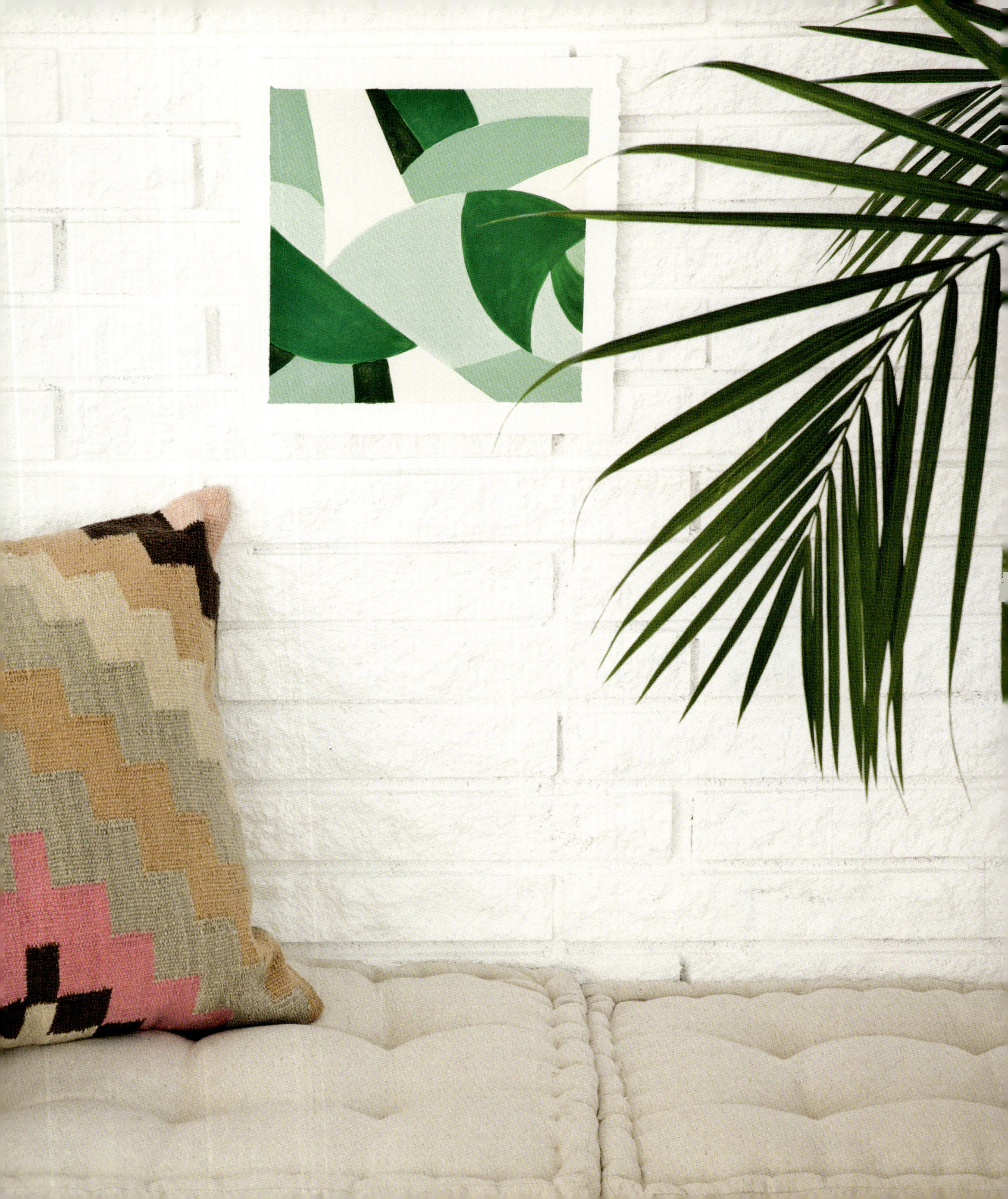

CHAPTER EIGHT

PERSPECTIVES ON COLOR

"Color helps to express light, not the physical phenomenon, but the only light that really exists, that and the artist's brain."

—HENRI MATISSE

Color plays an important role in abstract and contemporary art. Yet with all the factors that involve the use of color, such as chroma, saturation, hues, complementary colors, and color mixing, the use of color can be a daunting one. Even if you are a fan of neutrals or monochromatic colors and tones, it is important to practice and appreciate the use of all colors and what they can evoke in the viewer.

The next two exercises give a basic introduction to the language of color and a bit of history on some of the masters who prominently showcased color in their work.

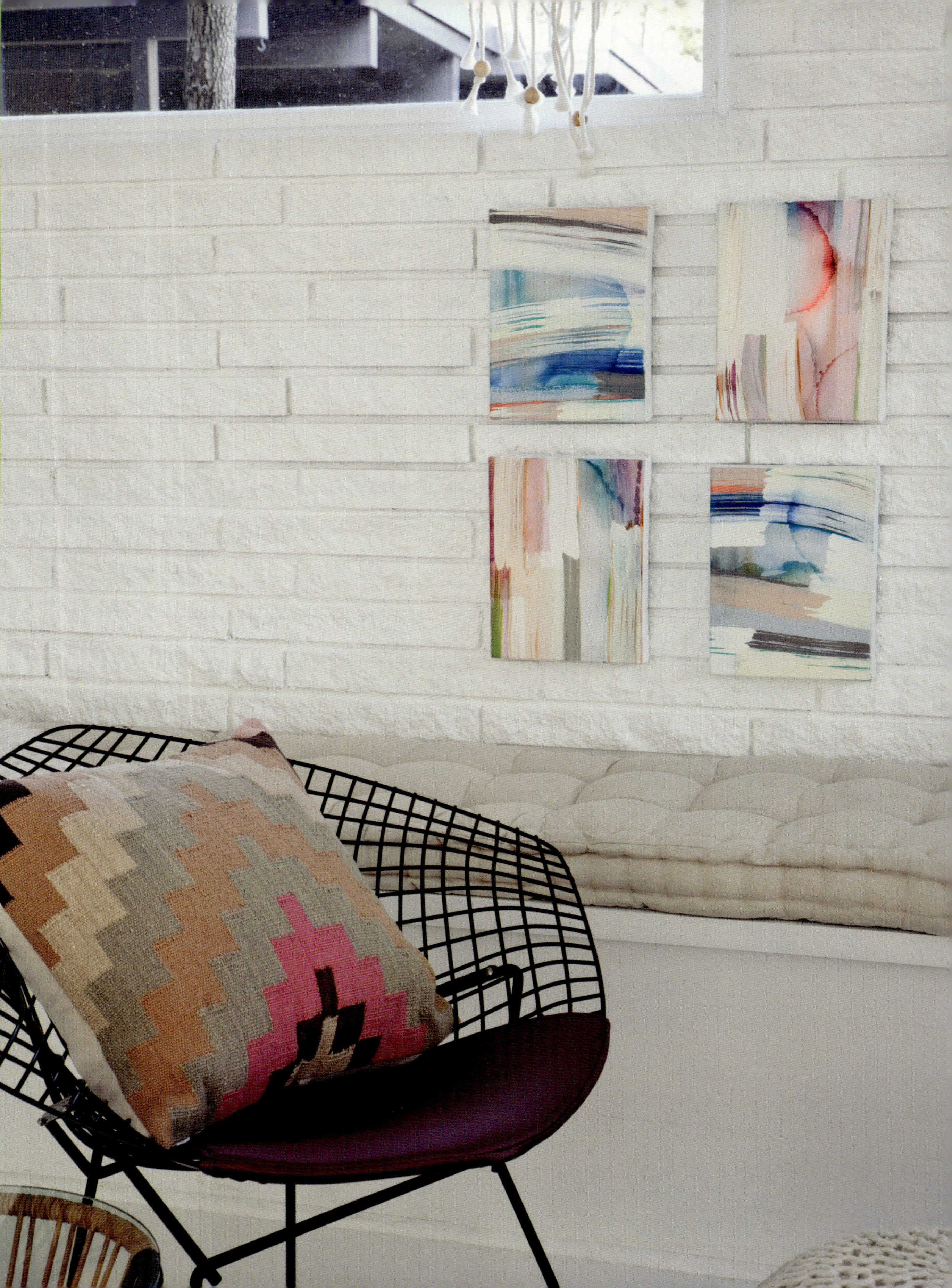

EXERCISE SEVENTEEN

the language of color

using contrast to learn about color

MATERIALS

- several small- to medium-size round and flat brushes, such as sizes 4, 6, and 8
- three 12" × 12" (30.5 × 30.5 cm) sheets of heavyweight mixed-media art paper
- 1" (2.5 cm) wide painter's tape
- white and black paint
- your three color choices
- 12" (30.5 cm) ruler
- no. 2 mechanical pencil

One cannot deny the weight that simple color can carry in abstract art and painting. It evokes emotions and memories. Color conveys messages and can even create a particular state of mind. In every culture, different colors symbolize a variety of things. When talking about color as a visual language, using cultural symbolism is one way to relay a message.

Another way is by homing in on the emotions and sentiments that colors can generate. In Western cultures, red typically represents passion, love, or anger. Blues often symbolize water or sky and produce a sense of calm and well-being. For this exercise, I want you to choose three colors from the following list of six.

Color choices:

- → Red
- → Orange
- → Yellow
- → Green
- → Blue
- → Purple

TIP ▸ Mechanical pencils are handy when sketching out ideas. The lead is fairly hard, which makes a light line. It also creates a line of constant width without having to keep sharpening a standard drawing pencil.

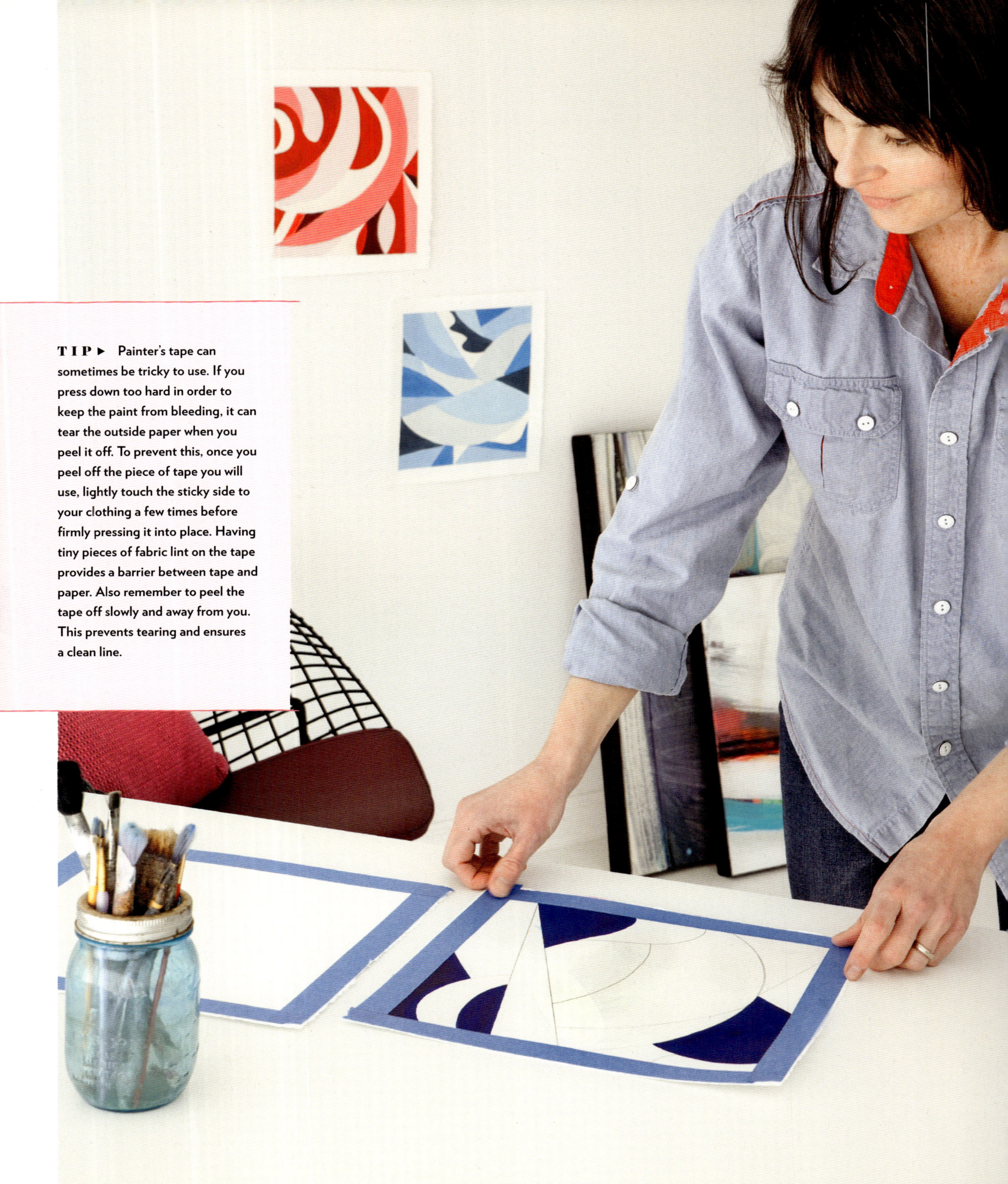

TIP ▸ Painter's tape can sometimes be tricky to use. If you press down too hard in order to keep the paint from bleeding, it can tear the outside paper when you peel it off. To prevent this, once you peel off the piece of tape you will use, lightly touch the sticky side to your clothing a few times before firmly pressing it into place. Having tiny pieces of fabric lint on the tape provides a barrier between tape and paper. Also remember to peel the tape off slowly and away from you. This prevents tearing and ensures a clean line.

prepare

→ On your three pieces of paper, measure off a 10" × 10" (25.5 × 25.5 cm) square in the middle. Use the painter's tape to tape off the square, pressing firmly.

create

→ Once you've prepared the paper, lightly draw fifteen to twenty geometric or organic shapes on each piece. Vary them in size. Each square will be dedicated to one of your color choices.

→ You'll use the white and black paint to adjust your colors, making them lighter or darker to suit your preference. This is a very basic technique of changing a color's contrast, but it is instructive in better understanding the "language" of your base color. You can certainly make blue-greens, orange-reds, and other combinations, but in doing this, you are altering the pure quality of the original color. By using black and white, you only vary the contrast—or value—of the color as opposed to changing its foundation.

→ Now fill all of your shapes while varying the contrast of each one with different amounts of black or white. You will begin to see and feel how the original color can be manipulated to represent its unique language.

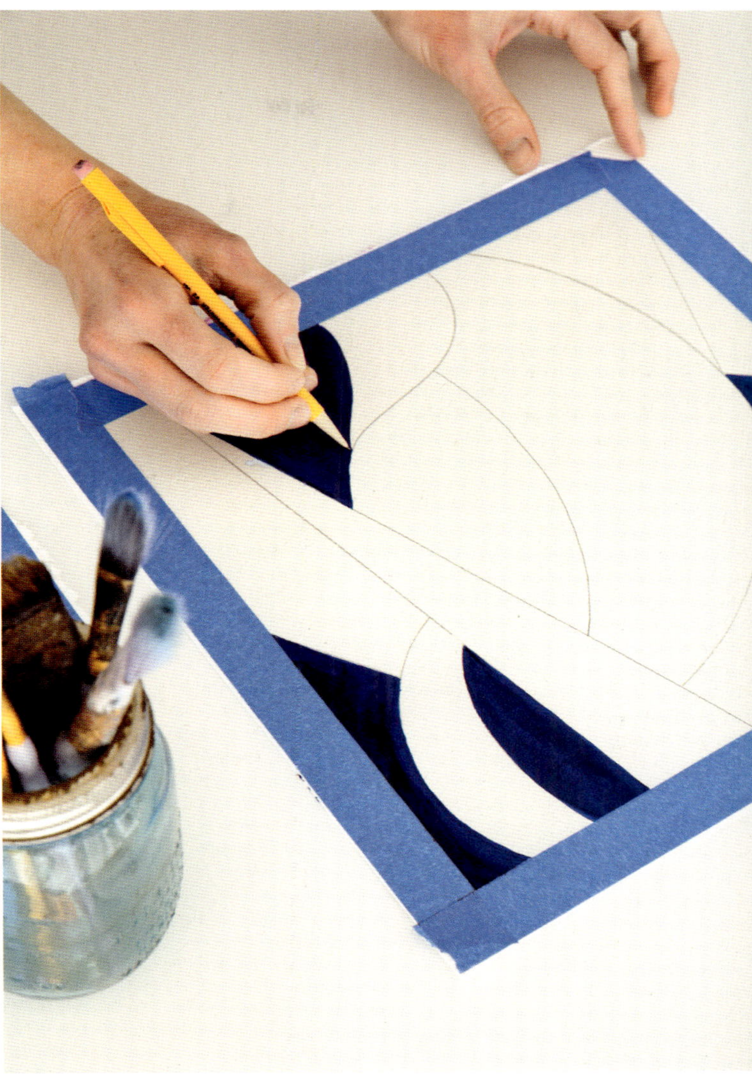

TIP ▸ In terms of composition, keep in mind that lighter colors recede from the eye and darker color advance toward the eye.

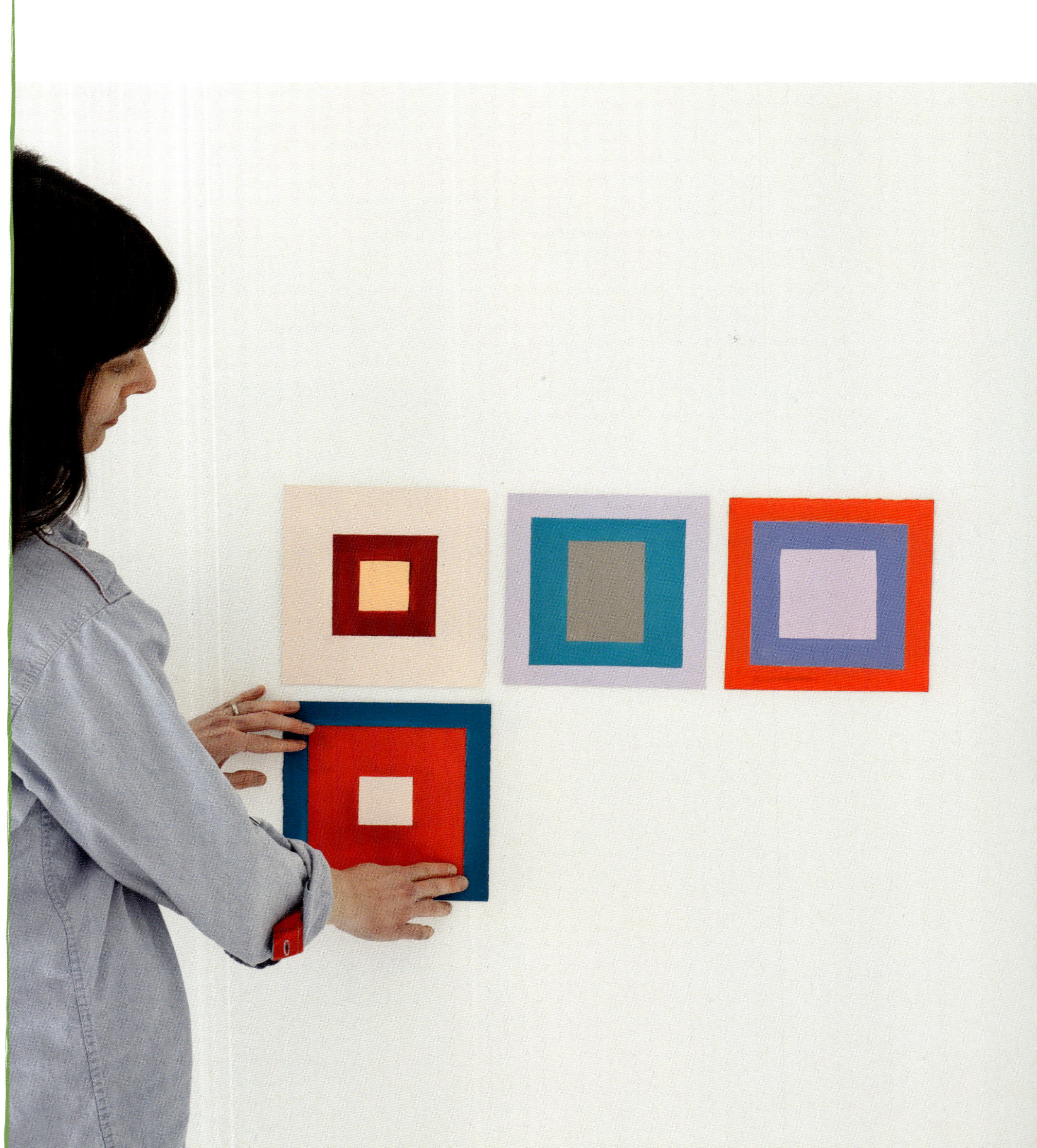

EXERCISE EIGHTEEN

learning how colors work together

imitating two color masters

MATERIALS

- one sheet of 140 lb (300 gsm) hot-press watercolor paper or smooth mixed-media paper
- mechanical #2 pencil
- 1" (2.5 cm) painter's tape
- 15–20 matte acrylic paints
- two or three flat synthetic short hair paintbrushes

josef albers and mark rothko

As this chapter is about color, I wanted to talk about Josef Albers (1888–1976) and Mark Rothko (1903–1970), two modern abstract art masters, who dedicated their lives to the study of color and its function. Their careers were long and successful, and even though both men were prolific, they focused on one certain style and series later in their careers.

Rothko was always interested in the study of color, but only through significant evolution in his work did he start to create his well-known color fields. These vertical large-scale paintings were composed of rectangular blocks of complementary colors that were meant to overwhelm and envelop the viewer. In some of his work, the colors almost seem to vibrate, and in others, he creates an optical flicker through his use of color. I love this quote from Rothko about color as a language of art: "[I'm interested] only in expressing basic human emotions—tragedy, ecstasy, doom, and so on. And the fact that a lot of people break down and cry when confronted with my pictures shows that I *communicate* those basic human emotions... The people who weep before my pictures are having the same religious experience I had when I painted them. And if you, as you say, are moved only by their color relationship, then you miss the point!"

Albers began a series in 1949 that explored chromatic interaction and was called *Homage to the Square*. He worked on this particular series for more than twenty years and created each piece using basically the same format. They consisted of three to four squares nested inside of each other, yet not overlapping. He executed this by using a palette knife to apply the paint as thinly as possible onto wood panels. His color choices were meant to evoke different moods and visual effects similar to Rothko.

This next exercise focuses on Albers' *Homage to the Square* series and calls for you to create your own studies. The simplicity of his compositions and repetition of the same format helps in focusing on the color combinations and seeing how they relate and interact.

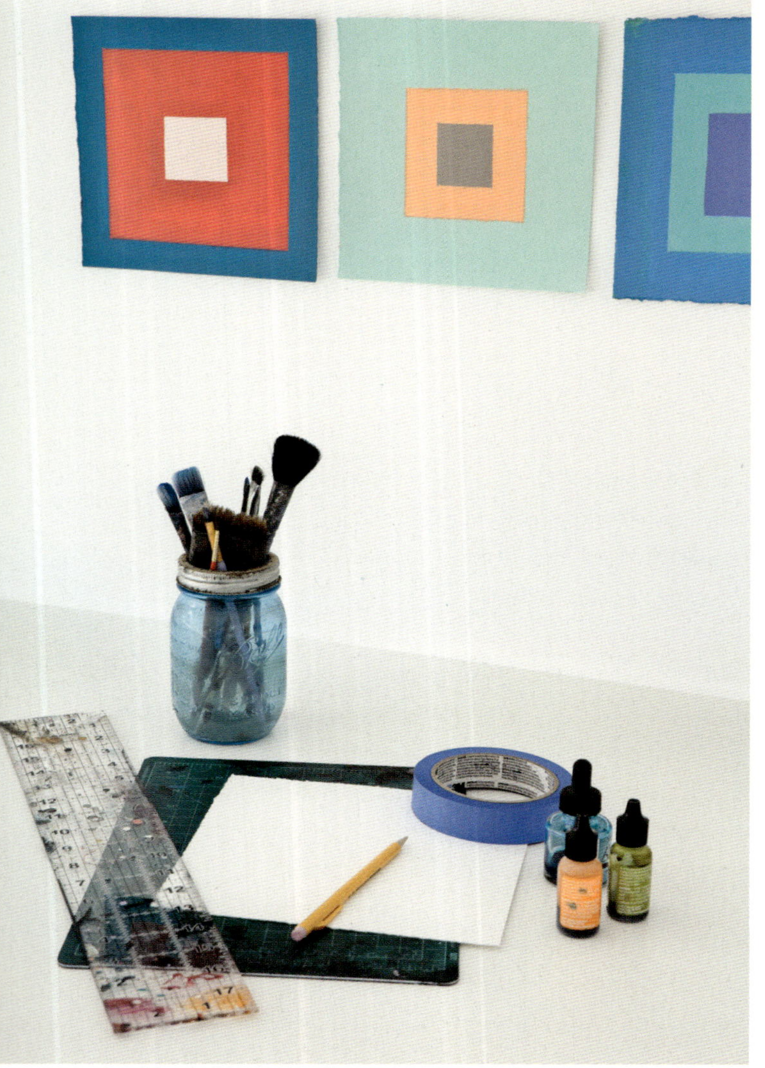

prepare

Albers created his *Homage to the Square* series on panel and by using a palette knife. Both these materials require some practice, and this exercise is focused on learning about color relationships, not about mastering certain paint tools. So I decided it was best to stick with paper and brushes.

- Cut or tear six 8" × 8" (20 × 20 cm) pieces of your chosen paper
- Tape off and size your paper into a 6" × 6" (15 × 15 cm) square.
- Lightly draw three or four squares inside of your 6" × 6" (15 × 15 cm) frame. Use one of Albers' designs and be sure not to overlap them.
- Albers' paint choices were flat and matte, devoid of any shading or visual brush strokes or texture. So choose paint colors that you will be using directly from the tube with no mixing, blending, and so on.
- I recommend using small, short, flat brushes for this exercise. The shorter the bristles, the easier it will be to control your lines. I also prefer synthetic hair brushes, as they typically allow for easier blending and your goal here is to make each color square uniform.

TIP ▸ Go ahead and draw all six square compositions because you will be rotating through them as you go. As one square dries, you can work on another and so forth in order to maintain a fluid process.

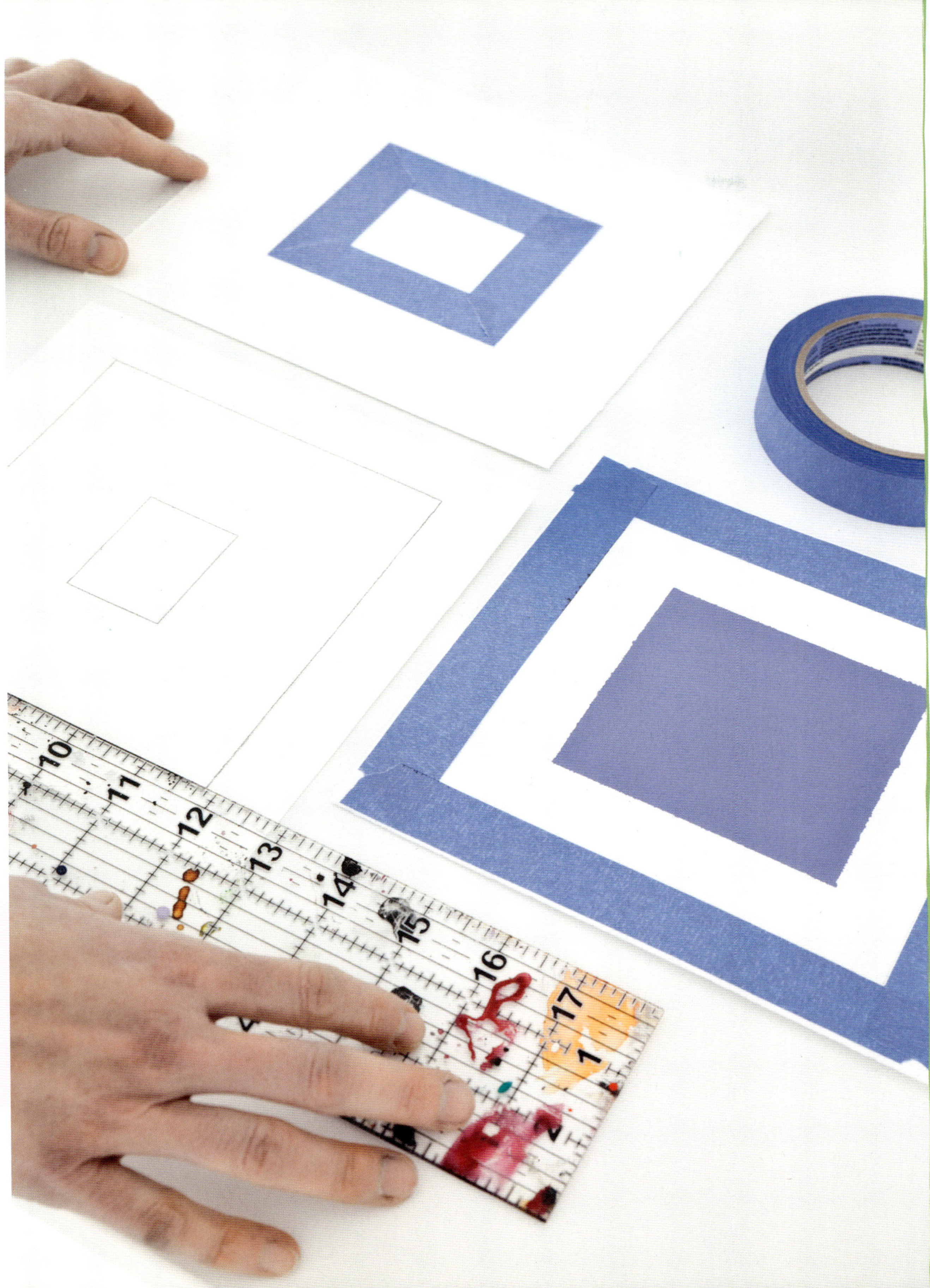

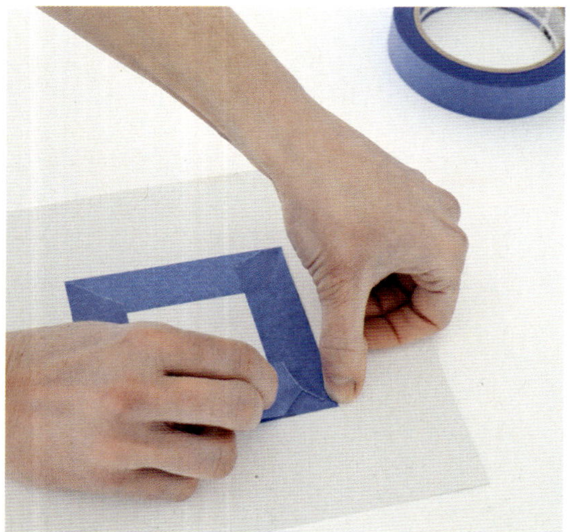

create

- Once all your squares are drawn, choose a color and begin to paint a square in each one. Alternate between them as others are drying. You may either do this freehand or use your painter's tape to tape them off individually.
- Experiment with your color choices for each square. For one, stick with monochromatic colors, and for others, strongly vary your usage of color.
- Create at least six squares so that you can begin to appreciate and see the different relationships among your color choices in the repetition.

TIP ▸ To tape off the inside section of a square using your painter's tape, place the tape on the inner square. Then press your thumbnail onto the corner of the square and tear the tape at a downward angle. Continue doing this with each corner and you will have a clean square.

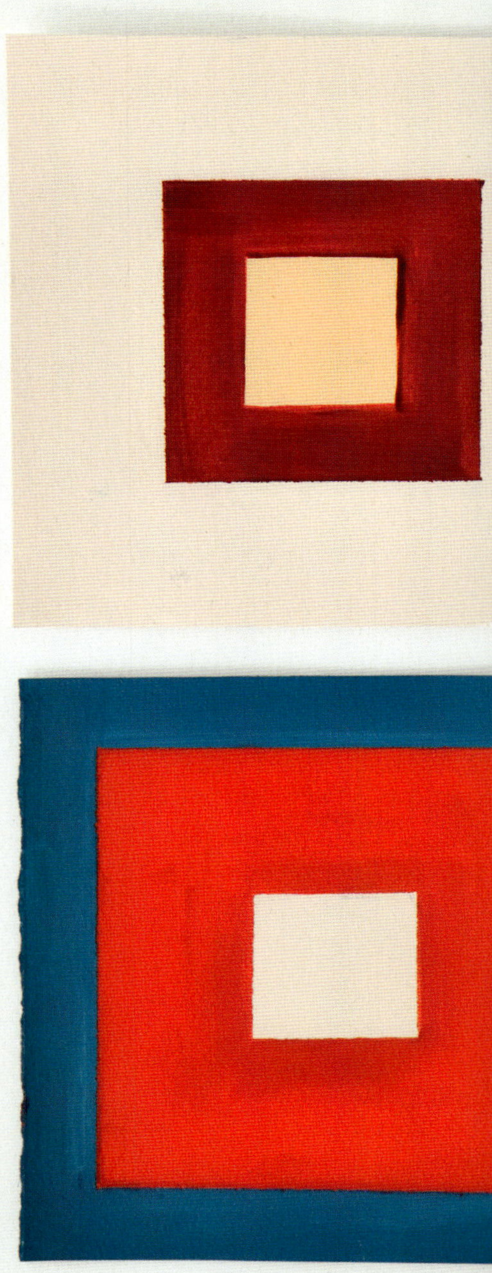

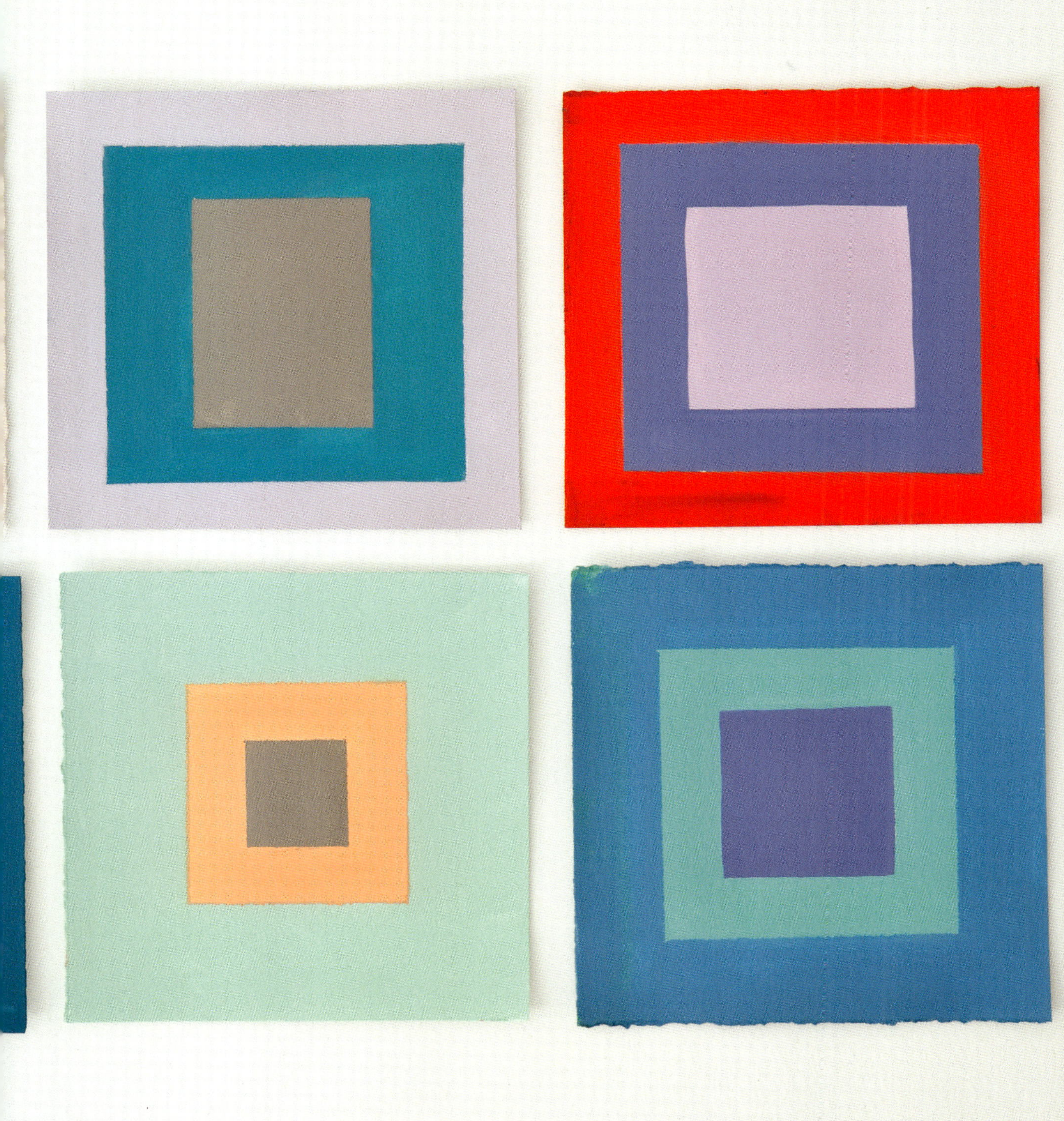

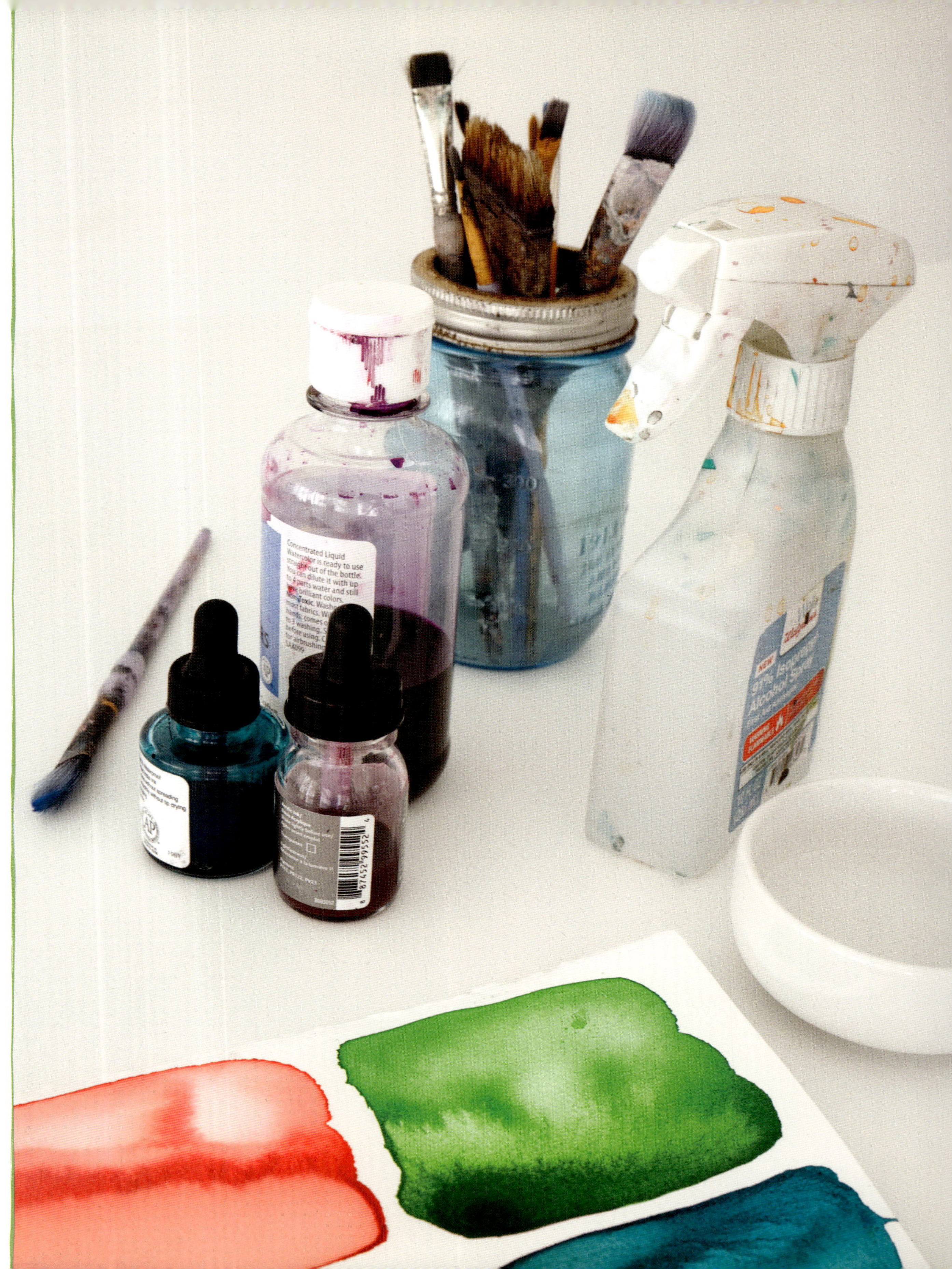
Concentrated Liquid
Watercolor is ready to use
straight out of the bottle.
You can dilute it with up
to 4 parts water and still
brilliant colors.

resources

supplies

Cheap Joe's Art Stuff
www.cheapjoes.com

Dick Blick Art Materials
www.dickblick.com

Ultrecht Art Supplies
www.ultrechtart.com

Fredrix Artist Canvas
www.fredrixartistcanvas.com

Sax Arts and Crafts Supplies
www.saxarts.com

Golden Artist Colors
www.goldenpaints.com

Binders Art Supplies and Frames
www.bindersart.com

Moleskine
https://us.moleskine.com/home

Dr. Ph.Martin's
www.docmartins.com

Sam Flax
www.samflax.com

INTERNATIONAL RESOURCES

FRANCE
Rougier & Plé
www.roucier-ple.fr

GERMANY
Boesner
www.boesner.com

UNITED KINGDOM
Jackson's Art Supplies
www.jacksonart.com

acknowledgments

I first must thank my editor, Mary Ann Hall. She believed in me and helped to guide me through this exciting endeavor of writing my first book. This is certainly a task I never dreamed I would accomplish. I will say, though, as the project began to unfold, and after a lot of inner reflection and focus, I realize there was actually a lot about art and being an artist that I wanted to share. I am so grateful that Mary Ann had the foresight to notice this because writing this book has been a blessing to me professionally and personally.

I could not have undertaken this project without the help of the extremely talented photographer, Christina Wedge. This is a visual book, and her skill and artistic vision are seen on every page. I think of this book as a collaboration between the two of us, and I could not be happier that our paths have crossed.

I must thank my loving and supportive family. They have never questioned my desire to become an artist, even though, as I mentioned before, this career choice can be a risky one. My parents enrolled me in private art classes when the public schools offered nothing and always exposed me to the arts and art culture. My supportive husband typed the entire manuscript for the book. He has been one of my most devoted and sincere fans and believed in me even when I did not. I feel like a lot of artists, including myself, are their own worst critics. So to have the outside support of my family has led me to where I am today.

Last, but certainly not least, I wanted to mention my beautiful son Bay. He has brought joy and happiness to my life that I would never have imagined possible. Every day he allows me to see the world in a completely new and vibrant perspective. Seeing his imagination at work and viewing life through his young eyes has gifted me as a human, a mother, and profoundly as an artist.

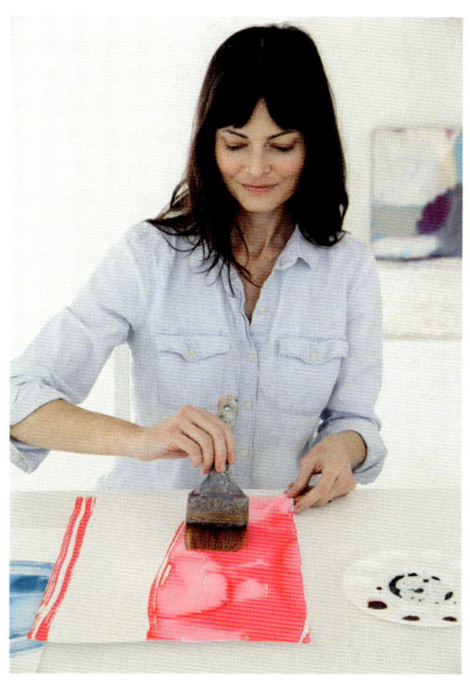

about the author

Eva Magill-Oliver is a professional artist currently living and working in Atlanta. She received a B.F.A. from the University of Georgia in Athens. Following her degree, she worked as an in-house artist and designer for a fine arts publishing company in Atlanta before pursuing a career as an independent artist. She is represented by several galleries nationwide and has been part of several art and design collaborations with prominent established brands and companies, including Anthropologie, Sylvie Thiriez, Schoolhouse Electric, Clémence, Seaworthy Jewelry, and Laura Cooke Ceramics. She has also had her work published in several national publications, including *Flow*, *Jezebel*, *House & Garden*, *HGTV*, and *Topiary* (Stanford University literary journal).

also available
FROM QUARRY BOOKS

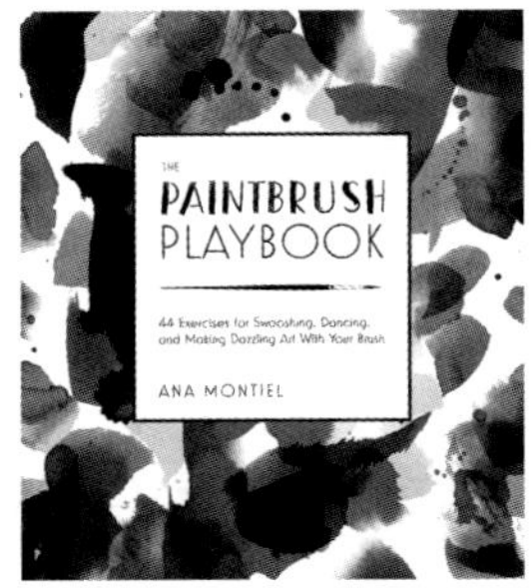

The Paintbrush Playbook

978-1-63159-046-7

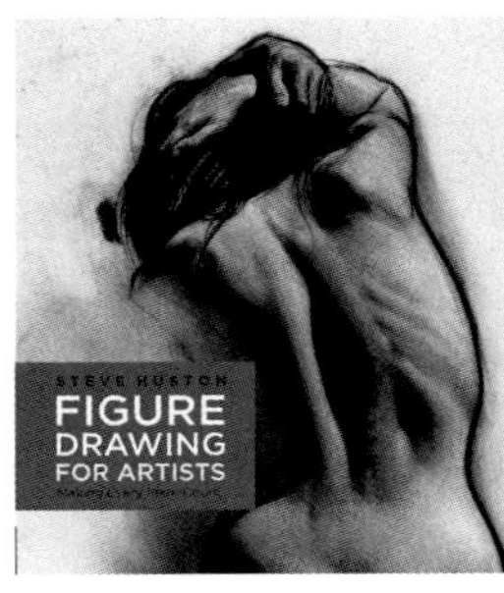

Figure Drawing for Artists

978-1-63159-065-8

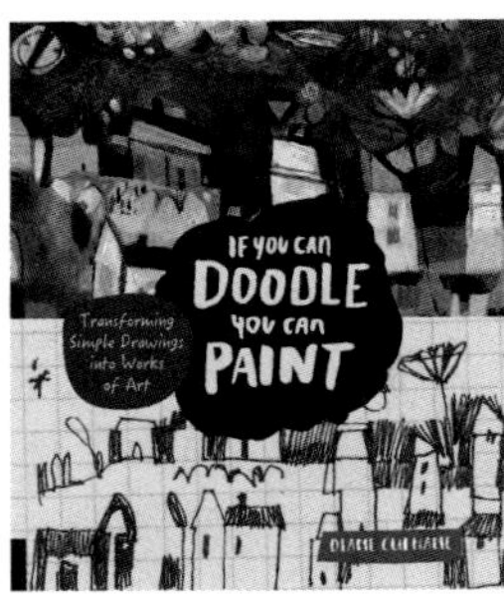

If You Can Doodle, You Can Paint

978-1-63159-289-8